NEGOTIATING CIVIC LIFE

For Bill Connolly

NEGOTIATING CIVIC LIFE

LITERATURE, FILM,
POLITICS

Michael J. Shapiro

EDINBURGH
University Press

Edinburgh University Press is one of the leading university presses in the UK. We publish academic books and journals in our selected subject areas across the humanities and social sciences, combining cutting-edge scholarship with high editorial and production values to produce academic works of lasting importance. For more information visit our website: edinburghuniversitypress.com

Edinburgh University Press Ltd
13 Infirmary Street
Edinburgh EH1 1LT

First published in hardback by Edinburgh University Press 2025

Typeset in 10/12.5pt Sabon by
Cheshire Typesetting Ltd, Cuddington, Cheshire

A CIP record for this book is available from the British Library

ISBN 978 1 3995 4574 7 (hardback)
ISBN 978 1 3995 4577 8 (paperback)
ISBN 978 1 3995 4575 4 (webready PDF)
ISBN 978 1 3995 4576 1 (epub)

EU Authorised Representative:
Easy Access System Europe
Mustamäe tee 50, 10621 Tallinn, Estonia
gpsr.requests@easproject.com

CONTENTS

FIGURES

ACKNOWLEDGMENTS

Because the ideas and sentiments in this book have been incubating for many decades, I want to acknowledge an old debt before identifying recent ones. During my first sabbatical, which I spent as a Guest Professor at the Institute for Sociological Research at the University of Bergen during the 1972–3 academic year, I was introduced to the Norwegian sociological imagination in a country where many academics were active within civil society. Some were supplementing the scholarship they published in academic presses and journals with social activism, often taking the form of *Kronika* (opinions) published in major newspapers. As I was working on what I conceived as "social control ideologies," I reached out to three sociologists who were deeply concerned with the politics and sociology of incarceration. Thanks to their collegial generosity, I learned from the Norwegian sociologists Vilhelm Aubert, Nils Christie, and Thomas Mathiesen about the connections between the conceptual thinking that constitutes social theory and attunement to the many voices involved in the ongoing negotiations that constitute the civil order. Inspired in particular by their attentiveness to Norwegian crime control as it existed and as it could exist otherwise, I sat for many hours as a guest of the Oslo newspaper *Dagbladet* reading and copying *Kronika* addressed to the problem of *narkotikamisbruk* and *avhengighet* (drug abuse and addiction) written by Norwegians in academia, in politics, in bureaucracies, in student life, and in diverse occupational positions. Reflecting a nationwide concern that drug dependency "calls for thinking" (to evoke Heidegger's famous phrase), the issue was being negotiated broadly within civil society. I remain indebted to my late Norwegian sociology colleagues and to the Norwegian society as a whole for acquainting me with what it can mean to be involved in civic life.

My current debts are to those who have either enabled and/or reacted to the formulations of the diverse civic life negotiations I treat in my chapters. A prototype of Chapter 1, "The Civic Lives of Grief," was solicited for presentation at a mid-November 2023 conference at Johns Hopkins University in honor of William Connolly's retirement. Thanks are owed to the graduate student organizers Blaz Skerjanec and Tvrtko Vrdoljak for the invitation and management of the occasion, and to Bill Connolly whose many years of productive scholarship inspired much of the way the chapter thinks.

The compositional structure and conceptual framings in all the chapters benefited from reactions by colleagues, students, and others, among whom were discussants and interlocutors at subsequent conferences where I presented two of the chapters. Thanks are owed to Matt Davies, James Der Derian, Shree Deshpande, Gitte Du Plessis, Jenny Edkins, Nate Gorelick, Jairus Grove, Elisabeth Heradstveit, Jef Huysmans, Rohan Kalyan, Sophie Kim, Carol Lau, Charles Lawrence, Daniel Levine, Ali Musleh, Sam Opondo, Kandida Purnell, Olivia U. Rutazibwa, Claire Sagan, Jerry Shapiro, Delacey Tedesco, Ritu Vij, and Beto Yamato. Special thanks are owed to my wife Hannah Tavares who introduced me to Dwayne LeBlanc's documentary film *Civic* which inspired the chapter titled "Civic Automobility," and to my Edinburgh University Press acquisitions editor Ersev Ersoy and two anonymous reviewers whose reactions and suggestions helped me shape the "Civic Empathy" introduction. Thanks are owed as well to Edinburgh's welcoming and efficient production staff, Sam Johnson and Joannah Duncan, and to Caroline Richards for outstanding copyediting.

This book is dedicated to Bill Connolly whose thinking, writing, and friendship enrich me.

INTRODUCTION: EXPLORING CIVIC EMPATHY

A POINT OF DEPARTURE

I closed a recent book-length investigation by reflecting on a question that I suggested requires more exploration.[1] Because much of the focus of that monograph is on both the rise of fascism in the twentieth century and the rise of white supremacy movements in the twenty-first, I was intrigued by a question Hannah Arendt raised after witnessing the trial of Adolf Eichmann. Heeding the words Eichmann evinced in his defense, which she rendered as an unthinking "adherence to standardized codes of expression," she followed up her account of his trial in *Eichmann in Jerusalem* by wondering whether those able to think critically would be unlikely to do evil:

> Does the inability to think and a disastrous failure of what we commonly call conscience coincide? The question that imposed itself was: Could the activity of thinking as such, the habit of examining and reflecting upon whatever happens to come to pass, regardless of specific content and quite independent of results, could this activity be of such a nature that it conditions men against evil-doing?[2]

Unconvinced by her surmise that Eichmann was a pawn in a violence-legitimating thought system he could not find words to oppose – a view that is belied by what is known about his crafty calculations, scrupulous mass murder

"

techniques, and "excess of enjoyment"[3] of his role – I turned to Robert Musil who posed a similar question. He too tries to make sense of a moral monster on trial, in his case by introducing Christian Moosbrugger, a fictional version of an actual "sex murderer" in his epic *The Man without Qualities* (hereafter *Qualities*).[4] Unlike Eichmann's disingenuous, responsibility-denying testimony, Moosbrugger proudly takes credit for his murderous deed. What stands out in Musil's rendering of the character is that rather than judging Moosbrugger's act with resort to transcendental moral principles, Ulrich, the novel's main protagonist through whom Musil filters his perspectives on persons and events, concerns himself with the experiential conditioning of Moosbrugger during the historical period in which his grievances developed. Viewing Moosbrugger through the lens of an "invigorating fever [that] rose all over Europe (out of the becalmed mentality of the nineteenth century's last two decades),"[5] Ulrich tries to understand the "dimly discernible principle"[6] on which Moosbrugger bases his defense. Articulating that "principle" loquaciously within a complex discursive framing, Moosbrugger

> wanted his deeds understood as the mishaps of an important philosophy of life. He hated no one as fervently as he hated psychiatrists who imagined they could dismiss his whole complex personality with a few foreign words ... [and] never missed a chance to demonstrate in open court his own superiority over the psychiatrists, unmasking them as puffed up dupes and charlatans who knew nothing at all.[7]

The textual form of Musil's solicitous attitude toward Moosbrugger matches the style with which Anton Chekhov's stories articulate an ethical sensibility. As Aleksandar Hemon puts it, Chekhov's

> gaze does not seek the moral center, because his mind does not care about the absolute, he sees the insignificant, he detects the minute and magnifies it because he senses the smallest quivers of the human soul ... his sensibility, his kindness allows him to pay extraordinary attention to his characters' idiosyncrasies.[8]

The historical event on which Musil bases Moosbrugger has been disclosed in much of Musil criticism: "In October 1911, a Bavarian carpenter by the name of Christian Voigt was indicted for killing a prostitute in Vienna's Prater Park."[9] The Voigt case was a media sensation drawing the attention of journalists, medical professionals, and the general public. Throughout the novel Musil provides an expansive language through both his characters and his authorial meta-statements that exceeds the reductive protocols of both criminal codes and psychiatric discourse. In another text he supplements the novel's ethics of form by returning to the Voight case. Writing with an explicit ethical focus Musil mirrors his protagonist Ulrich in *Qualities* with empathy for the perpetrator:

> Even a sex murderer is, in some cranny of his soul, full of inner hurt and hidden appeals; somehow the world is wronging him … In the criminal there is both a vulnerability and a resistance against the world, and both are present in every person … Before we destroy such a person – however despicable he may be – we ought to accept and preserve what was resistant in him and was degraded by his vulnerability. And no one does morality more harm than those … who in tepid horror over the form of a phenomenon, refuse to touch it.[10]

Musil's use of the second personal plural along with his reference to morality makes his essay a mandate about the appropriate collective civic response to "evil" deeds. His explicit statement of empathy in the essay and the aesthetic form in the novel with which he brings insights to the problem of negotiating the judgmental aspects of civic life are among the inspirations for the ethos guiding my inquiry. Heeding "the capacity of literary forms … to enter civic life,"[11] in this Introduction I pursue the form–ethos connection by revisiting Musil's ethical sensibility and supplement his empathetic approach to those peopling the Austrian civic sphere he constructs (criminal perpetrators among others) with attention to two other fiction writers who respond empathetically to violence in their national settings, Vasily Grossman, whose *Life and Fate* is situated on the Russian front during World War II's Battle of Stalingrad, and William Faulkner, whose *Light in August* is situated in the American South at the height of the Jim Crow period. Their texts implement the presumption that "[t]he arts … bear the pedagogical potential for activating an ethical mode of encounter with violence."[12]

To initiate an analysis of the way empathy is articulated through literary form I offer a brief contrast in my reading responses to two texts. Like Musil, the speculative fiction writer Octavia Butler was concerned with empathy, expressed in her case through the character Lauren Olamina in *The Parable of the Sower* who describes herself as having "hyper empathy syndrome."[13] When I read a passage in which Olamina describes a naked woman walking by her and responds empathetically by speculating about what the woman is experiencing, wondering whether she had just been raped or if she is high on a drug, I found myself pondering an ethical question. I wrote in the margin, "What do we owe to those we don't know but whose suffering is called to our attention?"[14] In contrast, while reading Musil I recognized his empathy as well, but instead of pondering a direct ethical question I found myself raising a meta-ethical one; I was prompted to ask how his approach, in which his protagonist does not explicitly nominate himself as empathetic, encourages thinking about empathy nevertheless. As I have suggested, the empathy that is conveyed by Musil's novelistic style is Chekhovian. He encourages speculative inquiry into the relationship between aesthetics and ethics through the sympathetic way he directs the gaze.

MUSIL'S MOOSBRUGGER AND THE PHENOMENOLOGY OF THE GAZE

As was the case with the actual murderer on whom he is based, Moosbrugger's crime draws the attention of disparate types. Focusing on "both rationalists – criminologists, psychiatrists, lawyers – and moralists … *Qualities* describes the faltering efforts of both of these groups to make sense of it."[15] For all of them, irrespective of whether he's regarded as worthy of either sympathetic understanding, punishment, or both, Moosbrugger is someone to be understood. In Foucault's terms he is a "criminal" in the sense in which that persona emerged in the mid-nineteenth century as an object of knowledge rather than merely an object of retaliation by the state. Foucault points out that prior to the mid-nineteenth-century the administration of criminality had no such persona. The official discourse on crime was exhausted by the catalogue of crimes and penalties without registering anything personal pertaining to the perpetrator (motives, biography, self-understanding, penchant for delusions, and so on).[16]

In the novel, although Moosbrugger's personhood becomes an incitement to knowledge for disparate individuals and groups distributed throughout social and professional orders, there is reflection and discussion but no consensus with regard to judging his responsibility for the killing. Musil's perspective is less concerned with what goes on in the courtroom than with "how large groups negotiate responsibility"[17] during a historical period of ideological ferment taking place amidst centrifugal social forces. His approach to that concept begins allegorically. As the novel opens a crowd has gathered around a truck that has struck a curb and a pedestrian whose body is lying in the street. Some, showing uncertainty about how to exercise their public responsibility, approach and handle the body by moving it tentatively and then returning it to its position, while some remain as bystanders and turn to each other in search of ways to put the event into a discourse that will justify their inaction. One bystander, a woman who "had a queasy feeling in the pit of her stomach, which she credited to compassion, although she mainly felt irresolute and helpless," is able to relax when a man next to her explains, "The brakes on these heavy trucks take too long to come to a full stop. This datum gives the woman some relief, and she thanked him with an appreciative glance. She did not really understand, or care to understand, the technology involved, as long as the explanation helped put this ghastly incident into perspective by reducing it to a technicality of no direct personal concern to her."[18]

As the narration proceeds Musil occasionally addresses the responsibility issue explicitly in the novel's meta-narrative moments. However, his main approach to the concept is implicit, expressed through literary form. The novel's "essayism ... [a narrative composed in the form of a long essay that thinks about responsibility] stresses the confluence of ethics and aesthetics."[19] As Musil puts it in a brief statement in another text, "For me, ethics and aesthetics are associated with the word *essay*."[20] Whereas Fredric Jameson has famously instructed about "the ideology of form,"[21] much of Musil's instruction in *Qualities* is about the *ethics* of form.

As for the frame within which Musil constructs an ethics, the text both states and stylistically shows how he regards the binary of good versus evil. He treats "Good and evil, duty and violation of duty [ontologically rather than moralistically as] ... forms in which the individual establishes an emotional balance between himself and the world."[22] Expressing that ambiguous binary phenomenologically through his characters as well as through meta-narrative interventions, insofar as *Qualities* references an evil act taking place it is ascribed not to the essential character of the perpetrator but to a moment of imbalance. As Musil states in a meta-narrative pause in the account of Moosbrugger's deeds, "Human nature is as capable of cannibalism as it is in the Critique of Pure Reason; the same convictions and qualities will serve to turn out either one, depending on circumstances, and very great external differences in the results correspond to very slight internal ones."[23] For Musil, "evil is not the opposite of good, or its absence; evil and good are parallel phenomena. They are not fundamental or ultimate moral antitheses."[24] As he ascribes radical contingency rather than enduring character to violent acts, Musil uses his own voice, that of his main protagonist, and textual form to evince an empathy toward moral monstrosity (a topic that is a main focus in Chapter 5). At one point, for example, he likens a criminal act to a "horse that goes berserk every time someone attempts to mount it" and goes on to point out that rather than receiving punishment "it is treated with special care, given the softest bandages, the best riders, the choicest fodder, and the most patient handling."[25]

Contrary to Musil's solicitous view of Moosbrugger, in *Qualities* the wide variety of types within the city, all fascinated by Moosbrugger's crime, are "reluctant to give up the idea of a villain, to banish the incident from their own world into the world of the insane," even though they are as much intrigued as they are censorious: "'finally something interesting for a change' ... While these people – ranging from 'busy officeholders to fourteen-year-old sons to house-wives befogged by their domestic cares' – sighed over such monstrosity, they were nevertheless more deeply preoccupied with it than with their own life's work."[26] It becomes evident as the Moosbrugger narrative thread progresses that Musil uses the Moosbrugger case to explore the diversities and vagaries of human subjectivity in general, which he renders as a delicate balance that "keeps the world in a transitional state between imbecility and sanity."[27] Figuring subjectivity as a "small basin hollowed out … [into which] many streamlets … trickle," he notes, "the inhabitant of a country has at least nine characters: a professional, a national, a civic, a class, a geographic, a sexual, a conscious, an unconscious, and possibly even a private character to boot."[28]

Ultimately, the way he invents the character of Ulrich is Musil's primary way of thinking about self-regarding versus other-regarding empathetic subjects. Ulrich's lack of his *own* qualities positions him as a mirror to reflect existing ideational versions of personhood. By inventing an empathic subject, a man without his own qualities, Musil has a detached medium through which to observe and evaluate – without a strong phenomenological inflection – the multiplicity in the range of characters his protagonist encounters. Nevertheless, that detachment is not ethically neutral. Exhibiting kindness rather than condemnation, Musil's Ulrich recognizes that Moosbrugger, a monster with a "pathological nature," had aspired to "a stronger and higher sense of himself" while caught in "a comically and distressingly clumsy struggle to gain by force a recognition of this sense of himself."[29] Moosbrugger is an extreme case of what is a more general society-wide struggle for recognizable personhood at a historical moment in which formerly stable markers for self-recognition have become unmoored. Characterizing the period, the sociologist Abram de Swaan refers to changes in "the canons of affect," a time in which "intimate relations have become less predictable because they no longer depend on the commands of social canons." Instead, "Relations between people are increasingly managed through negotiation rather than through command."[30] Among what are negotiated are changing norms with respect to what everyone owes others, as at individual and social levels people seek to negotiate civic normativity. Musil's novelistic embrace of empathetic kindness follows those negotiations while resisting adherence to a binary of good versus evil. Resistance to that binary is also a primary feature of Vasily Grossman's *Life and Fate*.

LIVES AND FATES

As is the case with the ethos articulated in Musil's *Qualities*, a Chekhovian sensibility shapes Grossman's novel. As *Life and Fate*'s translator Robert Chandler suggests, a "subtlety of moral understanding is one of the many qualities that link Grossman to a writer who worked in a very different scale: Anton Chekhov. Many individual characters in *Life and Fate* are surprisingly like Chekhov short stories."[31] That Grossman had Chekhov as a model is voiced by one of his novel's characters. In a conversation among several of them about the comparative value of famous Russian writers, one of them, Sokolov, says, "Chekhov's done the best of all … [he] took Russian democracy on his shoulders, the still unrealized Russian democracy … [his] path is the path of Russian freedom," and goes on to list Chekhov's "heroes" which include every possible social and occupational type and the "prisoners on the Sakhalin islands" (a gulag Chekhov visited to write a literary ethnography focused on their suffering).[32]

While Musil's novel has its monster, Moosbrugger, Grossman's has many, among whom are Zhuchenko and Khemlkov, soldiers in charge of herding Jews from a railway station to a concentration camp, the former with undisguised enjoyment, the latter going through the motions to survive, but both involved in unspeakable atrocities in the process. Much like the way Musil treats Moosbrugger, "Grossman enters into his most despicable characters" with "profound empathy." He treats his monsters "as men whose flaws and weaknesses have been exploited in the name of ideology."[33] His empathetic sensibility also gives the reader a deep appreciation of the mentality of those who are able to evince extraordinary kindness, for example the Russian Jewish doctor Sofya Levinton, who while incarcerated in a concentration camp neglects her own survival to bring comfort and assistance to others. Chekhov is Grossman's exemplar of an ethos of kindness; there is no category of person toward whom Chekhov doesn't feel a sense of moral solicitude. Grossman's character Ikonnikov is the voice through whom he privileges a Chekhovian kindness over adherence to "Good." Speaking to a fellow inmate in a prison camp, Ikonnikov says, "I saw the sufferings of the peasantry with my own eyes – and yet collectivization was carried out in the name of Good. I don't believe in your 'Good'. I believe in human kindness.'"[34] To Illustrate the difference, he juxtaposes "terrible Good with a capital 'G'" with "everyday kindness … private kindness of one individual towards another; a petty, thoughtless kindness; an unwitnessed kindness. Something we could call senseless kindness. A kindness outside any system of social or religious good."[35]

To situate the initial expression of Ikonnikov's version of kindness as "senseless," the novel refers to a thesis he wrote in which it is the main ethical perspective he hopes can endure against the ideological appropriation of "Good." It has to stand its empathetic ground, he says, "whenever we see the dawn of a an eternal good." Proceeding to postulate an ethically attuned historiography, Ikonnikov voices Grossman's main ethical observation. "Human history is not the battle of good struggling to overcome evil. It is a battle fought by a great evil struggling to crush a small kernel of human kindness."[36] As for how that small kernel is kept alive, the novel's ongoing narrative of the war implies that "Only individuals … can keep this kernel alive, and it can be spoken of only in language that has not been appropriated by state ideologies."[37]

The spaces of association in *Life and Fate* are also integral to the way the novel thinks about the conditions of possibility for empathetic conviviality in the midst of totalitarian violence. While urban space is the primary venue of interpersonal association in Musil's *Qualities*, in *Life and Fate* it's a warscape within which city boundaries have been effaced. However, within that warscape there is one administered space that is simultaneously the epitome of degradation and an arena of conviviality. It's a prison camp for Germany's war prisoners in view as the novel opens with a lyrical description of its setting:

> There was a low mist. You could see the glare of headlamps reflected in the high-voltage cables beside the road. It hadn't rained, but the ground was still wet with dew; the traffic lights cast blurred red spots on the asphalt. You could sense the breath of the camp from miles away.[38]

When Grossman then brings readers inside the camp, they become witness to an extraordinary temporary society of nationally and occupationally diverse prisoners who by necessity have transcended the usual strictures of social stratification:

> People unable to understand one another were bound by a shared fate. Specialists in molecular physics or ancient manuscripts lay on the bedboards beside Italian peasants and goat shepherds who were unable to sign their names. A man who used to order breakfast from his cook, worrying his housekeeper with his bad appetite, walked to work beside a man who had lived his life on a diet of salt-cod. Their wooden soles made the same clatter on the ground and they looked round with the same anxiety to see if the *Kossträger* [food distributer] were coming around with their rations.[39]

Despite lacking a shared language, that society of imperiled individuals manages a conviviality that revokes the usual class antagonisms and petty animosities pervasive within the social formations of national societies:

> in a language composed of smiles, glances, slaps on the back and ten or fifteen words of atrociously mangled Russian, French, German and English, [they] were able to discuss comradeship, solidarity, fellow-feeling, love of one's home, love of one's wife and children [using] … words that had originated in the camps themselves which were enough to express everything of real importance in the simple yet bewildering life of the prisoners.[40]

A page later, Grossman composes a telling juxtaposition:

> The Soviet prisoners-of-war were unable even to agree among themselves … The more they talked and argued, the less they understood each other. In the end they fell silent, full of mutual contempt and

hatred. And in this silence of the dumb and these speeches of the blind, in this medley of people bound together by the same grief, terror and hope, in this hatred and lack of understanding between men who spoke the same tongue, you could see much of the tragedy of the twentieth century.[41]

What we are encouraged to infer from the contrast is that the possibility of an ethical conviviality, a reciprocal exchange of empathetic recognition, requires separation from one's usual affiliations.

The multinational subsection of the prison camp that Grossman describes is the kind of space to which Foucault refers as a heterotopia, a space of otherness. Heterotopias, which are "absolutely different from all the sites that they reflect and speak about," function as venues of critique. They are spaces that defamiliarize the ordinary spaces containing the habitual, institutionalized relationships of the officially and popularly sanctioned life world.[42] The prison scene Grossman observes and characterizes, "People unable to understand one another were bound by a shared fate," is an ethical crucible and a microcosm of a possible world of empathetic intimacy that had been abrogated in the rest of the warscape that Grossman fastidiously observes and interprets. Written in the midst of a world of proliferating antipathies and compromised intimacies that Grossman encountered as a war journalist, his text wears its heart on its sleeve.

FAULKNER'S EMPATHY OF FORM

By way of transition, I suggest that finding the empathetic heart in Faulkner's novels is more difficult because they feature an ironic structure in which there exists what Wilson Harris labels a "sabotage of moral intention," each containing a "story … written one way while the moral intention tries to point to another."[43] Faulkner rarely makes authorial remarks in his novels. "Most of his stories," as Warren Beck points out, "[are] devoted to dramatic form and to the perspective it supplies"; they are "told largely through the consciousness of participant characters."[44] However, the spaces of experience and enunciation are also crucial to how and about what his novels think. My analysis here is focused on his *Light in August* (1932) because of the way the narrative trajectory, which is mainly concerned with the fate of the novel's protagonist Joe Christmas, maps the Jim Crow South's racial-spatial order while concerned, as are Musil's and Grossman's novels, with evil – a "theatring of evil" in Faulkner's words.[45] It is a work in which Faulkner articulates an anti-racist ethos through the way he treats the many voices and behaviors of the characters. Joe Christmas, whose appearance and biography defy the white–black binary that defines the South's racial order, is a disconcerting presence wherever he goes because he cannot be definitively coded. He is light-skinned enough to pass as white, and there is no information about his ancestry to make a case for either a white or black parentage. One of the places in which Christmas resides provides a bridge between Grossman's and Faulkner's novels because the prison where he is incarcerated briefly toward the end of the novel is the only space in the journey Faulkner invents for him that is not racially segregated. The prison as a Southern social institution is comparable to the prison camp that Grossman treats in *Life and Fate* because it's a heterotopia that deviates from other Southern institutions. It provides a space from which to reflect on the other normalized spaces in the South's racialized society.[46]

Before Joe Christmas appears, the novel explores other lives in a series of portraits of individuals who ultimately connect enough to give the novel's main drama social coherence. The primary narrative thread, focused on Christmas's fate, is an aspect of the text that much of Faulkner criticism takes up, but none more exhaustively and style-attuned as James Snead's. Noting the way Christmas's presence is socially destabilizing wherever he goes, Snead captures the essence of his role: "Throughout the novel, Christmas is the sign of resistance to fixed signs. He is the quintessence of indeterminable essence … ambiguous from his first description: 'the stranger … looked like a tramp, yet not like a tramp either.' We never discover his true age."[47] When he is killed (having decided not to hide from the pursuit led by the violent Percy Grimm), "the men who come to brutalize him; they certainly want to harm him but their motives are in large part definitional."[48]

While Christmas is a disconcerting enigma for the novel's other characters, for Faulkner he is a thought vehicle that enjoins the novel's writing problematic as well as its ethos. As Snead recognizes, "Joe Christmas is an idea rather than a person, a character who remains almost completely opaque … [he] avidly resists the properties and effects of written imprintation."[49] Put differently (as a commentary on Deleuzian philosophy suggests), "The person [Christmas in this case] is not a 'subject' but a device or contrivance … [a character that provides] a profoundly aesthetic account of the masks that define civil and juridical existence."[50] Faulkner's protagonist is thus comparable to Musil's Ulrich; he's an ideational device who, as Maurice Blanchot characterizes the latter, is "a living presence that becomes a thought"[51] (although Ulrich is more purposive and verbally performative than Faulkner's Christmas who lives his existence in the novel ascriptively as a series of abjections). While, as Blanchot notes, Musil's Ulrich becomes "a theory of himself,"[52] Christmas is an object of the way others conceive him. "From the moment Joe Christmas appears, he is seen as what others say about him, he is only a thought in other people's minds."[53] Nevertheless, Faulkner lends agency to Christmas. Although he dwells on his character's ambiguity, which is disconcerting for the people in the town, he also composes the way Christmas responds to it:

> All his life people attempt to force him to be what they insist he must be ... in the fifteen years of wandering he tries life as a black man living with Negroes, and as white man attempting to live with whites. But ultimately he chooses to be neither – he will simply be himself.[54]

As is typical of Faulkner's compositional strategy, those who populate the novel *speak* their minds. While he shows the way the South's racial division is spatially constituted, he also has it repeatedly realized in conversations. As Richard Godden puts it, "For Faulkner decisions about identity are communal and collaborative; as such they issue from a debate whose nature is most apparent in vocal acts."[55] Inasmuch as Faulkner's authorial voice is largely absent from the novel, which is dramatic rather than essayistic, the empathy he shows toward his tragic protagonist is compositional. He repeatedly turns to the spaces of social negotiation where people attempt to make sense of Christmas. The fraught speculations on Christmas's race take place among

> wives and families about supper tables in electrically lights rooms and in remote hill cabins with kerosene lamps, and on [a] ... slow, pleasant Sunday while they are squatted in their clean shirts and decorated suspenders, with peaceful pipes about country churches or about shady dooryards of houses where visiting teams and cars were tethered and parked along the fence and the women folks were in the kitchen, getting dinner, they told it again: "He don't look any more like a [n-word] than I do."[56]

Because his antagonists cannot legally invoke Christmas's racial ambiguity as a reason to attack him, they turn to subterfuge, pursuing and killing him for alleged criminal and immoral acts. There is inconclusive evidence that he has murdered the woman Joanna Burden on whose property he has lived (and with whom he has been sexually intimate, it is rumored). However, doubtless more important as regards their killing rage is his seeming to act as if he enjoys white privilege:

> He went into a barbershop like a white man, and because he looked like a white man, they never suspected him ... For him to be a murderer and all dressed up and walking the town like he dared them to touch him when he ought to have been skulking and hiding in the woods, muddy and dirty and running. It was like he never even knew he was a murderer, let alone a [n-word] too.[57]

How then can one identity Faulkner's ethical point of view? Unlike Musil and Grossman who have spokesmen deliver theirs, Ulrich and Ikonnikov respectively, in Faulkner's case, "which of his spokesmen [convey his point of view] cannot be decided except in terms of the preponderance and system of his ideas."[58] Certainly there are hints articulated through the "compassionate observers" through whom Faulkner enacts empathetic moments – for example, the defrocked minister Hightower in whose presence Christmas is murdered.[59] However, it is mainly through narrative form and allegorical intention that one can discern the ethical perspective implicit in Christmas's story. Certainly, Faulkner evinces empathy for the way his early maltreatment and the subsequent continuous abjection wherever he has gone has made him vulnerable and prone to acting out violently. However, inasmuch as Christmas is more an idea than a person, Faulkner's empathy is directed toward the Southern society as a whole which he saw as tragically caught up self-destructive impulses for which there is a lack of self-understanding. Christmas is a victim of a society-wide will to racial truth.

As for the meta-ethics of Faulkner's writing, the narrative offers no direct evaluation of Christmas's fate. The text thinks about it obliquely. On the one hand, there is the distorted biblical allegory – Joe Christmas has the same initials as Jesus Christ – but on the other, rather than being a martyr who redeems a sinful order, he is a victim. Denied *more than* "three times" (Matthew 26:34), his fate exposes an irrational order that doesn't know itself. Insofar as Christmas's abbreviated life has a lesson, it is less about the injustice of racial segregation than about the will to racial truth that sustains it. Faulkner's approach to a point of view is to explore the problem as a novelist. Frustrating the reader's search for a definitive conclusion, the novel's approach to civic empathy consists in the way the reader is implicated in the text; she is enjoined to engage in self-reflection. As Snead puts it, while "Christmas's tragic death provides the gruesome climax of the novel," what is more important is the way the novel's "syntax" yields ambiguity. "Joe is the uncertainty that resists being made into writing. He is more an absence than anything else."[60] The ethos that emerges, Snead suggests, lies in literary form. "The uncertainties surrounding the meaning of Joe Christmas's murder, implicate author, town, and reader in that same web of guilt. We all owe a debt, of sorts, to any victim."[61]

By way of transition from what I learn from Musil's, Grossman's, and Faulkner's compositionally articulated empathy to the chapters that follow, I want to repeat the question I raised in reaction to the empathetic moment in Octavia Butler's *The Parable of the Sower*, "What do we owe to those we don't know but whose suffering is called to our attention?" Apart from the object of the sentence, "suffering," there are two other words with crucial implications for this book's civic life inquiry, the pronoun "we" and the possessive "our." Those grammatical choices elevate the mentality-related concepts – a sense of one's debt to alterity ("owe") and the demands on one's awareness ("attention") – to the level of collective and civic as opposed to individual responsibility. Heeding the implications of how I was prompted to respond to that textual moment sets up the way I want to characterize the explorations of civic life in the chapters by highlighting some of the crucial protagonists in each of them.

CHAPTER 1

The main intention sustaining the textual itinerary I curate in Chapter 1, "The Civic Lives of Grief," is to make civically relevant a human experience that has been privatized as an asset for the "health" profession, psychiatry. No one has provided a more compelling rationale for such a conceptual move than Judith Butler, who evinces a Faulknerian sensibility about the vagaries of a social unconscious:

> Many people think that grief is privatizing, that it returns us to a solitary situation, but I think it has and can furnish a sense of political community of a complex order ... it seems that what grief displays is the way in which we are in the thrall of our relations with others in ways that we cannot always recount or explain, in ways that often interrupt the self-conscious account of ourselves we might try to provide, in ways athat challenge the very notion of ourselves as autonomous and in control.[62]

In accord with Butler's statement, the main contention in Chapter 1 is that rather than a clinical disorder, "prolonged grief" – recently added to the American Psychiatry Association's manual of mental disorders (DSM-5) – should be regarded as an asset. When experienced by those who have the ability to compose reactions to their grief in compelling, publicly available texts, grief gives rise to an important politico-aesthetic intervention in the civic sphere. Among the protagonists treated in the chapter is the late Argentine expatriate poet Juan Gelman, whose son and daughter-in-law were murdered during Argentina's Dirty War (1976–83) and his grandchild (a granddaughter with whom he was eventually reunited) sent off to Uruguay for adoption. Written while in exile in Mexico, Gelman's poetry indicts the acts of a murderous regime, discloses the effects of their actions on his family's fate, and assembles an archive of commentary on events. He contributes a poetic historiography to be shared among other victims as well as with the world community as a whole. In Gelman's published work the world has received a treasure chest of civically relevant feelings and ideas, which, had the expression of his "prolonged grief" been treated as a clinical disorder, would have been confined to the notes of a professional "healer" who is paid by the hour.

CHAPTER 2

Atom Egoyan's film *Ararat* (2002) is among the several texts explored in Chapter 2, "Civic Cleansing," which is concerned with the way states engage in willful amnesia, officially deleting historical events and periods that weigh against the national image they wish to perpetuate. Although the Armenian Genocide, an event that Turkey enduringly refuses to acknowledge, provides the historical basis of the film, Egoyan's concern is mainly with the event's afterlife as it persists in discourses and registers itself in contemporary bodies. As I note in the chapter, the film is "less concerned with disclosing the historical truth of an event, which Turkey steadfastly misrepresents, than with sorting the way experiential truth resides in the afterlife of the event." I suggest that the film's key moments occur "when bodies are affected by scenes and events that nudge ... buried pain and trauma ... to the surface."

While the film shows many bodies experiencing buried pasts at such moments, the most affecting scenes involve the painter Arshile Gorky (Simon Abkarian) who went into exile without his mother with whom he had a close bond. Two of his gestures articulate his embodied recollection of a traumatic past. In one scene he is shown redoing a portrait he had painted based on a photograph of himself as a young boy with his mother. Because his mother died while still in Turkey, leaving him to go into exile without her, he expresses his lament about having lost the feeling of her caresses by erasing the hands from the portrait. The other gesture hits the viewer suddenly. At one point, as he is painting in his studio while listening to the Armenian music he heard in his youth playing on his record player, he stops painting in mid-brush stroke, backs away from his easel, and executes dance steps that are part of his muscle memory. For Egoyan, bodies in general and Arshile Gorky's in particular are among the main texts through which his *Ararat* testifies to what he calls "the truth" of the event. The truth of history according to Egoyan lies in what remains sensible and figurable to those who experience it, not in a narrative's fidelity to historical events.

CHAPTER 3

Dwayne LeBlanc's documentary film *Civic*, the featured text in Chapter 3, "Civic Automobility," illuminates aspects of Los Angeles's Black civic life from the space of Booker's (Barrington Darius) car. Situating the viewer in the back seat of what becomes a mobile civic space, the film narrative follows Booker's return to LA after years away. Driving through his former neighborhood streets, picking up passengers (mostly his former friends and acquaintances), he is brought up to date on the experience of being Black in LA and schooled on his civic responsibilities. His last passenger, Harmonie, is the most challenging. Dismissing such Booker subterfuges as "I just came back to check on my mom" by a young man who ultimately confesses identity confusion, Harmonie (to quote from the chapter) "draws him toward a more civic self-understanding, realized in his old LA neighborhood's participation in what Achille Mbembe refers to as 'the collection of voices, pronouncements, discourses, forms of knowledge' that constitute 'Black reason.'" Subtitled "Driving White, Driving Black," among what the chapter contrasts is the unalloyed civic eligibility of white drivers, while Black drivers have found automobility to be both liberating and perilous, a peril exemplified in the chapter by the fate of Coalhouse Walker, Jr. in E. L. Doctorow's novel *Ragtime*, who is victimized because he acts as if he "didn't know he was a Negro."

CHAPTER 4

Chapter 4, "The Civic Lives of Things," a chapter that emphasizes non-human protagonists, is composed to show the way clothing fashions, what Roland Barthes calls "vestimentary signs," are statements about their wearers' location within social and civic orders.[63] By way of a brief illustration, I select two scenes the chapter rehearses, one from Martin Scorsese's film *The Age of Innocence* (1993), an adaptation of Edith Wharton's late nineteenth-century "jazz age" novel by the same name, and one from Jane Campion's film *The Power of the Dog* (2023), which depicts ranch life in early twentieth-century Montana. In Scorsese's film there's a stunning bowler hat scene. Right after a scene that shows the protagonist-would-be lovers, Newland Archer and Ellen Olenska, departing after one of their desire-inhibited encounters, there's a cut to a large phalanx of hunched-over men in bowler hats marching along a Manhattan sidewalk. Shot in slow motion, the scene foregrounds their bowler hats slowly bobbing up and down in a shared rhythmic choreography. The hats are a fashion development that became pervasive during the belle époque (1890–1910) and were worn by tradesmen, businessmen, servants, clerical workers, artisans as well as laborers, a fashion that distinguished them from the leisure class, indicated by a prior scene in which men of a leisure class are at a garden party wearing straw boaters. In contrast, the vestimentary homogeneity of the leisure class is more explicitly symbolized by women's white silk gloves. As the film narrative turns to a party in an upper-class mansion, the camera cuts away from the arriving guests and does a long take of several pairs of the gloves on an entry table. They have been shed by the female guests on their way to the main rooms to join their hosts at a wealthy family's party. The shot is also historiographic, in this case registering an alteration in the fashion system. At the end of the 1800s, it was no longer fashionable for the leisure class to wear their gloves indoors.

A different cinematic historiography structures a glove scene in Jane Camion's *The Power of the Dog*. The film's setting, a Montana ranch in the 1920s, registers the end of the Euro-American "ethnogenesis,"[64] the whitening of the American continent which destroyed what the fictional Mason and Dixon in Thomas Pynchon's novel recognize as another "civic entity."[65] As (Shoshone) Native Americans Edward Nappo and his son pass by the ranch owned by the Burbank brothers, George Burbank's wife Rose rushes to catch up with them and offers them cow hides that her brother-in-law Phil – an exemplar of what Herman Melville refers to as "the metaphysics of Indian hating"[66] – has refused to make available. Nappo accepts the hides and has his son give Rose a pair of gloves that they have made from cow hide. That exchange turns back the historical clock to a period before the money form had largely displaced the exchanges involved in Native and Euro-American reciprocity. The encounter calls attention to a period in which gift exchanges, as Marcel Mauss famously points out, involved the creation of symbolic capital and the establishment of civic bonds. As I note in the chapter, less important than the materials exchanged were the intersubjective relations they established.[67] The glove scene enacts one of the film's allegorical intentions by turning what had seemed to be primarily a family drama into a reflection on a repressed history, a period in which Euro- and Native Americans negotiated a shared civic life.

CHAPTER 5

The textual itinerary in Chapter 5, "The Civic Lives of Gender," which addresses historical and contemporary reactions to transvestite and transgender persons, begins with an analysis of the concept of monstrosity elaborated in the writings of George Canguilhem and Michel Foucault. Extensive space is allocated to the latter's analysis and illustration of official and civic reactions to the case of Herculine Barbin, a nineteenth-century hermaphrodite who was driven to suicide. The chapter moves ultimately to an analysis of the hospitality toward transvestites, non-binary, and transgendered persons in Pedro Almodóvar's films, calling special attention to two of his characters. One is Juan Agrado in *All About My Mother* (1999), a trans person who does an improvised standup comedy routine for a theater audience in Barcelona that was about to leave because a theatrical performance of Tennessee William's *A Streetcar Named Desire* had been cancelled. After going on stage to offer a substitute act, she (a former he) retains most of the audience with a comical tale of the many surgeries she needed to accomplish becoming a woman. Doing a parody of commitments to the authenticity of gender roles, she says, "It costs a lot to be authentic but one can't be stingy with these things." Like Canguilhem and Foucault, Almodóvar's Agrado introduces the concept of monstrosity but in a satiric mood that solicits laughter rather than obloquy. Referring to her chest surgeries she says, "Tits, two because I am no monster, 70,000 each."

The other character receiving substantial attention is a hospital nurse, the sheltered, socially and romantically inexperienced Benigno (Javier Cámara) in *Talk to Her* (2002), who while caring for his love object, the comatose Alicia

(Leonor Watling), impregnates her, loses his job, and ends up in prison. As it's put it in the chapter, Benigno's monstrousness suits Almodóvar's cinematic critique of normalizing gender protocols because he's a "monster" who "reveals the unpredictability of categories, bodies, narratives and lives." As Almodóvar states in a reflection on the monstrosity he lends to Benigno, the film is in part "about madness, about a type of madness so close to tenderness and common sense that it does not diverge from normality." I suggest that Chapter 5's "assemblage of multiple gender tonalities in a montage of media genres" does what the prior chapters do. It provides a view of civic life that (quoting Hil Malatino) challenges the "monotone of the state," which, caught up in the management of its population, "'privileges' and 'fetishizes the eternal and stable ... fixed, immutable and essential understandings of being.'"

NOTES

1. Michael J. Shapiro, *Aesthetics of Equality* (New York: Oxford University Press, 2023).
2. Hannah Arendt, "Thinking and Moral Considerations: A Lecture," *Social Research* 38, no. 3 (Autumn 1971): 418.
3. Slavoj Žižek suggests that those performing as part of the bureaucratization of genocide derived an "additional kick," a "*jouissance*" from the performance of "killing as a complicated administrative-criminal operation": *The Plague of Fantasies* (New York: Verso, 1997), p. 55.
4. Robert Musil, *The Man without Qualities*, trans. Sophie Wilkins (New York: Picador, 2017).
5. *Ibid.*, p. 39.
6. *Ibid.*, p. 39.
7. *Ibid.*, p. 52.
8. Aleksandar Hemon, "Introduction" to Anton Chekhov, *The Duel*, trans. Constance Garnett (New York: Modern Library, 2003), pp. xiv–xv.
9. Gabriela Stoicea, "Moosbrugger and the Case for Responsibility in Robert Musil's *Der Mann ohne Eigenschaften*," *The German Quarterly* 91, no. 1 (Winter 2018): 49.
10. Robert Musil, "Moral Fruitfulness (1913)," in *Precision and Soul*, ed. and trans. Burton Pike and David S. Luft (Chicago: University of Chicago Press, 1990), p. 39.
11. I am borrowing that apropos phrase from Steven N. Zwicker, "Reading the Margins," in Kevin Sharpe and Steven N. Zwicker (eds.), *Refiguring Revolutions: Aesthetics and Politics from the English Revolution to the Romantic Revolution* (Berkeley: University of California Press, 1998), p. 102.
12. Marco Abel, *Violent Affect: Literature, Cinema, and Critique after Representation* (Lincoln: University of Nebraska Press, 2007), p. 189.
13. Octavia E. Butler, *Parable of the Sower* (New York: Grand Central, 1993), p. 277.
14. As Desiderius Erasmus famously suggested, "Reading worked best when it was conducted with pen in hand and notebook at the ready; the goal was not simply to commune with the past but to translate its idioms into one's own." Quoted in

Catherine Nicholson, "Livelier Than the Living," *The New York Review of Books* 711, no. 11 (June 20, 2024): 8.

15. Zeynep Talay-Turner, "Musil on Ethics and Aesthetics: Essayism as a Way of Living," *Philosophy and Literature* 39, no. 1A (September, 2015): 50.

16. See Michel Foucault, "About the Concept of the Dangerous Individual in Nineteenth Century Psychiatry," *International Journal of Law and Psychiatry* 1, no. 1 (1978): 1–18.

17. Stoicea, "Moosebrugger and the Case for Responsibility," p. 58.

18. Musil, *The Man without Qualities*, p. 7.

19. Stoicea, "Moosebrugger and the Case for Responsibility," p. 49.

20. Robert Musil, "On the Essay," in Pike and Luft (eds.), *Precision and Soul*, p. 48.

21. See for example Fredric Jameson, "The Ideology of Form: Partial Systems in 'La Vieille Fille'," *SubStance* 5, no. 15 (1976): 29–49.

22. Musil, "Moral Fruitfulness," p. 37.

23. Musil, *The Man without Qualities*, p. 268.

24. Musil, "Moral Fruitfulness," p. 38.

25. Musil, *The Man without Qualities*, p. 179.

26. *Ibid.*, p. 39.

27. *Ibid.*, p. 178.

28. *Ibid.*, p. 24.

29. *Ibid.*, p. 50.

30. Abram de Swaan, *The Management of Normality* (New York: Routledge, 1990), pp. 155–6.

31. Robert Chandler, "Introduction" to Vasily Grossman, *Life and Fate*, trans. Robert Chandler (New York: NYRB Classics, 2006), p. 370.

32. Grossman, *Life and Fate*, p. 282.

33. The observation belongs to Tess Lewis, "The Captive Soul: Vasily Grossman's Life and Fate," *The Hudson Review* 59, no. 2 (Summer 2006): 338.

34. Grossman, *Life and Fate*, p. 29.

35. *Ibid.*, p. 407.

36. *Ibid.*, p. 410.

37. Chandler, "Introduction," p. 356.

38. Grossman, *Life and Fate*, p. 580.

39. *Ibid.*, p. 604.

40. *Ibid.*, p. 32.

41. *Ibid.*, p. 33.

42. See Michel Foucault, "Of Other Spaces," trans. Jay Miscowiec, *Diacritics* 16, no. 1 (Spring 1986): 22–7.

43. Wilson Harris, "Preface: Cross-Cultural Community and the Womb of Space," in Andrew Bundy (ed.), *Selected Essays of Wilson Harris* (New York: Routledge, 1999), p. 70.

44. Warren Beck, "Faulkner's Point of View," *College English* 22: 2 (November, 1960), 88.

45. The Faulkner quote is in Richard Chase's reading of *Light in August*: "The Stone and the Crucifixion," *The Kenyon Review* 10, no. 4 (1948): 539.

46. For a similar analysis see Martin Stray Egberg's Master's thesis in English Literature at The Arctic University of Norway: "Racialized Space in William Faulkner's *Light in August*," at https://munin.uit.no/bitstream/handle/10037/13726/thesis.pdf?sequence=2&isAllowed=y (last accessed August 27, 2024).

47. James Snead, *Figures of Division: William F. Faulkner's Major Novels* (New York: Methuen, 1986), p. 88.

48. *Ibid.*, p. 93.

49. *Ibid.*, p. 89.

50. Edward Mussawir, *Jurisdiction in Deleuze* (New York: Routledge, 2011), pp. 22–3.

51. Maurice Blanchot, "Musil," in *The Book to Come*, trans. Charlotte Mandell (Stanford, CA: Stanford University Press, 2003), p. 140.

52. *Ibid.*, p. 142.

53. Alfred Kazin, "The Stillness of *Light in August*, in O. W. Vikery (ed.), *Light in August and the Critical Spectrum* (Belmont, CA: Wadsworth, 1971), p. 263.

54. John L. Longley, Jr. "Joe Christmas: The Hero in the Modern World," *Virginia Quarterly Review* 33, no. 2 (Spring 1957): 233.

55. Richard Godden, "Call Me [N-word]: Race and Speech in Faulkner's 'Light in August'," *Journal of American Studies* 14, no. 2 (August 1980): 236.

56. William Faulkner, *Light in August* (Digital Fire ebook, 2022), p. 349.

57. *Ibid.*, p. 350.

58. Beck, "Faulkner's Point of View," p. 88.

59. *Ibid.*, p. 90.

60. *Ibid.*

61. Snead, *Figures of Division*, p. 97.

62. Judith Butler, "Violence, Mourning, Politics," *Studies in Gender and Sexuality* 4, no. 1 (2003): 13.

63. See Roland Barthes, *The Fashion System*, trans. Matthew Ward and Richard Howard (Berkeley: University of California Press, 1990).

64. The expression belongs to William Boelhower, *Through a Glass Darkly: Ethnic Semiosis in American Literature* (New York: Oxford University Press, 1987).

65. See Thomas Pynchon's *Mason & Dixon* (New York: Penguin, 2012), p. 649.

66. See Herman Melville, *The Confidence-Man* (New York: Harper Perennial Classics, 2014).

67. See Marcel Mauss, *The Gift: The Form and Reason for Exchange in Archaic Societies* (New York: W. W. Norton, 2000).

1. THE CIVIC LIVES OF GRIEF

As Henri Bergson instructs us, people are durational subjects whose perceptions are shaped by accumulated memories. As a result, the apprehension of events is suffused with recollection; "it … is the recollections of memory that link … instants to each other and interpolate the past in the present."[1] Crucially as well, as Stefanie Fishel reminds us, "We are all bodies, but we are often not aware of how corporeality matters."[2] Noting the effects of that corporeality on consciousness, William Connolly refers to "the role of affect in perception and thought"[3] and adds complexity to the memory–recollection relationship:

> Memory itself is essentially layered: one dimension takes the shape of recollection images; another of unconscious dispositions and habits without recollection consolidated from past shocks, joyous events, and routines; yet another of residues, traces, or scars in which, for example, an incompletely formed intention previously blocked from consolidation festers again in a new setting. So only one dimension of memory takes the form of recollection, and even recollections vary among themselves in the extent and ways to which they are affect-imbued.[4]

Taken together, those instructions tell us that recollection gains affective density over time because an essential aspect of embodiment is an increasing capacity to be affected and to affect others. As Brian Massumi puts it, "the capacitation of the body as it's gearing up for passage toward a diminished or augmented state is completely bound up with the lived past of the body."[5] The composer/vocalist Ray Charles effectively acknowledges that observation, remarking that affective density increasingly manifests itself in a singer's voice: "singers don't reach their full potential until 50, because a whole life shows up in the voice."[6] Expressed similarly, albeit in a different artistic medium, the painter Francis Bacon attests to it as well. Asked why he "didn't start painting full-time till quite late," he said, "I couldn't. When I was young I didn't, in a sense, have a real subject. It's through my life and knowing other people that a subject has really grown."[7] Although it's evident that accumulated experiences create a fuller embodied archive on which creative work can draw, there is a sense in which a young person's relatively small archive can be an asset for critical interpretation. Describing what he refers to as "the uncluttered mind of a young person," the standup comedian Steven Wright says, "A kid is like an alien who just got off a spaceship and is looking around."[8] His implication is that because young people have yet to build a deep reservoir of experience, they are less afflicted by recollections that invade perception and are thus enabled to see things in new ways.

That exception noted, many of my pedagogical experiences attest to the positive effects of accumulated affective density, which migrates into perceptions and produces empathic modes of reception. I have often taught film courses at the University of Hawaii at Manoa (my home institution) to a mixed audience of registered undergraduate students and older citizens from town who can attend courses in a program that welcomes interested *kupunas* (the Hawaiian word for elders). When I have shown a film that has strong emotional resonances, as the film ends and the lights go on it is mostly I and some of the (other) *kupunas* who show signs of having wept. Why? Doubtless because we have more accumulated grief. As Amanda Petrusich points out in her review of the song "The grief it gets me, the weird goodbyes" by The Sad Dads, there is an "ambient sadness … We are always losing, or leaving, or being left, in ways both minor and vast … a person you once loved but lost touch with, A friend moved to a new own … An old dog. A former colleague."[9] Connolly suggests that in the face of such losses, "it is wise, perhaps, to write them up, to encourage them to play positive roles in life rather than to sink into sealed vessels or slink into other darker places awaiting them."[10] Heeding Petrusich's observation and Connolly's suggestion, this chapter's inquiry is concerned with the ways that grief shapes civic life by inspiring not only creative artistic expression but also productive reception.[11] With regard to the latter, on such classroom occasions I share my perspective that grief is a powerful resource for affectively attuned interpretation. The more one has accumulated – the more filled up is one's personal "encyclopedia," as Umberto Eco puts it[12] – the more likely it will manifest as an embodied resonance, a capacity to be affected that impacts one's reception of a film narrative and encourages critical reflection. Yet at the same time I want to acknowledge that I have been edified by the observations of those with less "cluttered minds," who see things that my years of investment in interpreting my experiences with a "prepopulated mind"[13] have me missing.

Because those pedagogical moments dividing the film reception of my viewing audience have enabled me to appreciate how prolonged grief (my own as well as that of others) can be a vital interpretive resource that attunes one to what others are experiencing, I was intrigued when I read about a professional organization's appropriation of grief: "After more than a decade of argument, psychiatry's most powerful body in the United States [The American Psychiatric Association] has included a controversial addition in their diagnostic manual, 'prolonged grief disorder.'"[14] That notable event in the contemporary history of psychiatry is an instance of what Michel Foucault refers to as the "productivity of psychiatric power."[15] It's an instance of what he identifies throughout his corpus as power-produced *assujetissement* (subjectivation), a paradoxical form of selfhood assignment that "denotes both the becoming of the subject and the process of subjection."[16] It is also an instance of the profession's economic self-interest. Through the creation of grieving client eligibility for psychiatric counseling, secured when such grieving was included in the March 2022 edition of the American Psychiatric Association's diagnostic manual, the DSM-5 (often referred to as "psychiatry's bible"),[17] psychiatry augments its position in the dispensing of health care, allowing "clinicians [to] … bill insurance companies for treating people for the condition."[18] As Jacques Donzelot points out in his historical analysis of psychiatry's imperial ambitions, by the late nineteenth century "its whole theoretical effort … was to consist in trying to align their own reasons for wanting to extend their work beyond the asylum to the social body as a whole."[19]

THE DIAGNOSTIC MANUAL'S PSYCHOANALYTIC PATRIMONY

The diagnostic contributions of the acknowledged father of psychoanalysis Sigmund Freud are largely absent from the current version of the manual. Although "Freud was the first to introduce the concept of grief into the psychological lexicon,"[20] pathologizing melancholy but insisting that mourning, however prolonged, "never occurs to us as a pathological condition" to "refer to medical treatment,"[21] the APA's Diagnostic and Statistical Manuals of Mental Disorders (DSMs) ultimately adopted "neutral language that did not endorse specific and controversial theoretical viewpoints (Freudian, psychoanalytic theories among others)."[22] The scientific aspirations of the APA have not been compatible with what I will call Freudian poesis. Although, as I've noted elsewhere, Freud's texts are "epistemologically urgent" – they abound in what Roland Barthes refers to as epistemological codes – the textual practices with which he vindicates his interpretive claims are framed within a story, a "family romance" running through many of his case studies. Operating within an aesthetic register, it's a drama of the way a developing ego emerges within a family dynamic.[23] Although Freud employs a grammar that allocates that story to a psychic reality (with such sentences as "the schema presents"), the story is his and as literature it is richly figured and elaborated. Alerted to that feature of Freudian analysis, Shoshana Felman suggests, "Psychoanalysis is not what it should be ... without this cultivated receptivity to literature." Because it requires "an analytic literary ear, a tuned in analytic listening, attentive to the resonances and to the nuances of the patient's language, [it] requires ... something like poetic intuition."[24]

Nevertheless, a literary framing "is never explicitly programmed by Freud, even though literature imposes itself periodically with insistence within the totality of the Freudian context."[25] In his case studies he represents his patient's recollections with borrowed figures incorporated within the "family romance" he composes. It's a story, or what Peter Brooks calls a "master plot," in which the dynamic of "life" for Freud is the condition of possibility for the narrative articulated in each individual plot.[26] Moreover, a review of Freud's texts reveals borrowed figures from "multiple sign systems ... optics, thermodynamics, neurophysiology, zoology pharmacology, anthropology, archeology" on the one hand, and "some textual and bibliographical" sources on the other: "(oneirocriticism, biblical and classical literary criticism)" as well as from "the occult (telepathy, totemism, animism, magic)."[27] For Freud, as is the case for other versions of "first psychoanalysis, literature seems to play a decisive, catalytic role,"[28] even though in Freud's case, as he incorporates "repeatedly thematic interpretation of literary texts,"[29] he remains ambivalent about "poetic effects."[30] He occasionally "places literature on equal footing with psychoanalytic theory, yet without inferring all the possible consequences of the equality."[31] As a commentator notes, "Freud, with his interest in archaeology worked like a novelist to recreate the past ... using interpretations to give [his patient's stories] new meaning, and creating form and significance out of the of the chaos of the unconscious."[32] By the time Freud got to his most notable late thinking in *Beyond the Pleasure Principle*, his writing, as Jean Laplanche puts it, is "only sporadically and superficially subordinated to logical principles"[33]; it is, among other things, a "vast ... metabiological fresco."[34]

In contrast with the poesis of Freud's texts, consisting in figuratively rich narratives of the dynamics of psychic life, which attest to psychoanalysis's historiographic potential (to which I refer later in the inquiry), are the texts of the German psychiatrist Emil Kraepelin (1856–1926) which bring that dynamism to a halt in figuratively barren classificatory inventories. Yet it was

"Kraepelin's 'new way of classifying illness' [that] became the foundation for the development of the psychiatry association's DSM."[35] Constructing "psychiatric disorder as discrete entities," Kraepelin's rather than Freud's writings serve as the dominant patrimony of the diagnostic manual as it has developed over the years.[36] While Freudianism has disappeared from the APA manual's treatment of disorders, Kraepelin's influence persists. The manual's architects and users have regarded his classification system as the fulfillment of a scientific approach to mental health – "science in the service of medicine," as one practitioner puts it.[37]

Considering the stylistic difference between Freud and Kraepelin, I suggest that to distinguish Freudian psychology from the contemporary Kraepelin-influenced psychiatric perspective one should heed Foucault's insight (in his *Madness and Civilization*) that Freud had attempted to "reinstate the dialogue with unreason that had been broken off by positivist psychiatry,"[38] and attend to a juxtaposition, that between what Franco Berardi refers to as poetry and financialization. As Berardi puts it, while "poetry is the reopening of the indefinite, the ironic act of exceeding the established meaning of words," in the contemporary situation of financialization, "the economy is the universal grammar traversing the different levels of human activity."[39] Siding with the way poesis challenges the "established meaning of words," as I pursue alternatives to the way the current version of the American Psychiatric Association's handbook constructs "prolonged grief" as an asset for the profession, I turn to the works of two poet/writers, the Argentine Juan Gelman and the Chilean Ariel Dorfman. In both cases, most of their work, inspired by *their* "prolonged grief," has been produced from exile after escaping state terror in their home countries.

In accord with Berardi's juxtaposition of financialization and poetry, Gelman refers in the opening and closing lines of one of his poems to the inherent hostility of poetry to capitalism.[40] However, more crucial to the point of my focus on his life and writing are what he experienced while he was in exile, first in Europe and subsequently in Mexico during Argentina's "Dirty War." Gelman's son and daughter-in-law were murdered and his granddaughter Macarena (with whom he was ultimately reunited) was sent off for adoption to Uruguay.[41] Rather than doing what a therapeutic approach to "healing" does – what Freud famously called "grief work" (*Trauerarbeit*) – Gelman did grief-inspired work, writing elegiac verse that translates loss into politically attuned aesthetic apprehension. Instead of seeking the resolution typical of memorial rituals, he wrote to "sustain bereaved pain as a means to acknowledge the social politics and personal ethics entailed in loss."[42] Figuring himself as an invalid in his one of his poems, his grief is articulated as wakefulness as he refers to sipping the night slowly while imagining his missing family in it somewhere.[43]

Although Dorfman also wrote from exile (in the United States), he hadn't lost family members. Rather, he regards his exile as a form of death he has shared with those who had been "disappeared" after the 1973 coup in Chile, orchestrated by U.S. intelligence agencies and led by General Augusto Pinochet. As he puts it, "To go into exile is to go into the country of the dead."[44] His poem "Red Tape" exemplifies his creative response to the grief he shares with those who have lost relatives as he laments being unable to bury one of his.[45] Preserving the rest of my engagement with Gelman's and Dorfman's writing for later in the inquiry, my immediate concern in the next section is with the political implications of psychiatry's way of "making up people."[46]

THE POLITICS OF THE PSYCHIATRIC PROFESSION

Psychiatry's construction of "prolonged grief disorder" has both micro- and macropolitical effects. As part of its current micropolitical agenda, the inclusion of prolonged grief as a disorder enhances psychiatry's position in contemporary struggles over financing health care and at the same time expands its power struggle to secure a client base. As Foucault observes, psychiatric power has been involved in a history of "struggles and confrontations in which points of resistance – counter maneuvers – are present at every moment."[47] For insight into the macropolitics of the contemporary event in the expansion of psychiatric power there is no more instructive investigation than Foucault's extensive inquiry into the event-driven history of medical perception.[48] There he points to "the specific constitution of psychiatry's disciplinary space," which differs from all others because "it has a medical stamp."[49]

Once he abandoned his early fascination with phenomenological psychiatry and turned from "psychology to history,"[50] Foucault launched his archaeological method. Here my focus is on the application of that method to the development of the clinic, a historical and spatial investigation of changing medical practices, within which he identifies a "mutation" taking place in the last years of the eighteenth century when an altered "alliance was forged between words and things," changing the discourse of disease and reorganizing clinical space.[51] It was an event in which "medicine made its appearance as a clinical science,"[52] a historical break in which the medical gaze was no longer merely the doctor's look. The patient had become a political subject within an epistemological field associated with a new form of governance. When the hospital (as a scientifically ordered "clinic") became a concrete actualization of the state's concern with public health, the patient became a source of knowledge to be assessed with reference to the population as a whole (for example, providing insight into contagion) rather than simply an individual seeking to be cured. The same reigning governmentality gave rise to another reconfigured subject. Whereas in previous centuries there were merely crimes and penalties, the nineteenth century witnessed the emergence of the "criminal," who like the patient became a pathologized object of knowledge. As a result, conversations about the criminal/subject began taking place between doctors and jurists. Psychiatry entered the courtroom because it was part of a reconfigured medical practice focused on "a sort of public hygiene" applied to a new target of governance, the social order.[53] As Foucault summarizes the main political implication, medicine – psychiatry included – had become "a task for the nation."[54]

To situate the result of reoriented medical perception that Foucault's investigation of the clinic discloses, as the medical gaze displaced the healer's look the patient was turned into a semiotic object inspected for signs that would yield knowledge with collective implications. No longer merely subject to individual care, the patient had become someone to be interpreted and managed within a health assemblage, an "ensemble of discourses, and agencies of implementation,"[55] which include government bureaucracies, health professions, scientific discourses, apparatuses of data collection and patient management accounting procedures, and so on. As for Foucault's other main focus, medicine's re-spatialization of disease, he maps an alteration in what he refers to as a disease's "spatial requisites."[56] There are three: disease exists first of all in the space of "classificatory thought"[57] within which it is located in a series of homologies; second, it appears in the body, "a quite different configuration: the concrete space of perception"[58]; and third, it is located in a multi-agency apparatus, each with its discursive protocols, an ensemble tasked with control over the vitality of national populations.

That third space is a configuration that Foucault was subsequently to identify in later investigations as a *dispositif*, a conceptualization captured in Giorgio Agamben's commentary on Foucault's analytic turn from discourse to apparatuses. An apparatus, for Foucault, is "anything that has in some way the capacity to capture, orient, determine, intercept, model, control, or secure the gestures, behaviors, opinions, or discourses of living beings."[59] Thus inasmuch as disease had become a national policy problem, policing agencies as well as political and administrative ones are articulated with medical authorities. As Foucault sums up the apparatus–space relationship resulting from medicine's altered situation, officially sanctioned civic space invades the private space of the family. "The medicine of individual perception, of family assistance of home care can be based only on a collectively controlled structure, or on one that is integrated into the social space in its entirety."[60]

Since Foucault's identification of the "collective controlled structure" to which he refers, the locus of control over health has changed. The patient, whether psychiatric or otherwise, has become a commodity rather than merely a case added to the population's level of health. As health care has become increasingly privatized, with large U.S. corporations buying "primary care practices at a rapid pace" and with health care premiums increasingly controlled by private insurers that are "mostly investor-owned, for profit businesses," the main endeavor in the industry is "to keep premiums down and profits up by stinting on medical services."[61] In much of the contemporary world of health care, medicalization is less a reflection of the "task for the nation" than a field of investment opportunities. The medical gaze has been increasingly diverted from patients to insurance and pharmaceutical corporations as "the insistence on revenue and profits has accelerated."[62]

However, quite apart from the commoditizing aspect of the psychiatry profession's share of the health system, in which psychological issues are increasingly monetized, is the critical interpretive practice to which psychoanalysis contributes. Although I have implied that psychoanalysis and literature are radically opposed ways of interpreting grief – pathologizing versus politicizing it respectively – as regards practices of memory they converge in critical ways, especially in their shared emphasis on witnessing. Demonstrating that convergence in their inquiry into acts of witnessing, literary theorist Shoshana Felman and psychiatrist Dori Laub – the former involved in a practice of reading and the latter in one of listening – collaborate in a text that alternates between literary and clinical perspectives. Their aim is "to articulate the obscure relation between witnessing events and evidence" by posing the questions "what does literature tell us about testimony" and "what does psychoanalysis tell us about testimony?"[63] as each bears on "the meeting point between violence and culture."[64] Specifically concerned with the "traumas of history,"[65] as she ponders those questions Felman poses a politically attuned one: "by virtue of what sort of agency is one *appointed* to bear witness?"[66] "An appointment to bear witness," she adds, "is paradoxically enough, an appointment to transgress the confines of [an] isolated stance to speak *for* other and *to* others." Scanning diverse literary examples, she suggests that a literary version of testimony "does not offer a completed statement, a totalizable account of ... events,"[67] hence the productive engagement she stages with her co-author/ clinician.

Picking up on her complementary role in the inquiry, Dori Laub evokes the vicissitudes of listening in her clinical practice and responds to the question she and Felman pose about what psychoanalysis can tell us about witnessing. Faced with a mind in disarray as a result of trauma – for example that of a Holocaust survivor – she suggests that the listening clinician is seeking to evoke an "event [that] has not been truly witnessed." In such a case, rather than doing "grief counseling," which is in Foucault's terms a coercive "technology of the self,"[68] the clinician becomes a "participant and co-owner of the traumatic event," helping to bring memory into a revivified existence, rather than merely uncovering one that has already taken place.[69] Laub's observation about overcoming deferrals in one's claiming of traumatic experiences is an issue I take up at the end of the chapter with examples from a social science and a literary text. At this juncture I want to re-evoke the issue of civic space.

Spatiality in the Politics of Prolonged Grief

Hannah Arendt famously addressed herself to the relationship between the household and public space:

> The emergence of society – the rise of housekeeping, its activities, problems, and organizational devices – from the shadowing interior of the household into the light of the public sphere, has not only blurred the old border line between private and political, it has also changed almost beyond recognition the meaning of the two terms and their significance for the life of the individual and citizen.[70]

Reflecting on Arendt's insight in an earlier investigation, I analyzed what I referred to as a "topological drama," which I want to recall for this inquiry as an example of the politicization (in contrast with psychiatry's "medicalization") of grief. In 2005 while grieving over the loss of her son Casey, a casualty in the U.S.'s second Gulf War (2003–11), Cindy Sheehan initially camped outside the White House to protest the war and then set up an encampment she named "Camp Casey" on several acres she purchased in the town of Crawford, Texas in the vicinity of President George W. Bush's ranch. She and other mothers she assembled at the site and sought a conversation with the President about the domestic costs of the war. Delivering a speech at a Camp Casey rally, she said:

> The president says he feels compassion for me, but the best way to show that compassion is by meeting with me and the other mothers and families who are here. Our sons made the ultimate sacrifice and we want answers. All we're asking is that he sacrifice an hour out of his five-week vacation to talk to us, before the next mother loses her son in Iraq.[71]

As I noted in my prior analysis of Sheehan's encampment protest, she had indeed moved from "the shadowy interior of the household into the light of the public sphere."[72] By purchasing space in the vicinity of the Bush ranch she had migrated from being a trespassing subject to a propertied one with rights of self-assertion. What had been a mere residential area, a pattern of private holdings outside of the Bush ranch, became politicized civic space by dint of the content of Sheehan and her cohort's claim on the President's attention. In contrast with "prolonged grief" turned into a financial asset for psychiatrists, Sheehan and other protesting mothers had turned their prolonged grief into a political initiative, an exemplary political act involving both voice and space. With respect to the former, it was, in Jacques Rancière's terms, "politics" as a "mode of subjectification ... the production through a series of actions of a body and a capacity for enunciation not previously identifiable within a given field of experience."[73] It's a case of *assujetissement* as self-fashioning rather than a form of subjectivity imposed by authorities, an enactment that Julia Kristeva has identified as "women's desire to lift the weight of what is sacrificial in the social contract from their shoulders."[74] With respect to the latter, it was "politics ... not as the exercise of power or a struggle for power" but as "the configuration of a space as political."[75]

Two aspects of historical contingency speak to the space–grief relationship. First, all models of selfhood are constructed by the forces of their historical moments. As it's put in a commentary on Ian Hacking's concept of "making up people," "The subject is modeled in each epoch by the dispositive and the discourses of the moment ... The subject is a result of their time."[76] Second, as regards the relationship between subjects and civic life, there have been periods in which rather than resulting in a medicalized subjectivity, grief has been lodged in "the public eye." For example, an investigation about the disposition of grief in ancient Rome finds that "In the months after Cicero's daughter Tullia died in late January or early February of 45, his prolonged grief for her was judged by his contemporaries to be excessive and suspect." Prolonging his sorrow was regarded as a "weakness" by his peers, and his absence from public visibility while he sequestered himself to mourn was regarded as "anti-social behavior" and a dereliction of his civic responsibilities; "do not forget that you are Cicero" was among the reproaches.[77]

As the classical historian Paul Veyne points out, digging into Roman history provides a temporal poesis; it allows one to see what is peculiar to present practices. "There is a poetry of remoteness," he suggests,

> Nothing is further from us than this civilization of antiquity [and] ... Between the Romans and us an abyss has been hallowed out by Christianity, by German philosophy, by technologic, scientific and economic revolutions ... Roman history ... takes us out of ourselves and forces us to make explicit the differences separating us from it.[78]

In contrast with its civic relevance in Rome, grief in the contemporary era is mainly thought to belong in private space and if "prolonged" to be regarded as a mental health issue. That perspective was already developed during the Renaissance, articulated, for example, by the Oxford don Robert Burton (1577–1640), who "claimed that it was a disease."[79] Given the long tradition that treated prolonged grief as an abnormality, to deploy it in public space, abduct it from medical authorities, and turn it into a civic issue takes extraordinary initiative, precisely what has been ascribed to Sophocles' Antigone, who acted in "defiance" and "indifference" to her period's gender protocols: "It takes a lot to wrest such indifference before the edicts of the state into the realm of the political."[80] Among what it requires is the creation of what

Melissa Wright calls a "countertopography,"[81] an apt characterization of Cindy Sheehan's initiative.

Moving to a larger topography, an aspect of the current global situation with which my inquiry is concerned, there is an exemplary occasion for civically relevant grief. Widespread grieving is underway in an expanding geography of the "disappeared," people abducted and murdered in instances of state terrorism. By the beginning of this millennium there have been "accounts of tens of thousands of people who are known to have disappeared in Cambodia, Latin America, Iraq, Rwanda, the former Yugoslavia, Chechnya … Many relatives have searched in vain for their loved ones, year after year."[82] Here I turn to two notable Latin American cases in Argentina and Mexico, paying particular attention to politicized groups of protesting mothers who, rather than turning their grief into institutionalized mourning rituals (for example those sponsored by the church), have occupied public space seeking disclosure of the fates of "disappeared" family members (*los desaparecidos*).

MOTHERS' PROLONGED GRIEF AS POLITICAL ACTION

There's a similarity between the way mothers have been marginalized in both psychoanalysis and Latin American civic life. As for the former, "Freudian psychoanalytic theory has slighted the significance of the preoedipal experience [so that] profound ambivalence toward the mother, embedded both culturally and individually, has allowed continued insistence on the oedipal configuration as the key moment in the development of identity."[83] Referring to the identity impoverishment of mothers in psychoanalysis as their "unspeakably," Deborah Kloepfer pursues the writing of the former Freud patient H.D. (Hilda Doolittle) who took up the psychoanalytic vocation and filled the gap, "not a geographic locus but a space in language." It's a "'space' women had lost [because] … the semiotic registers pulses beneath the 'tin pan noises' of male discourse."[84] H.D. practiced a form of psychoanalysis construed as "a practice of negotiating the inevitable tension between being a subject (being subjected to the symbolic order) and being a unique individual (having a singular identity that somehow surpasses the parameters of that order)."[85] Opening up a space for critical self-fashioning, H.D., along with other women writers, sought "an 'inside', a semiotic locus or *chora* as 'woman's space,'" while thematizing "the position of women's language in a culture that does not admit it."[86]

As for the latter, among the most well known groups of protesting mothers are the "Madres de Plaza de Mayo," a group of middle-aged Argentine women who from 1976 to 1983 assembled weekly in a downtown square in Buenos Aries during Argentina's "Dirty War" to protest the disappearances of their sons and daughters, who were "disappeared (illegally detained, kidnapped, tortured and killed) as a result of state-sponsored terrorism in Argentina from the mid 1970s to the early 1980s."[87] "Boldly, mothers brought their private suffering into the open to confront the military dictatorships when no one else dared." No longer willing to "carry on their prescribed cultural roles ... they created a new collective motherhood devoted to human rights."[88] They were simultaneously "processing a wrong" and engaged in *subjectification*.[89] In opposition to male machismo, they manifested what Evelyn Stevens calls "*'marianismo'*[90], ... a kind of 'mother cult' which cherishes the qualities of women-as-mothers: moral superiority, spiritual strength, and an infinite capacity for humility and sacrifice."[91]

Crucial to an appreciation of the Argentina madres' political initiative has been their "refusal to mourn." Instead, they have politicized their grief and defied an Argentine cultural prescription in which a social majority has "wanted to move on and who thought the mothers should mourn privately and keep silent."[92] Unlike the concentrated space of Cindy Sheehan's and other assembled mothers' protest outside President Bush's Texas ranch, the madres' protest created a "disparate network"[93] and an expanded generational participation: "as the first group of Madres met in Buenos Aries, other women started to mobilize in cities across the country,"[94] among whom were *Abuelas* (grandmothers). Led by Estela de Carlotto they began participating by 1977, protesting in the Plaza and doing research to discover the fates of kidnapped children who had been "given new identities and handed to new families after their parents were killed by the ... military junta."[95]

The other notable historical moment for protests by mothers in Latin America has been taking place in Iguala, Guerrero, Mexico in response to an event in which "Mexican police forces ... attacked and abducted four dozen students known as *normalistas* (student teachers) who commandeered several buses to travel to Mexico City for their annual commemoration of the anniversary of the 1968 Tlatelolco massacre.[96] "Some were killed on the spot and the rest were never seen again."[97] It's one case among many episodes of abduction and murder in a country in which, as the late Mexican writer Carlos Fuentes remarked in his last novel, *Destiny and Desire* (2008), "Today the great drama of Mexico is that crime has replaced the state."[98] For purposes of illustration, Fuentes speaks of state-promoted crime through one of his characters, Sangines, who says, "I grew up in a society in which society was protected by official corruption. Today ... society is protected by criminals ... Just yesterday ... a highway in the state of Guerrero was blocked by uniformed criminals. Were they fake police?"[99]

In the Iguala episode, the same ambiguous form of agency in the same state to which Fuentes' character refers – collaborative violence by government officials, the military, police forces, and criminal gangs in the state of Guerrero – turned out to be involved in the abduction and murder of the *normalistas*. In response to the atrocity, father-activists have also engaged in public protests on behalf of family grief while accompanied by mother-activists, who, like "mother-activists over the decades of activism against state terror in the Americas ... present their political demands within a representation of themselves as 'mothers looking for their children.'"[100] Among their staged events in which they constituted themselves as a "counterpublic"[101] was a Mother's Day march in May of 2022:

> Thousands of women in Mexico have spent Mother's Day marching in the nation's sprawling capital, chanting, carrying pictures of their missing relatives, to demand accountability ... "where are they, where are they? Our children, where are they?" the women shouted on Tuesday as they demonstrated with supporters along Mexico City's main avenue ... they were joined by a caravan of Central American mothers searching for loved ones who went missing on their journey to the United States.[102]

In his protest poetry, Juan Gelman, to whose writing I now turn, joins grieving mothers stylistically as well as ideationally. Speaking "to his dead son in a mothering tongue,"[103] he fashions himself as a surrogate mother by constructing "the poetic subject" as one who "adopts gender markings contradictory to those ordered by social norms."[104] Reflecting his distance from traditional paternal norms, he writes a poem/letter to his son in which he imagines cuddling him to his mother chest.[105]

The Political Poetics of Juan Gelman's Prolonged Grief

The grim family history to which Gelman's poetry was a response "became the source of a new phase in his work, in which after being forced into exile, he transformed the deepest sorrow into some of his best poetry."[106]

> In 1976, shortly after a coup that saw the president of Argentina, Isabel Martinez de Peron, replaced by a military dictatorship, [Gelman's] son and daughter-in-law – Marcelo, 20 and Maria Claudia, an 18-year-old expectant mother – were kidnapped, just two of approximately 30,000 people to go missing ... Gelman's subsequent investigation confirmed the worst: that both had been killed, but also that their baby had survived and had been taken in by foster parents ...[107]

Referring to the day of their disappearance, August 24, 1976, Gelman, refusing to accept public officials' avoidance of accountability and their attribution of the disappearances to a past from which they wanted to move on, wrote a poetic public letter in which he says he will not give his family members up for dead until he sees their bodies.[108] Nineteen years after the abductions and before his granddaughter, Macarena, was located (in 1999), Gelman, still refusing to mourn but not knowing the gender of his grandchild, wrote "An open letter to My Grandson or Granddaughter" entitled "I would like to give you your own history" in which he provides details of her birth – "Within the next six months you will turn nineteen. You would have been born in an army concentration camp" – describes her parents and their fates, indicates how he knows she is still alive – "The grandmothers are there with their flesh-and-blood data banks that enable them to determine with scientific precision the origins of the Disappeared" – and tells her, "I would like to repair somehow this brutal severance of silence."[109]

The open letter form is a frequent part of Gelman's grief aesthetic. Added to the above noted poetic open letter to his son is one on which he revives his son's presence to his father in an embrace as he imputes a temporal sequence to his son's days.[110]

As a translator himself (one of the ways he survived financially while in exile), Gelman understood his bilingual experience as constitutive of his poetry in general and his grief aesthetic in particular. To situate his style, I want to recall Berardi's above-quoted remark on poetry, "the reopening of the indefinite, the ironic act of exceeding the established meaning of words." Gelman's version of that perspective arises from his being always "between words," a bilingual situation within which, as a "two-worlded" writer, he is "birthing words." He refers to his style as "amphibian" to identify the "unstable condition" in which his words are "double-sided verbal inventions" operating throughout his *Carta Abierta* (Public Letter) to his son.[111] Self-aware and multi-genre influenced, his "poetry speaks of poetry; it takes it all on: the objective and subjective, the real and imagined, I and other. It ventures into virgin territory, on the outskirts of romanticism, realism, symbolism and the avant-garde."[112]

Observing Gelman's poetic responses to his grief opens a space for analyzing why a poetics is an especially appropriate way to give the grief that state terror causes the civic impact its publicity can render. To elaborate on that suggestion, I turn to a grief investigation that contains alternative publicity genres, two different aesthetic responses to the aftermath of an atrocity. It was photographed by a photojournalist and reflected on in a poetic commentary by a soldier, who witnessed the aftermath after the liberation of the German-occupied Ukrainian city of Kerch in January 1942. The scene is an anti-tank ditch that held thousands of bodies of executed women, children, and old men among others, with several bodies strewn around the ground nearby, left there because the ditch was too full to hold more corpses.

Only Verse Could Suffice

David Shneer's biography of a Kerch atrocity photograph tells the story of the career of the Soviet war photojournalist Dimitri Baltermants, whose iconic photograph is of grieving women identifying dead family members on the ground near the anti-tank ditch site of the executions. Thematizing "women in mourning," Baltermants "photographed … the women several times as he tried to capture their changing emotions as revealed in their bodies in various state of gesticulation."[113] Referring to the effect on the photographer, Shneer writes, "Baltermants left Kerch a changed person, one who used his photographic skills to tell a horror story."[114] As an approach to trauma and suffering, photography, like many other media genres, has a marked effect on others; it moves grief into public space where its implications become subject to public negotiation. As a result of his photographic work, the photographer was doubtless not the only person changed by what he witnessed.

Although Baltermants's photographic career subsequent to his Kerch images makes for a fascinating story about the impact of photojournalism, it is a different genre response to the atrocity that attracts my attention. Another witness to the scene, a Soviet soldier, Ilya Sevinsky, "saw the antitank trench first hand as he accompanied the troops liberating the city."[115] Recording the experience in his diary, he reports:

> I got to Kerch with the second wave of airborne troops. The city is half-destroyed. That's that – we'll restore it. But near the village of Bagerov in an antitank ditch – [where] 7000 executed women, children, old men and others. And I saw them. Now I do not have the strength to write about it in prose, Nerves can no longer react. What I could I have expressed in verse.[116]

As for the poem, as it is described by Shneer it is composed as a declaration on the value of witnessing versus hearsay with a focus on seeing something with one's own eyes.[117] Sevinsky's resort to poetry reveals something significant about poetry as a genre. Faced with what the painter Francis Bacon famously refers to as "the brutality of fact," Sevinsky chose a mode of expression that privileges how he was affected by the facts on the ground. It's a genre effect that Theodore Roethke ascribes to poetry. "The novel, he says, "can teach us how to act; the poem and music, how to feel."[118]

Having evoked Bacon's expression, I want to linger briefly with his genre sentiments because they suggest a relevant transversality from painting to poetry. Bacon introduces his famous expression in an interview in which he describes the difference he observes between Picasso and Matisse:

> I much prefer Picasso because he has the brutality of fact, compared to Matisse. Picasso is able very often to bring over the rawness of life at a very acute point, when I talk about the brutality of fact in Picasso, Picasso in a curious way was able to put it across more directly and with less expressionism in it. It seemed to be the fact itself without the will to express it.[119]

It's not a hidden brutality – for example, the way "capitalism sustains ... a vast ignorance of social realities ... with care and brutality"[120] – but a direct experience that cannot be conjured away with disingenuous narratives. Accordingly, Bacon says that he prefers a painting that has an impact "directly onto the nervous system" as opposed to one that "tells you the story in a long diatribe through the brain."[121] The impact that Bacon ascribes to some of Picasso's paintings applies to his own painting practice. As Deleuze points out in his analysis of Bacon's canvasses, the aim is to orient "its potential narratives into the sensation of witnessing."[122]

Deleuze's remark provides for a propitious return to Sevinsky's genre choice where we observe a similar effect. He turned to poetry to transmit "the sensation of witnessing" (his experience of being powerfully affected by a scene he said he "saw with my own eyes") into an aesthetic genre, poetry, which he felt was the only adequate form to capture the immediacy of his experience. Turning witnessing into expression he effectively moved along an affective narrative path that Deleuze shares with Bacon. In his commentary "Spinoza and the Three 'Ethics'," Deleuze refers to "passional affects," and states that they are the "precursors of ... notions, the dark precursors."[123] Bacon and Deleuze's shared narrative of the dynamics of apprehension as it applies to artistic composition and reception brings us back to Juan Gelman, who conceives his poetic process similarly. *His* word for "passional effects" is "obsession"; "Poetry, before being written," he says "is an obsession."[124]

Speaking of the waxing and waning of obsession and expression, Gelman notes the reversals. The process begins with the "obsession," which he says is at "'100 percent' at the outset and the expression is at zero." Then, "the obsession begins to dwindle and the expression has been achieved."[125] For Gelman, as is suggested in the Deleuzian narrative, affection drives the artistic practice as a precursor for its ultimate expression. Thus, for example, throughout the period of his exile while grieving for his former Argentine life, Gelman turns his obsession with his estrangement into an expressive poetics with which he imagines justice arriving as a new dawn in a country that had been emptied of love.[126] The longing for home expressed in lines from his poetry notwithstanding, exilic Latin American writers have had varying degrees of attachment to their native countries; the literary responses to exile have been varied. For example, the Chilean novelist Ana Vasquez found "that the form in which she felt herself most able to respond was that of the short story," thus her "'The Doubts of the Bigamist' [in which] the protagonist seeks out a bigamist relationship as a metaphor for biculturalism."[127] In Ariel Dorfman's case, the response to his grief resulting from continuing state terror after the Pinochet coup in Chile, leading to his exile (which continues as he has remained in the United States as an academic teacher/scholar), has taken many genre forms.

Ariel Dorfman's Cosmopolitan Responses

In his 2010 Annual Nelson Mandela Lecture in South Africa, Dorfman identifies "home" as an exemplary political life rather than a homeland: "It was only after Salvador Allende died in a military coup in 1973, only after I went into exile and started to wander this earth like a kwerekwere, that the name of Mandela gradually became a beacon of hope, a sort of home to me."[128] He then proceeds to ponder universal questions from the point of view of his role as a writer who militates against complacency: "what writers do," he suggests, is "plunge into the vast complexity of our human condition rather than be content with simple answers that leave us satisfied and comfortable." Like Gelman he has turned his experience of personal grief and vicarious empathy for the grief of sufferers into lyrical reflections on political life with a style that unsettles certainties. In the afterword to his play *Death and the Maiden* he ponders the problem of artistic truth, asking "How do we find a language that is political but not pamphletary? How to tell stories that are both popular and ambiguous."[129] Also like Gelman, he has used his exile as a creative platform for expression – a permanent platform in his case as he decided to remain in exile as a U.S. academic, after a brief return to Chile once the violence of the Pinochet years had ended.

Similarly as well, Dorfman endorses the affective narrative that Gelman has expressed. He too refers to the initiating force of what becomes a politically attuned artistic expression as an "obsession." Referring to his play *Reader*, which "began life as a story," he says:

> I came to it after having spent many years, like most exiles do, exploring the minds and bodies of the victims of terror, wondering how to give voice to what was suppressed back home ... A voice and, ultimately a place on stage: it was that *obsession* [my emphasis] which was to give birth to two other plays of mine.[130]

Moreover, in accord with the gendered way Gelman often constructed voices in his poetry, the most notable voice Dorfman places on stage belongs to Paulina, a victim of state terror in his play *Death and the Maiden*. As the play opens, Paulina, a survivor of torture and rape during Argentina's "Dirty War," is at home when her husband, whose identity as an activist she had not betrayed during her ordeal, and welcomes a motorist whose car had broken down into their home. Although she had been blindfolded during the abuse, she recognizes the visitor's voice and smell. He was the doctor, Roberto Miranda, who had treated her wounds and had also brutally raped her many times. During the dramatic action – vividly shown in Roman Polanski's 1994 film version[131] – she holds a gun, while her husband is witnessing the encounter, threatening Miranda on the edge of a cliff over the ocean, demanding his confession and at the same time demanding her husband's trust in the certainty of her senses. Indicating in an interview why he made Paulina's voice the play's dominant one, Dorfman says, "Paulina's voice is 'the voice of community,' a submerged voice" that challenges Chileans who find it "difficult to 'remember' the past, but even more difficult to watch a woman take power in a macho culture the way Paulina does ... Paulina refuses to be obedient [and laments her earlier capitulation]: 'I submitted too easily right away without even a gesture of defiance. All my life, I've been much too obedient."[132]

In his "Foreword" to a collection of his plays, which he entitles *The Resistance Trilogy*, Dorfman evokes two aspects of punishment. He ascribes one to "the different and converging ways in which the State in our sad age punishes those who have rebelled and warns others who may have not yet done so to be wary of trying."[133] The other he ascribes to his art. Having "watched my country being ravaged from afar," he writes, "I decided that this suffering could only be justified if we are able to turn it into something else ... to grow with it and from it [and] ... to punish with words the men we cannot punish with other means."[134] The problem he has faced, however, is that many of those who suffered have, along with the state that created the suffering, tended toward amnesia about the experience, traumatically induced for the sufferers and purposive in the case of many perpetrators and supportive officials steering the state in the aftermath of the Pinochet years. Consequently, Dorfman, who escaped state terror, has regarded his writing genres as ways to stage vicarious events of both memory and history in support of those who have been silenced. As he puts it in "Acknowledgements and an Afterword" to his play *Windows*:

> I was writing on a painful series of poems about missing men and women who, snatched from their homes by the secret police in the silence of the night, are never heard of again, the bodies denied to their relatives as if they had never existed. As I wrote, I could feel myself being turned into a bridge through which the living and the dead were trying to communicate, a burial mound where they could meet and mourn and touch.[135]

The bridge metaphor with which Dorfman connects the living with the dead also serves to connect his aesthetics with an ethics. As Mieke Bal puts it, "ethical unsettlement is the thrust of his work."[136] In his plays we observe characters whose traumatic memories are hidden: through traumatically imposed amnesia in the case of victims, and officially, through a national amnesia involving an erasure of parts of state history, actively enacted by perpetrators and passively welcomed by their supporters. What emerges in Dorfman's counter-historical challenges is a universalistic ethos; the issues they raise transcend particular nation-state experiences. Their focus is on intersecting temporalities, national times and biographical times especially, as they articulate the complex entanglements between memory and history. Heeding Pierre Nora's insight that memory is a "dialectic of remembering and forgetting, unconscious of its successive deformations, vulnerable to manipulation and appropriation, susceptible to being dormant and periodically revived,"[137] and his dictum that "history" involves the "conquest and eradication of memory,"[138] the ethical questions surrounding that intersection are about individual and official responsibility to acknowledge and restore the memories of people whose experience of suffering has not been granted a sufficient place in public history.

As my preceding inquiry suggests, that requires witnessing, which comes in the wide variety of genres that express the responsibility to restore experiences for public consumption, to re-enter events into history which for both personal and official reasons have been erased. Turning to two illustrations, I want to explore the ways such acts of restoration, writing events to which I refer earlier in the inquiry, have overcome those erasures. In both cases, the authors were affected by the grief of relatives. After deferring the writing for many years, they produced texts whose analyses turn the grief of others into conceptually rich narratives, one explanatory in structure, the other autobiographical.

Deferrals: Prolonged (Vicarious) Grief

Every critically attuned artistic genre encodes complex temporalities. Carlos Fuentes nominates the novel as the one best suited to capture the world's multiplicity of times,[139] Gilles Deleuze ascribes that capacity to cinema,[140] Art Spiegelman, whose graphic documentaries *Maus* I and II respond to his father's post-Holocaust grief, nominates the commixture of image and narrative in comic strips as the genre that best brings the past into the present,[141] David Shneer credits a photograph's ability to tell a vast and complex history, and, reflecting on "the political force" of Dorfman's theater works, Mieke Bal refers to theater as a "time-based art form" that is "eminently suitable" for "staging, and consequently exposing" subjects' affective experiences. Such art forms, she adds, "make History enter art and accordingly, suspend the unfortunate and damaging ... opposition between fiction and reality."[142] Jacques Rancière offers a similar observation about the fiction/non-fiction binary, noting that to create "the sense of reality produced by the cutting out of the scene, the identification of its elements and the modality of the description ... Politicians, journalists or social scientists must [also] use fictions ... whenever they have to say: this is the situation, these are the elements that compose it."[143]

In accord with Bal's and Rancière's resistance to the non-fiction versus fiction divide, I turn to both a social science investigation and a novel to elucidate aspects of grief-initiated deferral and other aspects of the temporalities that structure memory and history. The former, whose author Manus Midlarsky reports that he was profoundly affected by expressions of grief while among some of his relatives who lost family members during the Holocaust, is an inquiry that was deferred for decades. The latter, a novel by the Belgian writer Stefan Hertmans, is based on the author's receipt of his grandfather/soldier's diary of his World War I experience, which Hertmans deferred reading for thirty years.

Turning first to the social science investigation, Midlarsky's "Preface" provides an account of his deferral, which reads like the beginning meta-narrative of an autobiographical novel:

> I write this book after a 46-year gestation period. This does not mean that my thinking about the book spanned five decades. Instead, my experiences as a seventeen-year-old were formative and ultimately decisive in the decision to do the research and writing. For many years, I avoided the issue of the Holocaust, despite an intense training in Orthodox Judaism and a household deeply affected by the news of the Holocaust ... On Yom Kippur in Israel in 1954, I visited an uncle (through marriage) who escaped the Holocaust from eastern Poland with his immediate family ... Virtually all his relatives who remained in Poland perished in the Holocaust ... only the older people in [the transit camp where his uncle lived] remembered only too well the extent of their loses ... When it came time for the Memorial service for the Dead (Yizkor), the extent of their agony became abundantly clear, I have never before, or since, heard such anguished weeping ... Such intensity of feeling was too much for a seventeen-year-old ... For the next thirty years, I blocked out the memory.[144]

The memory became unblocked ("revived" as Midlarsky puts it) after he got an invitation to contribute an article on a Holocaust topic for a special issue of a journal.[145]

Once he decided to write about genocides Midlarsky's inquiry featured "the use of social science theory in an effort to generalize across three cases of genocide" (the Holocaust along with the Armenian and Rwandan genocides).[146] Like Hertmans his affective connection with his subject runs in part through a grandparent. He recalls his "Orthodox Russian born grandmother listening to Yiddish radio at the end of WWII remarking in horror, *zex millionan Yiden hut geshtorben*!! (6 million Jews had died)," and notes:

> This memory remained with me. However, as for choosing my way, in one respect this was made easier by the fact that I was putting together one of my edited Handbooks of War Studies and was researching my

chapter on the then recent Rwandan genocide. From there it was easier to access my own feelings on the Holocaust and other genocides.[147]

While those "feelings" (a vicarious experience of intense collective grief) were, as I have suggested, the affective precursors of Midlarsky's investigation, what results is a theory building project. The autobiographical observations in the Preface are not continued throughout the text. Moreover, unlike Hertmans's literary project, in which small details of bodily comportment and everyday scenes (including the grisly aspects of trench warfare) are abundant, Midlarsky sticks to a comparative explanatory inquiry across historical examples. "The analytic enterprise," he writes, "does not concern itself with ... micro-level aspects of mass murder."[148] Nevertheless, motivating the "analytic enterprise" was an ethical commitment. His inherited, deeply felt connection with grief-stricken Jewish relatives affected by the Holocaust did not exhaust his focus. Midlarsky expanded the historical geography of his inquiry and thereby its ethical framing. Asked, "What was involved in your ethical self-fashioning that directed the scope of your inquiry," he responded, "The need to provide understanding of the sources of genocide generally to perhaps prevent future occurrences."[149] The broad historical coverage that resulted speaks to the empathy his inquiry evinces. After constructing an investigative narrative that emphasizes the epistemological warrants for his conclusions, a sentence in his ending "Coda" expresses the empathetic sensibility implicitly present throughout the inquiry:

> A Jewish mother walking in the Ukrainian woods with her children in September 1941, an Armenian working on the Berlin–Bagdad railway in late 1915, a Tutsi sitting in a crowded Rwandan church in the spring of 1994, or a Cambodian teaching her class of twelve-year-olds in 1976 most likely would never be seen again. It is my hope that this book has accurately charted pathways from the mundane to the bizarre and unthinkable.[150]

I suggest that although the text is what he calls an "analytic enterprise," it began and was sustained at the level of affect. As a result, its ethos mirrors the ethical narrative that Deleuze extracts from David Hume's philosophy in which "affective circumstances" guide ideas so that the ethico-political problem is "to pass from limited sympathy to an extended generosity."[151]

My turn to Hertmans's novel *War and Turpentine* at this point is to explore with an alternative lexical genre the ways that vicarious grief is implicated in decades of a book's deferral. Based on a difficult legacy for the author to negotiate, the novel narrates the life of Urbain Martien, a painter-copyist and a World War I hero whose life was situated between two world wars. Before he died, Urbain entrusted his notebooks to Hertmans, his grandson, asking him to write his posthumous biography. Empathically attuned to the various sources of grief that had afflicted his grandfather's life – the death of his fiancée, severe war wounds, and lost comrades among other things – Hertmans, a poet, and novelist, felt a deep but daunting obligation to do justice to the biography. He held the notebooks for more than three decades before reading them: "For more than thirty years I kept and never opened, the notebooks in which he had set down his memories in his matchless handwriting ... I had resolved not to read his memoirs until I had plenty of time for them."[152] In a remark that mirrors Midlarsky's about finding "his own way," Hertmans refers to facing "the painful truth behind any literary work ... I first had to recover from the authentic story. To let it go, before I could rediscover it in my own way."[153]

In narrative threads that interweave his own biography with his grandfather's memoirs, Hertmans states as well that he was, "too scared to open them ... in the knowledge that this story would be a farewell to a piece of my childhood."[154] That admission early in the novel indicates the particular intersubjective way the text articulates history, precisely captured by what Cathy Caruth calls "the central insight" in Freud's *Moses and Monotheism*, "that history, like trauma, is never simply one's own, that history is precisely the way we are implicated in each other's traumas."[155] Adding to Hertmans's reluctance was an "instinct [that] warned him not only of the horrors he would discover, but also the crushing human personal grief."[156] He also deferred a communion with war deaths in general. "All those years, something kept me from paying a mandatory visit to the endless cemeteries of white gravestones around Ypres and Diksmuide and the painstakingly re-created trenches that offer historically minded visitors the most 'realistic' experience possible."[157] What ultimately enabled the writing of the novel was a visit that affected him powerfully, affording him a vicarious yet close feeling of what his grandfather had experienced:

[I]t was not until a few years ago, when I visited the Citadel of Dinant with my son, that for half an hour my grandfather's world seemed frighteningly close by. The claustrophobic atmosphere of the constructed trenches in the war museum, the dim lighting, the naïve but effective simulation of soldiers' lives in the war years – because of the bleak setting, where I had to grope my uncertain way down the slanting paths, I felt a sudden connection to my grandfather's fumbling steps in the dark.[158]

To borrow some apropos words from one of Proust's observations – when he too experienced an "involuntary memory" (a "lacerating recollection of his dead grandmother") – it was a moment in which the "calendar of feelings" had caught up with "the calendar of facts."[159]

Throughout the novel Hertmans uses a compositional structure (what Lars Bernaets calls "an empathic constellation"[160]) that "bring[s] himself and the reader closer to the world of his grandfather."[161] He inserts himself as the narrator in Part I of the novel, recreating a world, now lost, which had incubated his grandfather's rigorous comportment – for example, the way "he would roll up his short sleeves, or rather, he carefully folded them over, twice, to a point just under his elbow, each fold exactly the width of the starched cuff"[162] – manifest in his early life, in his war experience, and in his later family life, all framed by Hertmans's essayistic reflections on the more general issue of how historical time has levied a "yawning gap between our grandparents and ourselves."[163] Yielding to his grandfather as narrator of his war experience in Part II, Hertmans draws from the notebooks to engage in vicarious witnessing as Urbain describes the horrors of war and the pain of his injuries while nevertheless managing to exercise the keen observations of nature characteristic of his artistic sensibility: "The earth warms up; after the chilly morning hours, vapor rises from the miry fields which shine in the strange light."[164]

Once inflected by Hertmans, the notebooks provide a story not only of a long life of prolonged grief (vicariously shared by his grandson) but also a critical engagement with multiple temporalities to which Urbain contributes as Hertmans's mediated collaborator. What emerges is the rendering of a mixture of biographical time, geopolitical time, war time, and generational time in a story in which grief as a productive aesthetic is situated in the midst of a historically unfolding life world rather than simply in a psyche. This lyrical passage exemplifies the way Urbain's mediated voice contributes to the effects of war's punishing duration:

> Time rolls on into bland duration, loses direction, direction give way to stasis and boredom, boredom makes us sluggish and apathetic, the days creep through our fingers. There are, in fact, whole weeks when nothing happens, weeks when commanders try to distract the men with petty projects, like building a better dugout for the officers or putting on a "war circus" behind the front lines, where one summer we witness an absurd spectacle [an "infantryman dressed like "a grotesque ballerina"] ... The men roar with laughter ... An explosion of pent-up mirth, a liberation from the stifling apathy of time.[165]

"Time has abandoned us," he adds as he identifies the malaise resulting from long years of war, "we have slipped into a dim unreal fold in its fabric, with no beginning or end in sight ... we are old before our time, we behave like housebound, fatalistic children, numbed and indifferent to life and death."[166]

Once Hertmans takes over the narration again in Part III he exposes the hardships of Urbain's life by adding a visual experience to his otherwise lexical data. He refers to observing his grandfather's unclothed body, which before his war service had been subjected to the perils of industrial labor. The scene has Urbain undressing at his last bedtime before he dies:

> He took off his white shirt, and then his undershirt, revealing the blue indentations in his back, the scars of brutal years in the iron foundry. And when he took off his long underpants he uncovered another bluish indentation, this one in his sagging underbelly, right next to his groin, and yet another in his skinny thigh. The proud badges of his heroic acts, inscribed in his body.[167]

Urbain's body was the only visual war canvas he ultimately contributed himself. "He never painted a single war scene, nor did it occur "to him to draw the things he recalled from the war., and since his death. I have found no trace of the charcoal portraits of his comrades-in-arms that he mentions in his memoirs."[168]

In a reflection that expresses the novel's methodological contribution, an affect-attuned historiography based on grief-initiated recollections in which one member of a generation is obliged to look back at another to see what is singular about his present world, Hertmans turns specifically to what is different about contemporary forms of violence:

> Something about the lost ethos of the old-time is almost unthinkable to us today, in our world of terrorist attacks and virtual violence. The morality of violence has undergone a seismic shift. The generation of Belgian soldiers driven into the maw of the German machine guns in the first year of the war had been raised with exalted nineteenth century values with pride and honor and naïve idealism. Their military ethics were based on the virtues of courage, self-discipline, honor, and love of the daily march ... and the willingness to fight man to man.[169]

CODA: FROM DEMENTIA TO COLLECTIVE AMNESIA

Hertmans's observation notwithstanding, the anachronistic ethos to which he refers has had remarkable persistence, with devastating consequences. As Paul Fussell points out, when in 1940 World War II was on the horizon, "the Great War had receded into soft focus, and no one wanted to face the fact that military successes are achieved only at the cost of insensate violence and fear and agony, with no bargains allowed."[170] It took a while with the war underway for political and military leaders, who initially thought the new war involved what Fussell calls "light duty" – "finesse, accuracy, and subtlety"[171] – to acknowledge the reality, a "mosaic of misery,"[172] a prolonged slaughter that belied the romanticization and sacralization of war that had persisted through the interwar period. What had prevailed was what George Mosse refers to as the way "the reality of the war experience came to be transformed ... into The Myth of the War Experience,"[173] a transformation promoted by a variety of memorial practices: war memorials, military cemeteries, patriotic songs, and interestingly, with a form of poetry that contrasts markedly with the critical poesis which (as I have noted) has exposed and challenged state terror practices. In this case, it is a poetry, "fitted to build national self-consciousness," an emotion-stirring version aimed at stoking "militant nationalism."[174]

In Georgi Gospodinov's novel *Time Shelter*, the historically persisting amnesia about the nature of war toward which Fussell and Mosse point is generalized to cover the glaring erasures in geopolitical historicity in general. It's the last text I interrogate in the chapter's textual itinerary, conducted to engage the traumatic loses to which prolonged grief has been a memory- and history-recovering response. By way of a preface to the novel's innovative way of lending complexity to history as it moves from a focus on persons with dementia to nation-states involved in willful amnesia, I return briefly to the issue of missing people as they are distinguished in an analysis focused on different kinds of grief-inducing loss, "one in which the person is present but missing (as in dementia) and one in which the person is missing but present (as in cases of forced disappearance like those in Argentina)."[175] Gospodinov's novel begins with a project designed to treat the former kind of loss, persons present but missing because of dementia.

The project belongs to a geriatric psychiatrist named Gaustine (a name that intermixes political and theological activism, the G for his father's admiration for Garibaldi and the rest for his mother's following of Saint Augustine). Gaustine, who shares the narrator's "obsession with the past," is nevertheless "at home in all times," while the narrator states that he merely "knocked on the doors of various years."[176] Turning his obsession into a psychiatric practice, Gaustine founds a clinic with a series of therapeutic time shelters for patients with dementia. The clinic recreates for each patient "a lost world"[177] within a time period that matches the dominant internal time that remains for each patient. For example, a patient who can still connect with the 1960s lives in an environment with 1960s music and other cultural features of the period. Because the patients are also sheltered from memories that are disturbing, Gaustine's experiment become ripe for transmutation to forms of collective, national amnesia in countries motivated to dwell on happy times and erase disturbing or inconvenient pasts. The shelters initially designed to accommodate individual memory loss provide a template for collective historical erasure. There is, however, an intermediate step as Gaustine's clinical practice undergoes geographic expansion. Adjunct time shelters, "rooms and houses of the past begin popping up in various places," for example in Aarhus, Denmark (which actually has a museum of the past, *Den Gamle By* [The Old City]) where "groups from retirement homes, primarily those suffering from dementia can go into sections that feature the kinds of life worlds they remember, farmsteads for some, village life for some, and for others, an apartment, preserved just as it had been in 1974."[178]

As Gaustine's temporal practice expands and receives widespread publicity, the novel's "allegorical intention"[179] is realized. Individual dementia is translated into willful collective amnesia. Having decided to emulate the time sheltering applied to individuals within collectives, countries begin holding referendums to plot futures based on preferred pasts ("happy times"). Each nation chooses a past decade as the paradigm for freezing the national community in time. As the process unfolds, political parties compete to promote some decades and discard others (for example, France and Spain choose the 1980s, Portugal the 1970s). To the extent that there remains the possibility of a united Europe, "temporal alliances would form, while further down the line it would be possible to vote for a unified European time."[180] The main consequence of national time sheltering is the loss of decades, a massive erasure of much of European history. As the "headlines in European newspapers" banner it: "Total Recall: Europe Chooses its Past." Gospodinov figures the consequence of the historical moment he invents with a temporal retreat from elderly dementia to infancy: "People didn't stop to think that in and of itself, the nation was a bawling historical infant masquerading as a biblical patriarch."[181]

Although it's evident that Gospodinov has contemporary issues in mind, such as the impact of Brexit on European unity, more central to the novel's critical reflections is the prolonged grief associated with losing relationships:

> When people with whom you've shared a common past leave, they take half of it with them. Actually, they take the whole thing, since there's no such thing as half a past. It's as if you've torn a page in half lengthwise and you're reading the lines only in the middle, and the other person is reading the ends.[182]

While the collective amnesia that concerns Gospodinov is more focused on the displacement of history with "ersatz memory"[183] than on the erasure of records of violence from state terror in the countries from which Gelman and Dorfman were exiled, he nevertheless regards one of collective amnesia's consequences as a distraction from some contemporary forms of violence. He expresses that concern in the voice of his narrator who is reflecting on the pervasiveness of time sheltering:

> One afternoon … after yet another terror attack somewhere in Europe, I spent hours in the museum at the Hague. As if in a shelter from another time. It was full of people who had run away from the news of the day … I was standing in front of [Vermeer's] *Girl with a Pearl Earring*. I was a step away from them, not moving. Their faces one and the same. So time is merely a piece of clothing, an earring … The gallery guard resembled Vermeer.[184]

To close provisionally (much remains to be thought), I want to re-emphasize the role of psychiatry, one that begins in the novel as an application of geriatric therapy but then becomes an instance of what I have referred to above as "psychiatry's imperial ambitions." In this case the ambition is on a global scale. In the words of the narrator describing the effect of the expansion of Gaustine's project, "The world had become a chaotic open-air clinic of the past."[185] Certainly there are enigmas involved in Gospodinov's allegorical intention. For example, can one ask about the full slate of consequences of a country's erasure of parts of its past? That question evokes the problem of reading. Gospodinov's turn to allegory-as-textual-performance encourages a productive reading performance because he supplies no definitive or wholly "satisfactory answers to readers' interrogations."[186] Experiencing the way his text thinks, we are enjoined to keep thinking. I follow up on that mandate in Chapter 2.

NOTES

1. See Gilles Deleuze's rendering of Bergson on temporality: *Bergsonism*, trans. Hugh Tomlinson and Barbara Habberjam (New York: Zone Books, 1991), p. 26.
2. Stefanie R. Fishel, *The Microbial State: Global Thriving and the Body Politic* (Minneapolis: University of Minnesota Press, 2017), p. 25.
3. William E. Connolly, *Neuropolitics: Thinking, Culture, Speed* (Minneapolis: University of Minnesota Press, 2002), p. 14.
4. William E. Connolly, *Resounding Events* (New York: Fordham University Press, 2022), pp. 1–2.
5. Brian Massumi, *Politics of Affect* (Cambridge: Polity, 2015), p. 49.
6. Ray Charles, quoted by Dwight Garner in a book review: "A Biography of a Blues Legend, Five Decades in the Making," *The New York Times*, April 17, 2023, at https://www.nytimes.com/2023/04/17/books/mack-mccormick-robert-johnson-biography.html (last accessed August 28, 2024).
7. David Sylvester, *The Brutality of Fact: Interviews with Francis Bacon* (London: Thames & Hudson, 1987), p. 68.
8. Jason Zinoman, "Steven Wright: Master of the One-Liner, Tries His Hand at a Novel," *The New York Times*, May 16, 2023 at https://www.nytimes.com/2023/05/16/arts/steven-wright-comedy-books.html (last accessed August 28, 2024).

9. Amanda Petrusich, "The Sad Dads of the National," *The New Yorker*, April 28, 2023, at https://www.newyorker.com/magazine/2023/05/08/the-sad-dads-of-the-national (last accessed August 28, 2024).

10. Connolly, *Resounding Events*, p. 151.

11. I take the idea of a productive reception from Roland Barthes's approach to a text as a "methodological field" that engages a reader conceived as a producer rather than a passive consumer: Roland Barthes, "From Work to Text," in *Image, Music, Text*, trans. Stephen Health (New York: Hill & Wang, 1977), p. 157.

12. Umberto Eco, "Kant, Pierce, and the Platypus," in *Kant and the Platypus*, trans. Alastair McEwen (New York: Harcourt, Brace & Co,), p. 57.

13. Massumi, *Politics of Affect*, p. 51.

14. Ellen Barry, "How Long Should It Take to Grieve? Psychiatry Has Come Up With an Answer," *The New York Times*, March 18, 2022, at https://www.nytimes.com/2022/03/18/health/prolonged-grief-disorder.html (last accessed August 28, 2024).

15. Michel Foucault, *Psychiatric Power*, trans. Graham Burchell (New York: Picador, 2006), p. 355.

16. Judith Butler, *The Psychic Life of Power* (Stanford, CA: Stanford University Press, 1997), p. 83.

17. Allan V. Horowitz, *DSM: A History of Psychiatry's Bible* (Baltimore, MD: Johns Hopkins University Press, 2021).

18. See "Prolonged Grief Disorder" at https://www.psychiatry.org/patients-families/prolonged-grief-disorder.

19. Jacques Donzelot, *The Policing of Families*, trans. Robert Hurley (New York: Pantheon, 1979), p. 129.

20. Leeat Granek, "Grief as Pathology: The Evolution of Grief Theory in Psychology from Freud to the Present," *History of Psychology* 13, no. 1 (2010): 49.

21. Sigmund Freud, "Mourning and Melancholia," in *The Standard Edition of the Complete Works of Sigmund Freud* vol. XIV, trans. James Strachey (London: Hogarth Press, 1914–16), pp. 248–9.

22. See "The History of the Psychiatric Diagnostic System Continued," *MentalHelp.net* at https://www.mentalhelp.net/personality-disorders/history-of-the-psychiatric-diagnostic-system-continued/ (last accessed August 28, 2024).

23. Michael J. Shapiro, "Metaphor in the Philosophy of the Social Sciences," *Cultural Critique* 2 (Winter 1985–6): 197.

24. Shoshana Felman, "Preface (To Reopen the Question)," *Paragraph* 40, no. 3 (2017): xiii.

25. Jean-Michel Rey, "Freud's Writing on Writing," *Yale French Studies* 55/56 (1977): 301.

26. Peter Brooks, "Freud's Master Plot," *Yale French Studies* 55/56 (1977): 280–300.

27. Dianne Chisholm, *H.D.'s Freudian Poetics: Psychoanalysis in Transition* (Ithaca, NY: Cornell University Press, 1992), pp. 3–4.

28. Rey, "Freud's Writing on Writing," p. 303.

29. *Ibid.*, p. 310.

30. *Ibid.*, p. 312.

31. *Ibid.*, p. 327.

32. Al Alvarez, "Foreword" to Harnish Canham, *Acquainted with the Night: Psychoanalysis and the Poetic Imagination* (London: Routledge, 2003), p. xiii.

33. Jean Laplanche, *Life & Death in Psychoanalysis*, trans. Jeffrey Mehlman (Baltimore, MD: Johns Hopkins University Press, 1970), p. 107.

34. *Ibid.*, p. 106.

35. Granek, "Grief as Pathology," p. 56. The inner quotations are from Christopher J. Lane, *Shyness: How Normal Behavior Became a Sickness* (New Haven, CT: Yale University Press, 2007).

36. Stuart A. Kirk and Herb Hutchins, *The Selling of DSM* (New York: De Gruyter, 1992), p. 5.

37. *Ibid.*, p. 6.

38. Amy Allen, *Critique on the Couch: Why Critical Theory Needs Psychoanalysis* (New York: Columbia University Press, 2020), p. 173.

39. Franco "Bifo" Berardi, *The Uprising: On Poetry and Finance* (New York: Semiotext(e), 2012), p. 158.

40. Quoted in Ben Bollig, "What Do We Say When We Say 'Juan Gelman'? On Pseudonyms and Polemics in Recent Argentine Poetry," *Modern Language Review* 109 (2014): 125.

41. For a summary of the gruesome details of the Argentine junta's disappearance tactic, see Elvia Arroyo-Ramirez, "Radical Empathy in the Context of Suspended Grief: An Affective Web of Mutual Loss," *Journal of Library and Information Studies* 3, no. 2 (2021): 1–15.

42. That apropos line is borrowed from Tammy Clewell, "Mourning Beyond Melancholia: Freud's Psychoanalysis of Loss," *Journal of the American Psychiatric Association* 52, no. 1 (2004): 63.

43. Juan Gelman, "I Sit Here Like an Invalid," in *Dark Times Filled with Light*, trans. Hardie St. Martin (Rochester, NY: Open Letter, 2012), p. 9.

44. Quoted in Hernán Vidal, "Ariel Dorman: The Residue of Hope after Public Personae Construction," HIOL Debates, *Hispanic Issues Online* 5 (2012): 6.

45. Ariel Dorfman, *Last Waltz in Santiago: And Other Poems of Exile and Disappearance* (New York: Penguin, 1988), p. 5.

46. See Ian Hacking, "Making up People," in *Historical Ontology* (Cambridge, MA: Harvard University Press, 2002), pp. 99–114.

47. Foucault, *Psychiatric Power*, p. 362.

48. Michel Foucault, *The Birth of the Clinic: An Archaeology of Medical Perception*, trans. A. M. Sheridan Smith (New York: Pantheon, 1973).

49. *Ibid.*, p. 188.

50. Elisabetta Basso, *Young Foucault*, trans. Marie Satya McDonough (New York: Columbia University Press, 2022).

51. *Ibid.*, p. xii.

52. *Ibid.*, p. xv.

53. See Michel Foucault, "About the Concept of the 'Dangerous Individual' in 19th-Century Legal Psychiatry," *International Journal of Law and Psychiatry* 1, no. 1

(1978), at http://schwarzemilch.files.wordpress.com/2009/02/foucault_dangerou s_individual.pdf (last accessed August 29, 2024).

54. Foucault, *The Birth of the Clinic*, p. 19.

55. In Foucault's words, a *dispositif* is "a thoroughly heterogeneous ensemble consisting of discourses, institutions, architectural forms, regulatory decisions, laws, administrative measures, scientific statements, philosophical, moral and philanthropic propositions ... the said as much as the unsaid ... the elements of the apparatus." Cited in Michael J. Shapiro, "Foucault and Method," in Philip Bonditti and Didier Bigo (eds.), *Foucault and the Modern International*, at https://doi.org/10.1057/978-1-137-56153-4_7. Gilles Deleuze's Foucault-influenced version of the concept adds a crucial nuance that lends the *dispositif* its historical dynamism. He refers to the mutations in the assemblages constituting a *dispositif* – for example, those historical events that have shifted the "lines of force" involved in structures of command (over others and/or over oneself). See Gilles Deleuze, "What is a *Dispositif*," in *Two Regimes of Madness*, trans. Ames Hodges and Mike Taormina (New York: Semiotext(e), 2006), p. 342.

56. Foucault, *The Birth of the Clinic*, p. 3.

57. *Ibid.*, p. 9.

58. *Ibid.*

59. Giorgio Agamben, *What is an Apparatus?* trans. David Kishik and Stefan Pedatella (Stanford, CA: Stanford University Press, 2009), p. 14.

60. Foucault, *The Birth of the Clinic*, p. 20.

61. Marcia Anglell, "Privatizing Health Care Is Not the Answer: Lessons from the United States," *Canadian Medical Association Journal* 179, no. 9 (2008): 916.

62. Eyal Press, "Moral Wounds: The Moral Crisis of American Doctors," *The New York Times Magazine*, June 15, 2023, at https://www.nytimes.com/2023/06/15/magazine/doctors-moral-crises.html?searchResultPosition=1 (last accessed August 29, 2024).

63. Shoshana Felman, "Education and Crisis: On the Vicissitudes of Teaching," in Shoshana Felman and Dori Laub, *Testimony: Crises of Witnessing in Literature, Psychoanalysis and History* (New York: Routledge, 1991), p. 1.

64. Felman and Laub, "Introduction," in *Testimony*, p. xiii.

65. *Ibid.*, p. 3.

66. *Ibid.*, p. 2.

67. *Ibid.*, p. 3.

68. Catherine E. Foote and Arthur W. Frank, "Foucault and Therapy: The Discipline of Grief," in Adrienne S. Chambon and Allan Irving (eds.), *Reading Foucault for Social Work* (New York: Columbia University Press, 1999), p. 170.

69. Dori Laub, "Bearing Witness: Or the Vicissitudes of Listening," in Felman and Laub, *Testimony*, p. 57.

70. Hannah Arendt, *The Human Condition* (Chicago: University of Chicago Press, 1958), p. 31.

71. Cindy Sheehan, quoted in Michael J. Shapiro, "The Presence of War," in *Studies in Trans-Disciplinary Method* (New York: Routledge, 2012), pp. 137–8.

72. Shapiro, "The Presence of War," p. 139.

73. Jacques Rancière, *Dis-agreement: Politics and Philosophy*, trans. Julie Rose (Minneapolis: University of Minnesota Press, 1999), p. 35.

74. Julia Kristeva, "Women's Time," trans. Alice Jardin and Harry Blake, *Signs* 7, no. 1 (1981): 32.

75. Jacques Rancière, "The Politics of Aesthetics," quoted in Shapiro, *Studies in Trans-Disciplinary Method*, p. 139.

76. María Laura Martínez Rodríguez, "Making Up People: A Project of More than Three Decades," in *Texture in the Work of Ian Hacking: Michel Foucault as the Guiding Thread of Hacking's Thinking* (New York: Springer, 2021), p. 89.

77. Amanda Wilcox, "Paternal Grief and the Public Eye: Cicero 'Ad Familiares'," *Phoenix* 59, no. 3/4 (Fall–Winter 2005): 267.

78. Paul Veyne, "The Inventory of Differences," trans. Elizabeth Kingdom, *Economy and Society* 11, no. 2 (1982): 173.

79. Erin Sullivan, "Sadness, Selfhood, and Disease," in *Beyond Melancholy* (London: Oxford University Press, 2016), p. 25.

80. R. Clifton Spargo, "The Apolitics of Antigone's Lament (from Sophocles to Ariel Dorfman)," *Mosaic* 41, no. 3 (September 2008): 18.

81. Melissa Wright, "Against the Evils of Democracy: Fighting Forced Disappearance and Neoliberal Terror in Mexico," *Annals of the American Association of Geographers* 108, no. 2 (2018): 332.

82. Margriet Blaauw, "'Denial and silence' of 'acknowledgement and disclosure'," *IRRC* 84, no. 848 (December 2002): 767.

83. Deborah Kelly Kloepfer, *The Unspeakable Mother* (Ithaca, NY: Cornell University Press, 1989), p. 1.

84. *Ibid.*, p. 27, also quoting Hilda Doolittle, *Hermione* (New York: New Directions, 1981), p. 42.

85. Mari Ruti, *A World of Fragile Things* (New York: State University of New York Press, 2009), p. 110.

86. *Ibid.*, p. 26, also quoting Margaret Homans, *Beating the Word: Female Experience in Nineteenth Century Women's Writing* (Chicago: University of Chicago Press, 1986), p. 16.

87. Fernando J. Bosco, "The Madres de Plaza de Mayo and Three Decades of Human Rights' Activism: Embeddedness, Emotions, and Social Movements," *Annals of the Academy of American Geographers* 96, no. 2 (2006): 342.

88. Andrea Malin, "Mothers Who Won't Disappear," *Human Rights Quarterly* 16, no. 1 (February 1994): 188.

89. Rancière, *Dis-agreement*, p. 35.

90. Evelyn Stevens, "Marianismo: The Oher Face of Machismo," in Ann Pescatello (ed.), *Female and Male in Latin America* (Pittsburgh, PA: University of Pittsburgh Press, 1973), p. 94.

91. Malin, "Mothers Who Won't Disappear," p. 190.

92. Berber Bevernage and Koen Aerts, "Haunting Pasts: Time and Historicity as Constructed by the Argentine Madres *de Plaza de Mayo* and Radical Flemish Nationalists," *Social History* 14, no. 4 (November 2009): 395.

93. Bosco, "The Madres de Plaza de Mayo," p. 350.

94. *Ibid.*, p. 448.
95. "Grandmothers of Plaza de Mayo Identify 130th Missing Grandchild of Long Search," *Buenos Aires Times*, June 10, 2009, at https://www.batimes.com.ar/news/argentina/grandmothers-of-plaza-de-mayo-identify-130th-missing-grandchild-of-long-search.phtml (last accessed August 29, 2024).
96. To describe the event: Students expected the government to give in to their demands, but they were greeted with a clear message from the President: "No more unrest will be tolerated." The army proceeded in the following days to seize the National University, with virtually no resistance from the students, and later the National Polytechnic Institute, with active and violent student resistance. After these events, the students rapidly called for a new gathering, on October 2, at the Three Cultures Square in the Tlatelolco housing complex. Thousands of students showed up to get firsthand knowledge of the movement's next steps. As the gathering was ending, soldiers arrived to capture the movement's leaders. They were greeted by gunshots from the buildings surrounding the square. The troops then opened fire, turning the evening into a shooting that lasted nearly two hours. "Mexico's 1968 Massacre: What Really Happened?" *NPR*, December 1, 2008, at https://www.npr.org/2008/12/01/97546687/mexicos-1968-massacre-what-really-happened (last accessed August 29, 2024).
97. Wright, "Against the Evils of Democracy," p. 327.
98. Carlos Fuentes, *Destiny and Desire*, trans. Edith Grossman (New York: Random House, 2011), p. 382.
99. *Ibid.*
100. Wright, "Against the Evils of Democracy," p. 332.
101. *Ibid.*, p. 333.
102. "Mexico: Women March to Demand Justice, Answers for Disappeared," *Aljazeera*, May 10, 2022, at https://www.aljazeera.com/news/2022/5/10/mexico-women-march-to-demand-justice-answers-for-disappeared (last accessed August 29, 2024).
103. Lisa Rose Bradford, translator's introduction to *Between Words: Juan Gelman's Public Letter*, trans. Lisa Rose Bradford (San Francisco: Coimbra, 2010), p. 5.
104. Katherine M. Hedeen and Victor Rodriguez Nunez, translators' introduction, "Juan Gelman: 'There are hunger in the broken savor of the world,'" in *Juan Gelman: To World*, trans. Katherine M. Hedeen and Victor Rodriguez Nunez (Cromer, U.K.: Salt, 2014), p. xxi.
105. *Ibid.*, pp. xxi–xxii.
106. *Ibid.*, p. xxi.
107. *Letters of Note*, October 27, 2015, at https://lettersofnote.com/2015/10/27/i-would-like-to-give-you-your-own-history/.
108. Juan Gelman, *Between Words: Juan Gelman's Public Letter*, trans. Lisa Rose Bradford (San Francisco: Coimbra, 2010), p. 85.
109. *Letters of Note.*
110. Gelman, *Between Words*, p. 43.
111. Bradford, translator's introduction to *Between Words*, p. 2.
112. Hedeen and Nunez, translator's introduction, "Juan Gelman," p. xxvii.

113. David Shneer, *Grief: The Biography of a Holocaust Photograph* (New York: Oxford University Press, 2020), p. 51.
114. *Ibid.*, p. 53.
115. *Ibid.*, p. 36.
116. Ilya Sevinsky, *Wartime Diaries*, January 1942, cited in Shneer, *Grief*, pp. 36–7.
117. *Ibid.*, p. 37.
118. Theodore Roethke, *On Poetry & Craft* (Port Townsend, WA: Copper Canyon Press, 2001), p. 41.
119. Sylvester, *The Brutality of Fact*, p. 182.
120. Jacques Rancière, "Images Re-Read: The Method of Georges Didi-Huberman," *Angelaki* 23, no. 4 (August 2018): 16.
121. *Ibid.*, p. 18.
122. Tom Conley, "Afterword," in Gilles Deleuze, *Francis Bacon: The Logic of Sensation*, trans. Daniel W. Smith (Minneapolis: University of Minnesota Press, 2003), p. 138.
123. Gilles Deleuze, "Spinoza and the Three 'Ethics'," in *Essays Critical and Clinical*, trans. Daniel W. Smith and Michael A. Greco (Minneapolis: University of Minnesota Press, 1997), p. 144.
124. Lisa Rose Bradford, "Afterword: A Conversation with Juan Gelman," in *Between Words*, p. 91.
125. *Ibid.*, p. 92.
126. Gelman, "Alone," in *Dark Times Filled with Light*, 91.
127. William Rowe and Teresa Whitfield, "Thresholds of Identity: Literature and Exile in Latin America," *Third World Quarterly* 9, no. 1 (January 1987): 236.
128. Ariel Dorfman, "Whose Memory? Whose Justice: Meditations on How and When to Reconcile," Annual Nelson Mandela Lecture, South Africa, August 2, 2010, in *Campus, Academics, Global*, at https://today.duke.edu/2010/08/dorfman.html (last accessed August 29, 2024).
129. Ariel Dorfman, quoted in Carolyn Pinet and Carol Pinet, "Retrieving the Disappeared Text: Women, Chaos & Change in Argentina & Chile After the Dirty Wars," *Hispanic Journal* 18, no. 1 (Spring 1997): 91.
130. Ariel Dorfman, "Afterword," in *The Resistance Trilogy* (London: Nick Hern Books, 1998), p. 212.
131. For a feminist reading of the film version, see Orit Kamir, "Cinematic Judgment and Jurisprudence: A Woman's Memory, Recovery, and Justice in a Post-Traumatic Society (A Study of Roman Polanski's *Death and the Maiden*)," in Austin Sarat, Lawrence Douglas, and Martha Merrill Umphrey (eds.), *Law on the Screen* (Stanford, CA: Stanford University Press, 2005), pp. 27–81.
132. Pinet and Pinet, "Retrieving the Disappeared Text," p. 96.
133. Ariel Dorman, "Foreword," *The Resistance Trilogy*, p. vi.
134. *Ibid.*, p. ix.
135. Ariel Dorfman, "Acknowledgments in the Guise of an Afterword," *The Resistance Trilogy*, p. 75.
136. Mieke Bal, "Response: Ariel Dorfman's Quest for Responsibility," *The Art Bulletin* 90, no. 1 (2009): 50.

137. Pierre Nora, "Between Memory and History: *Les Lieux de Memoire*," *Representations* 26 (Spring 1989): 8.
138. *Ibid.*
139. Carlos Fuentes, "Writing in Time," *Democracy* 2, no. 1 (January 1962): 72.
140. See Gilles Deleuze, *Cinema 2: The Time Image*, trans. Hugh Tomlinson and Robert Galeta (Minneapolis: University of Minnesota Press, 1989).
141. See the commentary by James E. Young, "The Holocaust as Vicarious Past: Art Spiegelman's *Maus* and the Afterimages of History," *Critical Inquiry* 24 (Spring 1998): 666–99.
142. Bal, "Response: Ariel Dorfman's Quest for Responsibility," p. 49.
143. Jacques Rancière, "Fictions of Time," in Grace Hellyer and Julian Murphet (eds.), *Rancière and Literature* (Edinburgh: Edinburgh University Press, 2016), p. 26.
144. Manus I. Midlarsky, Preface to *The Killing Trap: Genocide in the Twentieth Century* (New York: Cambridge University Press, 2005), p. xiii.
145. *Ibid.*, pp. xiii–xiv. The invitation was from his wife, "Professor Liz Midlarsky of Teachers College, Columbia University … then in the midst of a research project on helping during the Holocaust (supported by The national Institutes of Health)."
146. Midlarsky, *The Killing Trap*, p. 14.
147. From my interview with Manus Midlarsky, June 15, 2023. To follow up and learn more about the writerly narrative path that Midlarsky shares with Gelman and Dorfman, a move from being initially affected to the construction of critical conceptual thinking, I approached him (a long-term acquaintance who was my classmate in the Political Science PhD program at Northwestern University in the mid-1960s) about an interview. The quotations of his responses to my questions are a result of his generous assent to the request. This is his response to my question, "Can you say something about the extent to which your sense of obligation to a suffering generation was involved in your deferral, and about the tension you might have felt between your obligation to them and one to your vocation. Then, speaking of the vocation … as a social scientist … what can you say about the process of finding '*your* own way' as you faced a huge Holocaust and genocide literature."
148. Midlarsky, *The Killing Trap*, p. 15.
149. The author's interview with Manus Midlarsky on June 14, 2023.
150. Midlarsky, *The Killing Trap*, p. 395.
151. Gilles Deleuze, *Pure Immanence*, trans. Anne Boyman, (New York: Zone Books, 2005), p. 46.
152. Stefan Hertmans, *War and Turpentine*, trans. David McKay (New York: Pantheon, 2016), p. 9.
153. *Ibid.*, 15.
154. *Ibid.*, p. 10.
155. Cathy Caruth, *Unclaimed Experience: Trauma, Narrative, and History* (Baltimore, MD: Johns Hopkins University Press, 1990), p. 24
156. Eileen Battersby, "*War and Turpentine* by Stefan Hertmans Review: Real, Raw and Powerful," *The Irish Times*, July 6, 2016, at https://www.irishtimes.com/

culture/books/war-and-turpentine-by-stefan-hertmans-review-real-raw-and-pow-erful-1.2712362 (last accessed August 29, 2024).

157. Hertmans, *War and Turpentine*, p. 264.

158. *Ibid.*

159. In *Search for Lost Time*, Proust writes, "It was only at that moment – more than a year after her burial, on account of that anachronism that so often keeps the calendar of facts from coinciding with the calendar of feelings – that I real-ized she was dead." Gilles Deleuze, *Proust and Signs*, trans. Richard Howard (Minneapolis: University of Minnesota Press, 2000), pp. 20–1.

160. Lars Bernaerts, *Narrative Constellations of Empathy in the Contemporary Novel*. An open access text at https://www.degruyter.com/document/doi/10.1515/9783110693065-014/html?lang=en (last accessed August 29, 2024).

161. *Ibid.*, p. 268.

162. Hertmans, *War and Turpentine*, p. 3.

163. *Ibid.*, p. 16.

164. *Ibid.*, p. 188.

165. *Ibid.*, p. 196.

166. *Ibid.*, p. 217.

167. *Ibid.*, p. 284.

168. *Ibid.*, p. 255.

169. *Ibid.*, p. 226.

170. Paul Fussell, *Wartime: Understanding and Behavior in the Second World War* (New York: Oxford University Press, 1990), p. 4.

171. *Ibid.*, p. 8.

172. *Ibid.*, p. 12.

173. George L. Mosse, *Fallen Soldiers: Reshaping the Memory of the World Wars* (New York: Oxford University Press, 1990), p. 7.

174. *Ibid.*, p. 21.

175. Alexa Hagerty, "The Melancholy of Bones: Forensic Exhumation as an Elegaic Transformative Experience," *Ethos* 49, no. 3 (2022): 266.

176. Georgi Gospodinov, *Time Shelter*, trans. Angela Rodel (New York: Liveright, 2023), 17.

177. See Basso, *Young Foucault*, p. 169, where she refers to Foucault's "demonstration" that the aphasic is one who has "lost a world in which he can orient himself."

178. Gospodinov, *Time Shelter*, p. 81.

179. The expression belongs to Walter Benjamin, *The Origin of German Tragic Drama*, trans. John Osborne (New York: Verso, 1998), p. 177.

180. *Ibid.*, p. 126.

181. *Ibid.*

182. *Ibid.*, p. 210.

183. *Ibid.*, p. 176.

184. *Ibid.*, p. 260.

185. *Ibid.*, p. 254.

186. Ismail Xavier, "Historical Allegory," in Toby Miller and Robert Stam (eds.), *A Companion to Film Theory* (Malden, MA: Blackwell, 1999), p. 340.

2. CIVIC CLEANSING: WILLED AMNESIA, ARTISTIC ANAMNESIS

SHELTERING

Georgi Gospodinov's novel *Time Shelter*, the last text I engage in Chapter 1, stages a global outbreak of national amnesia, the creation of time shelters within which nation-states select preferred periods of their histories. They each identify a decade as the paradigm for freezing the national community in what they regard as an uncontentious time and mandate a forgetting of other, less felicitous ones. As I put it in Chapter 1, "As the process unfolds, political parties compete to promote some decades and discard others (for example, France and Spain choose the 1980s, Portugal the 1970s)." Among what is implied in the selections are the notorious silences of European states about their colonial and postcolonial atrocities. They have the effect of striking from public recognition the narratives with which segments of their society identify themselves and seek to negotiate their place among the multiple stories that have shaped civic space. One can thus imagine why France would discard the 1960s, which featured the 1961 Maurice Papon-instigated Paris massacre of 200-plus French-Algerians involved in a peaceful protest. Their bodies ended up floating in the Seine, an event that has since been absent from official and popular versions of French history. In her historical novel concerned with the political choices of France's Algerian expatriates – some confined to camps in years following the massacre – Alice Zeniter provides an apt metaphor for the official silence. "Just as it stitches the borders of the resettlement camps with barbed wire, so France sews up its lips."[1]

Although the worldwide outbreak of amnesia that Gospodinov invents is a parody rather than a data-driven investigation of national policies, the gap between parody and reality is narrow. Nation-state temporality – that which is institutionalized as official history – has always involved a process of invention, reinvention, and suppression, the rhythms of which have tracked with changes in the kind of leadership steering the state. Of late, as is noted in a recent review of a Holocaust book, "Populist politicians everywhere, from Viktor Orban in Hungary to Donald Trump in the United States, are trying to remold their nation's history into an uncritically patriotic narrative that involves massive denial of its negative aspects and brazen rejection of historical truth."[2]

That aspect of temporal governance, one facet of what I have elsewhere called "cultural governance," is a practice with which states have perpetuated the myth that they contain a culturally unified and consensual people.[3] A look back over the centuries shows how state governments have striven to contain, at times violently and at times with subtle forms of control, history-attuned ideational disparities that deconstruct that myth.[4] Two periods in Soviet history provide illustrations of violent versus subtly coercive approaches to silencing equilibrium-disturbing voices. In an elegant passage in his *Life and Fate* (a novel treated in the Introduction), Vasily Grossman captures the former, commenting within the text on Stalin's purges of his Bolshevik co-revolutionaries, which began in 1936:

> The might of the state had constructed a new past. It had made the Red Cavalry charge a second time. It had dismissed the genuine heroes of long past events and appointed new ones. The state had the power to replay events, to transform figures of granite and bronze, to alter speeches long since delivered, to change the faces in a news photograph. A new history had been written.[5]

Exemplifying a subtle strategy decades later is the way the dissident writer Vladmir Nabokov achieved partial rehabilitation in Soviet Russia. A story excerpted from his 1954 book *Different Shores*, the first of his works to be openly published in his native land, appeared in a small-circulation chess magazine in 1986, nine years after he died.[6]

Gospodinov's allegorical intention, accomplished as a parody of state-level civic cleansing, calls attention to a wide range of amnesiac strategies accomplished through *sheltering*, a concept that for Gospodinov refers to both a geriatric practitioner's management of dementia at an individual level and the official management of collective historical time. Because he supplies no definitive or wholly "satisfactory answers to readers' interrogations,"[7] Gospodinov's turn to allegory encourages productive reception. Drawing in this chapter on a different concept of shelter, conceived and illustrated by Jeremy Eichler,

I respond to that implicit challenge with attention to an oppositional form of sheltering, historical restorations accomplished in artistic genres. In his investigation, *Time's Echo*, Eichler reviews musical compositions that thematize violence against civilians during World War II, the details of which states have since suppressed. Among them is Arnold Schoenberg's "A Survivor From Warsaw," *which evokes details of the Holocaust carried out in Poland,* and Benjamin Britten's "War Requiem," a musical meditation on the bombing of Coventry by the German Luftwaffe during the same period. Redemption-aimed rather than parodic, Eichler attributes the inspiration for his inquiry to Walter Benjamin's "vison of the true purpose of history: to sort through the rubble of earlier eras in order to recover those buried shards of unrealized hope, to reclaim and redeem them."[8] Integral to that aim is a one of Eichler's featured illustrations, a nuanced analysis of a Britten song cycle based on nine John Donne sonnets:

> The cycle ends with Donne's famous "Death be not proud," set in this case as a passacaglia in which a five-bar ground bass cycles through the song … Both the sonnet and the song end with the famous line "Death, thou shalt die" … To whom, one may ask, is this music's final reassurance directed? Perhaps to no one more than the deeply shaken composer himself. "Songs connect, collect and bring together," the critic John Berger has written, providing "a shelter" from the flow of linear time: a shelter in which future, present and past can console, provoke, ironize and inspire one another.[9]

As Eichler reflects on the ways musical compositions restore what state-level cultural governance neglects, over-codes, or erases, he evokes the present and future along with the past to enlarge the temporal frame within which forces of inclusion and exclusion contend. In what follows, I engage other such restorative temporal shelters in three artistic works, an Atom Egoyan film, a Judith McCormack novel, and an Octavia Butler work of speculative fiction, each of which is a historically attuned, amnesia-resisting contribution to the temporal enlargement of civic life. Egoyan's 2002 film *Ararat*, to which I turn first, addresses one of the most enduring cases of willed amnesia, Turkey's steadfast resistance to acknowledging the Armenian genocide which began in April 1915 (scholarly estimates put the number of victims to upwards of 1.2 million).[10] Despite Turkey's attempts to delete the genocide from history, using both internal and extra-territorial sanctions aimed at repressing details of the atrocities, intimate experiences of the event continue to surface, mainly through the attention drawn to it by diasporic Armenians in artistic treatments of its various afterlives.

Ararat

Egoyan's film is historiographic as well as thematic. As he attests, "In making *Ararat*, I wanted to show how the truth is not to be found in the epic scenes of deportation and massacre, but in the intimate moments shared by individuals."[11] Given that the dominant (Hegelian and neo-Hegelian) historiographies feature the nation-state as a culmination of collective belonging, *Ararat*, written and staged by one who belongs to a dissident "time scale,"[12] provides a diasporic temporal habitus whose collective coherence defies state-oriented identification; it is counter-historical in its locus of enunciation as well as its theme. Rather than dwelling on Turkey's willed amnesia, *Ararat* is a self-conscious meditation on the ways that history is constituted through stories in multiple artistic genres: biographies, films, photographs, theatrical performances, paintings, and bodies (experience-recalling feelings and gestural movements). As Egoyan has stated, he wanted to show "the importance of finding a way to articulate history – identifying what it means to you and what it means to others in the process."[13] With its emphasis on the vagaries of historical interpretation, the film is less concerned with disclosing the historical truth of an event, which Turkey steadfastly misrepresents, than with sorting the way experiential truth resides in the afterlife of the event, emerging in intimate spaces, especially in civically relevant conversations within families. In *Ararat* artistic displays and performances along with intense conversational engagements lead to recovered sensations associated with past events. The details surface when bodies are affected by scenes and events that nudge the buried pain and trauma with which they are associated to the surface.

At an interpersonal level the phenomenology of perception surrounds the spaces of interaction in the film, as stories are circulated and contested within families, testimony takes place at the border between arriving protagonists and a security-conscious customs agent, and historical events associated with the genocide are featured in public performances – a film, a public lecture, and a museum exhibition – all showing aspects of the way the Armenian genocide is continually (re)experienced. Crucial as regards comprehending *Ararat*'s complex temporality as it shifts among the past, present, and an imagined future is heeding its grammar. As Egoyan puts it, "The grammar of the film uses every possible tense and mood available to tell its story, from the basic pillars of the past, present and future to the subjective, the past-perfect, and past-not-so-perfect, and the past-would-be-perfect-if-it-weren't-so-conditional."[14]

Continually integrated within those complex grammatical rhythms are hands which serve as main protagonists. While many of the important scenes are filtered through tension-filled families, at the individual level bodies register Armenian history, most notably the painter Arshile Gorky's, whose painting of himself as a child with his mother, copied from a studio photograph, supplies

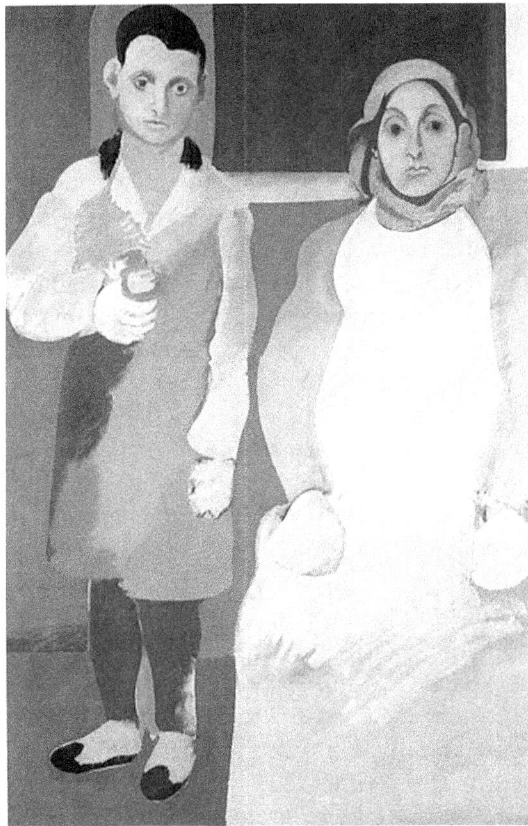

Figure 2.1 Portrait of Arshile Gorky and his mother in Atom Egoyan's 2002 film *Ararat*. Source: Alliance Studio, DVD, 2005.

the film's main iconography (Figure 2.1). Embodied memory, Gorky's and others', is at the center of the film's haptic events, those moments in which hands are the tactile media through which painful historical memories are recovered and intimacies are restored. To put the film's compositional practice figuratively, it's a meeting between the director's, Egoyan's, composing hands and his characters' hands.

An instructive way to frame that strategy is to turn to the jazz musician Thelonious Monk's keyboard style, which enacts a creative tension between melody and form. As one critic puts it, "Where other musicians played light chords with their left hand and quicker notes with the right, Monk played equally complicated notes with both hands."[15] His musical compositions, arranged as he played, simultaneously deliver melodies and dissonant chords that interrupt them with both sound and spacing strategies. For that, Monk's keyboard method frequently allocates one hand to playing an intelligible melody (the right) and the other to playing dissonant chords that generate tension (the left). Rather than offering a melody for the listener's enjoyment of something familiar, Monk introduces critical musical thinking, a demonstration that melodies are subject to a plurality of musical perspectives.[16]

Comparing Egoyan's cinematic compositional style with Monk's playing style, I suggest that while composing with one hand – the film-within-the-film directed by his character Edward Saroyan (Charles Aznavour), which offers an intelligible albeit fictionalized history – Egoyan's other hand is summoning the viewer's attention to details within a dissonant film grammar that thinks about history's alternative presences located in contemporary lived experience. As that second hand counters the first, which is delivering non-linear temporal and thematic juxtapositions, *Ararat* becomes a story that belongs to the film genre to which Gilles Deleuze famously refers as a "cinema of seeing." Juxtaposed to a "cinema of action" in which the viewer's problem is "'What are we going to see in the next image,'" the viewer's problem in a cinema of seeing is "'What is there to see in the image?'"[17]

That problem surfaces as the film opens. While the credits are run, the viewer is alerted to one of the film's multiple narrative threads, the creation of Arshile Gorky's (Simon Abkarian) painting of himself as young boy with his mother who died, leaving Gorky to make it out of Turkey alone. That painting is at the center of a story that participates in *Ararat*'s dual film narrative, the narrative supplied by a film-within-the-film, focused on the genocide as history, and the overall film narrative focused on how its aftermath is experienced, individually and in both intimate and contentious interpersonal encounters. After images of the painting launch the film, the following scene begins with a face shot of Saroyan who has just arrived in Toronto to direct the film-within-the-film. After a long take of his face there's a cut to a framing shot of the landscape leading up to Turkey's Mount Ararat before cutting back to where Saroyan is standing in the foreign arrivals section of the Toronto airport, where the camera zooms in on his carry-on bag. As the scene proceeds, David (Christopher Plummer), the customs inspector examining his luggage, takes a pomegranate out of the carry-on and says it's not permitted. Before the scene ends, Saroyan takes the pomegranate back and begins eating it, saying that the seeds bring him luck. His offer to David to try them is declined.

That sequence distills much of the film's compositional approach to the afterlife of the genocide. The cut from Saroyan's face to the Ararat landscape suggests that he carries the memory of his homeland with him as part of his mental baggage (as the metaphorical close-up of his carry-on bag, closely following the landscape scene, implies). David's remark that the piece of fruit is "not permitted" is another metaphorical gesture; it echoes Turkey's proscription on mentioning the Armenian genocide. When Saroyan then takes the pomegranate back and eats it, commenting that the seeds bring him luck, his body is yet another metaphor, a media genre that articulates the experiential aspect of his biography. That the interaction takes place at a policed border emphasizes the condition that characterizes diasporic Armenian civic life, which requires individual and collective management of the estrangement of going into exile. As he attests, Egoyan's film is his way of managing that estrangement. While the film-within-the-film provides a reading of the past, the overall film, "replete with mnemonic anchors tying the past to the present," reflects continually on "transgenerational trauma," which remains persistent for Armenian émigrés.[18]

Saroyan's filmmaking role is one of several plot lines that Egoyan composes, not, as he has said, to reveal what Turkey has striven to hide – he points out that despite how Turkey's "denial has been universally sustained and meticulously pursued," the events that took place are irrefutable – but to explore relationships between media and history. Egoyan's historiographic emphasis is on the genocide's afterlife as it exists in the stories, media images, emotions, and interactions of Armenians, Turks, others (and in himself as an émigré from Egypt). Exchanges of accusations, complaints, intimacies, and interpretive contention constitute, in his words, "the emotional foundations" that "persist in our culture today."[19] To map that pluralistic post-genocide afterlife while at the same time reflecting on the ways it is mediated by a variety of artistic genres, Egoyan weaves a complex tapestry of memory shelters.

One of the most subtle memory moments occurs in the film's footage of Arshile Gorky in his New York studio at the moment in which he is preparing to modify the iconic painting of himself as a child with his mother Shushan. As he approaches the canvas, Armenian music is playing in the background. Feeling the rhythm of the music, Gorky steps back and executes several dance steps which have lingered as part of muscle memory from his childhood, yielding an embodied response to the music (Figure 2.2). That moment is implicitly referenced in a later scene. While Gorky's dance testifies to the way that the aftermath of the Armenian diaspora persists as embodied memory, a later dance scene takes us back to atrocities visited on a group of Armenian women abducted by a Turkish regiment while they were on the road heading into exile. In Saroyan' s film-within-the-film, he casts the young Gorky as a witness to the coerced dance scene. As he watches from hiding, Turkish soldiers are whipping naked Armenian women, forcing them to dance before murdering them by pouring flammable liquid on them and setting them on fire.

The disparate dance scenes constitute one among several referential montages that are essential to *Ararat*'s compositional structure. This one testifies to the disjuncture between Saroyan's film-within-the-film and Egoyan's film. While Saroyan's narrates atrocities based on the journals of the American physician and missionary Clarence Ussher (Bruce Greenwood), an eyewitness

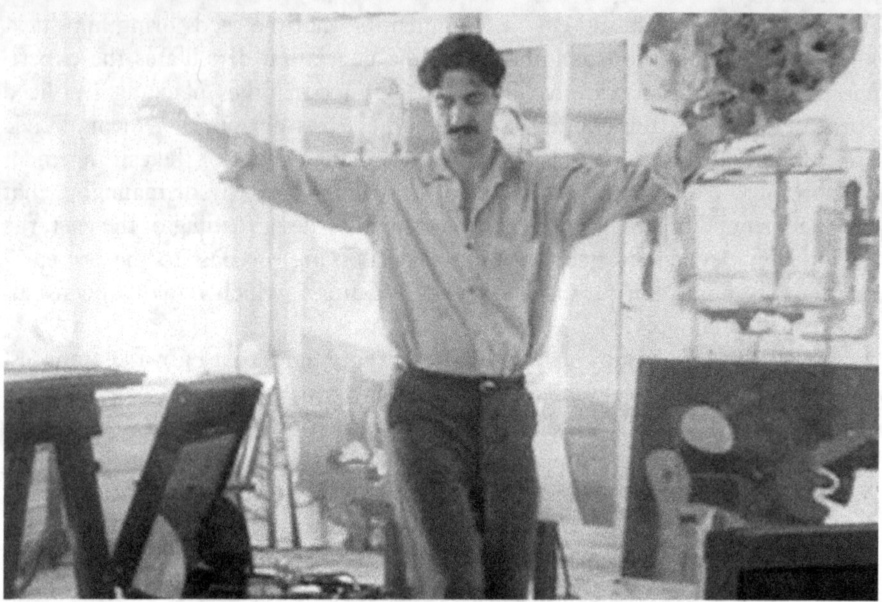

Figure 2.2 Arshile Gorky dancing to Armenian music in Atom Egoyan's 2002 film *Ararat*. Source: Alliance Studio, DVD, 2005.

to the genocide while living in Van (Gorky's home village), Egoyan's pursues the way that that past is lived in the present. Nevertheless, Egoyan implicitly endorses Saroyan's fictionalizing – to which Saroyan refers in a conversation within the film as "poetic license" – because the truth of history for Egoyan lies in what remains sensible and figurable to those who experience it, not in a narrative's fidelity to historical events.

The character who bears much of the burden of articulating Egoyan's version of truth is Raffi. Like Gorky, Raffi is a body that registers the sensations through which the genocidal event continues to be lived. However, Gorky's and Raffi's stories move in opposite directions, exemplified in the relationship of each with their mother's hands. Gorky's mother's hands show up in two ways in the Saroyan film. In one scene, as mother and son are walking in their village, Shushan's (Lousnak Abdalian) hands are continually caressing the young Arshile (Garan Boyajian), wrapped around his back, rubbing his shoulder, and rarely breaking contact. Later, in a scene in the photographer's studio, the camera zooms in on Shushan's hands before backing up to capture the mother-and-son tableau that Gorky's painting copies. In Egoyan's film, Shushan's hands show up in several repeated scenes in a museum where Raffi's mother Ani, an art historian, is lecturing on Gorky's life, once with the famous painting projected in the background and twice when the painting is displayed on the museum wall. The last two museum scenes are another of the film's referential montages. In the first one, Ani's stepdaughter Celia, from whom she is estranged, tries to attack the painting with a knife before being restrained by a museum guard. In a subsequent scene much later in the film, Ani approaches the painting, which is unguarded at that moment, and touches it, caressing Shushan's body and hands.

In between those scenes is the one in Gorky's New York studio when Gorky paints over Shushan's hands, obscuring them before weeping in despair. While the film leaves Gorky in a state of mourning – what Freud famously refers to as a reaction to a lost object, most prominently the lost mother – having realized that the comfort of his mother's touch is irretrievable, it gives Raffi the opposite mother–son temporal trajectory. In his first appearance, he's reading a poem from his book to women in his mother's reading group. Immediately afterwards, we become aware that Tolstoy's famous opening to his novel *Anna Karenina* about unhappy families – "All happy families are alike, each unhappy family is unhappy in its own way" – prevails. Raffi is sexually involved with his stepsister, Celia, he has serious disagreements with his mother, and Celia, who is fundamentally estranged from Ani, expresses her anger toward her stepmother (whom she accuses of causing her father's death) by attending her lectures and asking impertinent questions. Ani, in turn vexed by Celia's constant criticism, is unhappy about Raffi and Celia's relationship; she has admonished Raffi about the propriety of sleeping with his stepsister.

While Raffi is pressured by both Ani and Celia to take sides in their controversy, he is more preoccupied with recovering and publicizing the details of the Armenian genocide than with managing family tensions. As his body, like Gorky's, becomes a text registering the way the event lives in the present, the film uses his role to articulate Egoyan's reflections on historical truth. Two of Raffi's encounters are the vehicles for that articulation. The first is precipitated by his witnessing of the Saroyan film-within-the-film, in which the actor Ali (Elias Koteas) plays a convincing role as Jevdet Bay, the Turkish commander who bears much of the responsibility for the atrocities during the genocide. Assigned to drive Ali back to his lodging after the filming, Raffi, despite their contentious conversation in which Ali expresses support for the Turkish position, thanks him for his performance. After telling Ali that his father was killed trying to assassinate a Turkish diplomat, he says that watching him do such a convincing portrayal of Bay has made him experience a killing rage. Ali, he says, has helped him become attuned to what he's been feeling, the truth of the past that had been an "unclaimed experience."[20] Unmoved by the revelation, Ali simply says, "you're welcome," and as one representing the diasporic Turkish population's complicity in Turkey's denial of the genocide, urges him to put the past behind him.

In contrast, Raffi's next crucial conversation has a powerful effect on his interlocutor. In that scene, Raffi, having landed in Toronto after visiting Turkey and taking film footage of the terrain of the genocide in Khorkom, near Lake Van (where Gorky is from), is in front of David, the customs inspector who is suspicious about the film canisters Raffi has in his possession. When David asks him to open them, Raffi resists, saying that the film footage they contain would be ruined if exposed to the light. What follows is a long interrogation, punctuated by cuts to other narrative threads within the film-within-the-film and the overall film. As the interrogation proceeds, David, who begins as his old self, someone wholly unsympathetic toward anyone with a criminal past and anyone who is likely to be involved in a smuggling attempt (as well as one who is proud of his ability to detect lying), undergoes a transformation. After Raffi enlightens him about what had transpired during the genocide, and in particular the experience of Arshile Gorky, David becomes less interested in whether Raffi is smuggling heroin in the canisters (which he is) and more fascinated with Raffi's exemplary emotional commitment to preserving the memory of the Armenian experience. He becomes convinced that Raffi truly believes they contain film footage because he is an honest true believer in the necessity of publicizing the residual trauma of the genocidal event. The more he learns about Raffi and his family situation, the more he sees Raffi as a beloved son as well as one committed to historical truth. By the end of the interrogation, despite having learned that the canisters contain heroin, David treats Raffi as a son rather than as a smuggler and lets him phone his mother to come pick him up. When she does, a mother's hands once again come into play. Relieved that Raffi has not been arrested, she shelves her former discontent with her son and takes his face in her hands in a long caress.

A similar family scene follows when David's son Philip (Brent Carver) comes to pick *him* up at the airport. While David and Philip were estranged the first time we see them together, their second scene together revokes the first one. Whereas in an earlier car ride Philip tells his father that his rigid moral policing mentality was no longer welcome in his home because of its negative effect on *his* son, David's grandson, in this repeat ride Philip is incredulous that David has let a heroin smuggler go. "Dad, what came over you?" he says. David responds with, "I think it's hope, hope for human kind" and adds, "it's you Philip." Raffi's passion turns out to be contagious. It awakens something long buried and unclaimed in David, his love for *his* son. His family, like Raffi's (which had also been "unhappy in its own way"), has resolved its tensions. As for what is intended by David's transformation, I suggest that it affirms the value of the kind of truth to which Egoyan has dedicated his film. While his film rehearses the traumatic after-effects of the Armenian genocide, it also imagines conditions of possibility for the restoration of interpersonal intimacies that get obscured when the focus is on the evidence of who is responsible for what has been done to whom. To repeat the Egoyan quotation from above, "I wanted to show how the truth is not to be found in the epic scenes of deportation and massacre, but in the intimate moments shared by individuals." The text to which I turn next, another historiographic metafictional story of atrocities, also features a redemptive effect.

A "Singing Forest" in Belarus

Jill Jarvis provides an instructive prelude to Judith McCormack's *The Singing Forest*, a novel that uses the occasion of a legal case to resurrect a repressed historical event. Referring to literature's "unexpected, disruptive, and surreptitious power to make ghosts perceptible, and to make possible what state violence has rendered nearly unimaginable,"[21] Jarvis suggests that in contrast with "activist effort to instrumentalize the language of the law to compel the state to listen," literature does its work by "flagrantly disregarding and defying the language of the law."[22] McCormack's novel reflects on and complicates the law–literature binary that Jarvis proposes. A literary recreation of what had been for decades a hidden atrocity – thousands of people in Belarus murdered by Stalin's NKVD – the novel makes "ghosts perceptible" by staging the historical event as a crime story in which the main drama is the trial of a collaborator in the Stalin-ordered mass killing of (officially) 30,000 ("unofficially, two hundred thousand") residents.[23] Before it concludes, a novel that begins as a crime story thinks well outside of the issues of justice, crime, and punishment, as it constructs a series of dialectic inter-articulations between national histories and individual biographies.

The historical event on which the novel is based is the 1988 discovery of a killing field in Kurapaty, a village in Belarus. The more than 30,000 victims, almost all shot in the head by Stalin's NKVD, were part of a large-scale repression of the Belarusian people, which began in the 1930s and ended in 1941. Part of a purge that claimed at least 250,000 victims in Belarus, western Ukraine and other neighboring areas, the victims represented a broad swath of the population: intelligentsia, farmers, Polish residents, visiting Polish officers, most of the Jewish residents, and many others. The civic cleansing of inconvenient existences was based on the presumption that they were either unsuited for or recalcitrant to Stalin's image of a Soviet future.[24] McCormack's novel invents protagonists to imagine the initial experiences of perpetrators and victims as well as the continuing effects of that historical event, which Belarusian authorities have been reluctant fully to expose, part of a general "unwillingness of the post-independence government to pursue the harsher aspect of the Stalin era."[25]

The novel's drama is shaped by another discovery: a war crimes perpetrator, Stefan Drozd, is found living in Canada where he has worked in a glass-bottling plant throughout his adult life, a much longer career than the brief one he had in Minsk as a young man extracting confessions from prisoners prior to their executions (so employed because the NKVD had discovered that his brutal interactions with those selected for execution tended to produce quiescent acceptance of their fate). Now in his nineties, he's facing a trial in the country to which he has fled. While supplying the details through which Drozd became part of the killing machine, the novel, in alternating chapters, dwells on the contingencies that have shaped not only Drozd but also his adversary, Leah Jarvis, a young lawyer with Jewish ancestry, working in a law firm in which her older male colleagues have been withholding respect. With her professional worthiness at stake, she has the job of building the prosecution's case against Drozd.

The evidence demands for a war crimes prosecution, especially for crimes that took place many decades ago, turns Jarvis into a traveler and historiographer as well as a legal functionary. She journeys to Belarus to interview living witnesses to the atrocities. Compositionally, beyond its crime and punishment drama the novel enlists her within an ongoing *self*-conscious commentary on ethico-political questions surrounding such prosecutions. At one point, as Leah "glances at the man across from them [the prosecution team]," the questions the glance evokes are represented in free indirect discourse, a counter-ideological compositional form that resists identification between a character and author. It alerts the reader to a thought-provoking tension between what the novel wants to ask and the perspectives of the characters involved in the case:

> What does a war criminal look like? An alleged criminal that is, Stefan Drozd, a man in his nineties, his face cross-hatched with lines, the skin on his hands like cracked varnish. Sitting stoically as his lawyer makes his submissions ... The man the government – their client – wants to deport. Why now? A deterrent to others, to refugees who lie their way in. Or to keep him from benefiting from his crimes?

The novel doesn't answer those questions. It performs the way critically attuned literature can. "The role of the arts," as the novelist and screen writer Thornton Wilder puts it, "is not to answer questions, but to state them fairly."[26] Crucially, as regards the implicit question that passage raises about justice, whereas the case as it is litigated submits to legal temporality – it moves toward a closure that a verdict will impose in order to administer justice – the novel operates within a literary temporality within which the question of justice remains speculatively open. That clash of temporalities staged between law and literature as it comprises two different durational trajectories in the novel is precisely captured in Shoshana Felman's observations on the differences between legal and literary justice as they respond to traumatic historical events:

> In contrast to the 'legal justice,' dispensed at trials ('physical theaters of justice'), 'literary justice is a dimension of concrete embodiment and a language of finitude that in contrast to the law, encapsulates not closure but precisely what … refuses to be closed … It is to this refusal of the trauma to be closed that literature does justice'.[27]

Sorting the disjunctive temporalities between the juridical and literary approaches to events, Felman adds, "A trial … is a search for a decision … it seeks not simply truth but finality: a force of resolution. In contrast, a literary text is a search for meaning, for expression, for heightened significance, and for symbolic understanding."[28]

While composing the dual temporality between a trial headed toward a definitive outcome and a story of intersecting life worlds whose layers of experience raise questions that will remain despite that outcome, the novel contrasts two biographies. Stefan and Leah are involved in very different self-fashioning situations. To borrow a phrase from Nietzsche, while Stefan's today reproduces his yesterday, Leah's "today refutes" her "yesterday."[29] As the novel encourages the reader to ponder the different identity durations represented by the two protagonists, it becomes evident that the micropolitics of their differences implicates a macropolitical question. How does one negotiate the ethical responsibilities pertaining to civic spheres that host a variety of pasts within their present while having to adjust to the different ways that incommensurate durational selves participate contentiously or otherwise in a shared order in which interpersonal interactions and negotiations are constrained by reasons of state?

Stefan Drozd embodies a self that has been hardened by a childhood in which he has been continually disparaged and beaten by a brutal alcoholic father. Driven by fear and anger from early childhood on, cruelty combined with a survival instinct become his unchanging way of meeting the world. He has introjected the remorseless cruelty of his father, who is described as "not squeamish … he is hard, a hardness that has accumulated layer by layer, almost everything else is wasting away. Leaving only a stony sediment and a strand of self-pity." We first meet Stefan as "a small dirty faced son" trying to avoid the results of that hardness as he assists his father during a pig slaughter. As his father is slashing their throats with one hand, he's drinking alcohol with the other. While Stefan hurries to fulfill his role, building a fire for the cooking and helping prepare the pig meat for consumption – "only meat," according to his father who barks, "get moving" – he "tries to go faster, trying to avoid a kick or blow" before his next task, taking out the organs.[30] "He has learned to gauge the dangers – he knows instinctively how drunk his father is, how drunk he will be, and how brutal he is at each stage of his drunkenness." Needing to be alert to what might come, "Fear is his gauge, his understanding, his negotiation with the world."[31] Along with the fear and anger he accumulates from the abuse at his father's hand is the bigotry he adopts from a man who refers to Jews a "animals, pigs."[32] Decades later he repeats the disparagement while on trial, seeking to justify his role in the mass killings. "They were all enemies ... Jews are not really human. That is a proven fact. They are closer to animals."[33]

On the cusp of adulthood, Stefan flees to Minsk, bringing resources, money, and a horse and carriage he steals from a pastor who had taken him in. He also brings his fear-driven alertness to the work for which he is hired by the NKVD. Impressed by their arrogance, he manages to impress them as well. Using the survival instincts that served him at home, he watches the NKVD operatives closely, seeing "who mutters to someone under his breath, who snickers at someone's jokes, who nods or makes knowing gestures of derision, of malice. He fixes those tiny moments, this information in his mind, saving then for the day when they might be useful or necessary."[34] After he is hired as an interrogator, he brings his cruelty, the violence it has incubated, and his fear ("his old acquaintance") to his job. Intimate with that sensation, he discerns it in those he interrogates, "He watches their restless hand. Underneath the swagger, he can sense it ..."[35]

When he escapes to Canada after the war and marries, his cruelty annexed to his fear-driven alertness is deployed on his marriage:

> The first time he hits her, the expression on her face is stunned, hurt. She puts her hand to her cheek, and it comes away with a streak of blood ... This is your fault, he says. What was her sin? She bought a dress without asking him first. Without his permission. A bleak rage overwhelms him.[36]

When he "hits her again, and she screams ... [he calculates how far it is safe to go] measuring her reactions – so far and no further, a gamble on the chances of her leaving. He knows she has no money, no people here. And he has convinced her that staying here, her status in this country, is now dependent on him."[37]

How should one judge such a character whose behavior as a moral monster seems to exhaust his personality? While within the novel's account of the juridical process he is judged according to war crimes codes for his complicity in the Kurapaty mass killings, within a literary frame the judgment that emerges from the novel's compositional structure is speculative and complex. How and what the novel thinks about Stefan Drozd's acts as an NKVD employee is similar to the way Robert Musil's novel *The Man without Qualities* (treated in the Introduction) responds to the infamous character, the sex murderer Christian Moosbrugger. The novel's composition recreates the character's vulnerability which Musil's novel discloses in Moosbrugger.

At no point in McCormack's novel does Stefan Drozd judge himself. As unrepentant as Musil's Moosbrugger, he devotes his psychic energy to survival, externalizing without self-conscious inhibition the sedimented hurt he has accumulated. While Stefan Drozd is implacably "a stranger to himself,"[38] Leah Jarvis is continually involved in reflective judgments about herself, about Drozd, and about how to narrate the history, which through a series of contingencies finds them juridically connected as adversaries. Her negotiations with all those involved in the case are accompanied by continual negotiations with herself. Having moved from her earlier artistic vocation, Leah realizes that she has transitioned to operating within an impoverished discourse:

> She felt as if she has been exiled from a world of hues and pigments, and sent to a place of flat words, a place from which all the color had been leached. Banished to some arid country she had no idea existed.[39]

Ironically, Leah's problem with managing that "country" is similar to the one Stefan had faced in his management of his atrocity apprenticeship. As Leah's task proceeds, she experiences the same affliction visited on Stefan as a functionary within the NKVD's extermination campaign, worrying about the judgments of one's employers. To recall the perils of Stefan's wartime vocation: At one point, as he observes "a cluster of three officers, talking in low voices," he panics. He "skirts them, hoping to overhear something … Do they seem a degree cooler? Maybe. But if they are it will pass."[40] Like Stefan, Leah becomes an interrogator whose future is at stake, dependent on how her colleagues judge her performance. It "rests on these witnesses [the ones she finds on her evidence-finding trip to Belarus]. She drafts questions over and over to prepare them for testifying, hoping to find the perfect way to ask something, the perfect way to evoke the most persuasive – the most damning – answer." At the same time, she observes the ways her legal colleagues manage their marriages, other facets of their personal lives, and the justifications through which they run their professional lives – for example, one who has no difficulty assigning the concept of justice to the Drozd prosecution. "Surely a delayed justice, an old justice, is better than none at all," says one of them.[41] In comparison with the self-assurance that permeates the lives of her male colleagues, Leah's way of being resembles "an infinite rehearsal."[42]

Unlike Stefan, however, Leah's mental life, inspired by the interpersonal world she is negotiating, expands. It becomes increasing nuanced as she continually reimagines who she is and finds herself considering imperatives well outside of those governing the prosecution. As the novel proceeds, she manages to disinvest in the legal dynamic to which she has been assigned. While Stefan's preoccupation is confined to lamenting his situation – at one point he's "up on his feet shouting … his anger crackles across the room"[43] – and worrying about his "bleak future ... filled with endless proceedings, the threat of deportation constantly hanging over his head,"[44] Leah continually reflects on who she is as a subject that has been drawn into a process with a devastating finality, "extinguishing someone's citizenship ... depriving them of their right to be where they are, to exist where they are."[45]

Stefan Drozd is a moral monster, afflicted by a monster within. His affliction is a wound over which he has no conscious control. Reading such an affliction symptomatically, Julia Kristeva supplies instructive figuration, referring to it as a "structure within the body, a non-assimilable alien, a monster, a tumor, a cancer that the listening devices of the unconscious do not hear."[46] In contrast, Leah tames her inner monsters, negotiating with her selfhood while managing relationships with colleagues and the former victims and witnesses she interviews. The process through which Leah gets in touch with her unanchored self ultimately becomes the novel's main narrative thread. She ponders her Jewish ancestry, clearly manifested by her look, "a flood of dark curls down her back ... strands of DNA sliding down an ancestral ladder."[47] It begins pressing for attention as she sees how it had once imperiled thousands of victims and how in contrast it manifests in those who now exist unself-consciously outside of the historical atrocities. "She envies [a Jewish legal colleague] his careless Jewishness ... that he can pick it up or drop it whenever he wants, even waste it. Her own seems much less reliable."[48] As her work becomes increasingly punctuated with such reflections she feels temporarily stymied, "unable to think" until a moment in which she is overwhelmed by a sense of coherence." Although she, like Stefan, "has a damaged, obstinate heart," she realizes that "she still might survive it ... The future [which Stefan experiences as only bleak] becomes for her a snake, straightening itself out from a cramped position."[49]

It is through Leah that McCormack integrates interpretive reception into the novel. It is with descriptions of her explicit thoughts, with conversations between her and her legal colleagues and interviewees, and with subjectless reflections in free indirect discourse on what one might think as a representative of either the author or an autonomous voice outside the novel, that the novel ponders history-relevant civic issues that exceed its crime and punishment story. As Leah becomes self-conscious about the value of her role, she becomes open to thinking critically not only about the limitations of a juridical framing of violent historical events but also about the contingencies shaping the subjects involved in them, herself included. She, like the author who has invented her as an aesthetic subject, becomes affected by the story and is thereby able to accept a version of the self that remains "always unconsummated," a subject who is (in Bakhtin's words) "axiologically yet-to-be."[50] In the process, she embraces the contingencies of a changing self by recovering and renewing an aesthetic sensibility that she had been holding in abeyance as she entered the legal profession.

Developing an expansive civic awareness, Leah thinks her way out of a role suborned to "the doctrines [that had] lured her" into "a piece of reality that had been carved up and tied into a bundle, ideas exhaling the air of other centuries,"[51] and is able to imagine a life that exceeds the particular deeds for which the man, Drozd, is being prosecuted. At a crucial point that imagining is articulated in free indirect discourse through which the author participates along with her character to raise a crucial question that juxtaposes the temporality of legal justice with the temporality of a life: "is there anything more final than extinguishing someone's citizenship? Depriving them of their right to be where they are, to exist where they are. Interrupting a highly specific life, filled with accumulated circumstances, incidents, experiences."[52]

Through the narrative of Leah's self-fashioning, which runs in parallel with the legal process, McCormack executes a micropolitical politics of aesthetics that accompanies what the novel supplies at a macropolitical level: the exposure with perpetual experiential consequences of a genocidal event that the states involved would rather excise from their official histories. In a recent interview, in which he extolls the value of novelistic fiction, the writer Haruki Murakami provides a perspective on what McCormack's *The Singing Forest* accomplishes. The novelist, he suggests, uses fiction "to bring a truth out to a new location and shine a new light on it."[53] That observation applies as well to the text to which I turn next, Octavia Butler's *Kindred*, whose protagonist Dana Franklin time-travels from 1976 back to a plantation in the antebellum South in 1815 where her ancestry is located.

KINDRED

Butler's novel uses the occasions of her invented character Dana Franklin's travel back and forth between the present and a slave-holding past to provide a counter-history. Her use of speculative fiction, annexed to a "neo-slave narrative," "reconfigures generic conventions of the antebellum and post-emancipation slave narrative" by emphasizing intimate features of those enslaved while projecting them into a post-slavery subject by allowing her to personally experience her ancestor's past.[54] Butler's Dana, much like some of Egoyan's characters in *Ararat*, records the pain and trauma from the past with her body. As the novel mixes historical time with psychic and haptic time, it raises questions that perplex Butler's protagonist, which are succinctly posed by Julia Kristeva while thinking through the implications of Proust's epic reflections on time, "What is the time-scale that you belong to? What is the time that you speak from?"[55] *Kindred* enjoins the reader to ponder those questions.

As regards the novel's reception, Walter Mosely, who is best known for rehearsing aspects of the afterlife of slavery in his detective fiction, sees a similar effect in speculative fiction (which he refers to as "science fiction"). He suggests that it's a textual genre that holds special appeal for African Americans because they "have been cut off from their African ancestry by the scythe of slavery and from an American heritage by being excluded from history."[56] Like Mosley's detective fiction, Butler's novel challenges the presumption that the effects of slavery in the United States have no significant afterlife. She accomplishes a "revisionist historiography's decentering of a national narrative," which, as John Rieder points out (in his analysis of speculative fiction), is "too often monopolized by the perspective of white men in power."[57]

Ironically, the erasures and silences that impede recognition of the still violent afterlives of slavery in the U.S., "'the structural hold of racial slavery' on American life even after the advent of formal emancipation,"[58] has afflicted Butler's book. It has been banned in U.S. prisons. Whatever has been the rationale for official fears that *Kindred* might unsettle a prison population, its inter-articulation of genres – the neo-slave narrative and speculative fiction – defies the presumption that it lends itself to a stable and unitary form of reader reception. Rather than affirming a particular narrative of history, Butler's genre ensemble, a form of genre mixing which Edouard Glissant famously refers to as *métissage*, defamiliarizes both genres, interrupting (as Nadine Flagel suggests) "assumptions and expectations" of readers of each genre.[59] *Kindred*'s drama, which portrays racial and gender violence within a series of temporal paradoxes, yields no definitive conclusion. It affirms what Maurice Blanchot insists is "the purpose of literature ... to interrupt the purposeful steps we are always taking toward a deeper understanding and a surer grasp of things."[60] And it exemplifies the imaginative ability Toni Morrison assigns to the writer: "to familiarize the strange, and to mystify the familiar."[61]

To summarize the basic plot: The protagonist Dana Franklin, a 26-year-old Black woman in an interracial marriage, is an aspiring writer working in California in the mid-1970s. Suddenly, in the midst of a conversation with her writer husband Kevin, she experiences a dizzy spell before being projected back in time to the Weyland plantation in antebellum Maryland where in that and subsequent such journeys she learns about her ancestry and becomes involved in a temporal paradox, the felt need to be complicit with an atrocity in order to avoid what she fears would erase her present California existence.

As her time travel back and forth between her ancestral past and her present ensues, she brings home wounds that have given her a palpable, embodied experience of the violence visited on Black slaves. Her wounds, which are among the remaining after-effects of her time travel, are the subject of the novel's prologue, which reviews her condition after her last visit to a plantation past. She's back in California, hospitalized with her most grievous wound, the loss of part of an arm which occurred when her ancestor Rufus Weyland tried to hold on to her as she was about to be snatched back into her present life. Arriving back in 1976 California, she inexplicably finds herself at home with an injured arm that has to be extracted from a wall to which it is stuck.

That the arm has to be wrenched away from both her plantation and California homes turns the ambiguity of what constitutes being at home into a metaphor for the way African Americans continue the experience of being not-at-home in the United States.

The arm's painful adventure is also a materialization of Dana's paranormal and paradoxical temporal experience, which renders her hard pressed to explain the origin of the disfigurement to police investigators who assume that they're dealing with a typical case of a woman who has been battered by her husband:

> I lost about a year of my life and much of the comfort and security I had not valued until it was gone. When the police released Kevin, he came to the hospital and stayee with me so that I would know I hadn't lost him too. But before he could come to me, I had to convince the police that he did not belong in jail. That took time. The police were shadows who appeared intermittently at my bedside to ask me questions I had to struggle to understand. "How did you hurt your arm?" … Their words seemed to blur together at first … After a while I replayed them and suddenly realized that these men were trying to blame Kevin for "hurting" my arm.[62]

Dana's gender is crucial to the political contribution that Butler's innovative historiography makes. *Kindred* is best described as a feminist-attuned speculative fiction intervention into a neo-slave narrative of racial history. On behalf of that focus, the beginning and end of the novel are allegorical. That Dana is involuntarily whisked away at the outset of the narrative to a plantation in the antebellum South evokes the infamous Middle Passage in which Africans were involuntarily sent into servitude in the South's planation economy. That she returns from her last (of six) time travels to the Weyland planation disfigured, thus destined to live on as one not completely whole, has to evoke reflection on the privations that continue to afflict many of those living-while-Black in the United States.

Dana's initial surmise as to what had sent her into her ancestral past was a mission to rescue her ancestor, Rufus Weyland, whom she first sees after finding herself kneeling on the ground in an antebellum plantation as she regains consciousness. "Before me was a wide tranquil river, and near the middle of that river was a child splashing, screaming … Drowning!"[63] On that occasion, she rescues him with a mouth-to-mouth breathing assist, after which she wonders what would have happened if he had died, because if he didn't "survive to father Hagar [from whom Dana is descended] … I could not exist."[64] Pursuing that worry, she rescues him on subsequent occasions as well, once after finding him lying in a mud puddle with a broken leg and once when he has set fire to some curtains. Yet she knows she exists and must wonder what is therefore involved in her "imperative to help Rufus."[65] As Flagel suggests, the grandfather paradox that prompts Dana's questioning is a displacement for "Dana's terror of history – its linearity yet arbitrary impersonality – [which] leads her to try to bring the past under her control."[66]

More important than the paradox involved in the temporal trajectory that Dana's plantation ancestry creates is the way her treatment at the plantation mirrors the disempowerment of the slaves she meets. She incurs suspicion because she can read; she is regarded as insolent because she makes eye contact with the white planation family (Rufus's mother Margret and his plantation owner gun-wielding, whip-using father Tom); she cannot assume her role as Kevin's wife after he joins her in the time travel itinerary because she has to pretend that she is his property; and she is in fear for her safety after being beaten and bruised during an attempted rape by a patroller and having received a whipping by Tom Weyland. Although she is able to save herself every time she is imperiled, including the last time when she kills Rufus who is trying to rape her, by time-traveling back to contemporary California – accomplished each time she is injured (at times having to injure herself to manage it) – what she has learned about plantation life and its legacy provides the novel's main political pedagogy. Although the physical abuse Dana witnesses as well as experiences – beatings, whippings and rapes – are well-known features recorded in histories of the atrocities slaves faced in the antebellum era, even more telling with regard to the slaves' disempowerment was their inability to protect their family members. Slaves were faced not only with injury and premature death but also with being separated when at the whim of the plantation owner (at times as punishment), husbands, wives, and children were sold off to other plantations, never to be seen by their families again.

In conversations about Black families with two former slaves and one fugitive slave, in Russell Banks's novel *Cloudsplitter* (a novelistic biography of the abolitionist John Brown), Brown's son Owen, who serves as the novel's narrator, learns about that aspect of plantation life. In the last conversation in which he engages the fugitive James Cannon, he asks, "Who was your father … ? What happened to him?" "Don't know. Long gone … Same as my mother," is the answer. At the end of the conversation, Owen confesses, "I'd finally lost that punishing innocence, and I felt ashamed of my inquiry."[67] The innocence to which Owen confesses reflects a contemporary innocence, a failure of conventional U.S. histories to acknowledge the extent to which the plantation practice of separating slave families has yielded Afro-America's fractured and largely unrecoverable genealogies.[68] Emancipation did not result in a widespread reuniting of families.

Dana's ambiguous "home," divided temporally and spatially, allegorizes that historical atrocity, as does the grandfather paradox in her connection with the Weyland family. At a crucial moment, *Kindred* rehearses Dana's innocence, which mirrors Owens's in *Cloudsplitter*. While Dana is within what she naïvely regards as a safe feminine space, the plantation cookhouse run by the slave Sarah, we learn that Carrie working with her mother is Sarah's "fourth baby," and is "the only one Marse Tom let me keep."[69] Having already been warned by Sarah to be careful, Dana soon learns that a pervasively gendered space is no sanctuary from the brutality visited on slaves in the fields. While she had thought that the structure of domination was simply raced, it turns out to be gendered as well. Tom Weyland, upon entering the cookhouse and "catching Dana and one of her pupils with some books," becomes infuriated and "beats Dana mercilessly." Dana's naïveté, as Lisa Yaszek summarizes it, is that "in forgetting that the cookhouse is a both black and feminine space [she] ... also forgets that it is subject to masculine surveillance and penetration." She had bought into a narrative in which she was "a lone individual battling the abstract forces of history rather than someone enmeshed in familial and communal networks."[70] The bruised and battered body she brings back to present-day California is part of the price she pays for her naïveté as well as being the text she has preserved from her time travel to the antebellum South.

The marks on Dana's body turn out to be the most reliable way her experiences are recorded. In the novel's Epilogue, Dana and Kevin return to Maryland on a discovery mission, seeking details of the plantation to which they had time-traveled. The results are disappointing. They cannot locate the main house, and although there are some records in the local courthouse of the fates of slaves they knew – many were sold off when the owners died – there is no evidence of Rufus's grave in the area. The only reliable record of Dana's experiences is recorded on her body, expressed in one of her remarks: "I touched the scar Tom Weyland's boot had left on my face, touched my empty left sleeve."[71] By having that scar show on Dana in her present life Butler is implying that the gruesome past of slavery persists as scars.

THE PERSISTENCE OF THE PLANTATION

The scar as a trope, a visible sign of the lasting legacy of the planation period, is integral to the historiographic contribution of Butler's *Kindred*. As she has Dana's bruised and battered body existing in the present, her *Kindred* ends with the suggestion that the gruesome past of slavery has not been surpassed. The plantation effect remains alive, mainly as an update of forces that continue to perpetuate the perils and inequalities involved in living while Black. Before pursing the scar trope further, I want to reference texts that testify to the continuing presence of that plantation effect. What has been apparent to African Americans since emancipation – the extraordinary risks of being a young Black man – is now more generally known, in part as a result of the Black Lives Matter movement. As recent events attest, it is life threatening to be walking while Black (Trayvon Martin), jogging while Black (Ahmaud Arbery), or driving while Black (Michael Brown among others). A contemporary Black body-disciplining equivalent of the plantation's whip, wielded by owners, overseers, and patrollers, is the nightstick wielded by police officers. Aware of that equivalence and endeavoring to keep his Black son alive and whole, the writer Ta-Nehesi Coates includes, among the many instructions in his epistolary book *Between the World and Me* – composed as a letter to his son and designed to keep him alive – this warning: "The policeman who cracks you with a nightstick will quickly find his excuse in your furtive movements."[72] "The police departments of your country," he informs his son, "have been endowed with the authority to destroy your body." "Racism," he notes, "is a visceral experience … it dislodges brains, blocks airways, rips muscle, extracts organs, cracks bones, breaks teeth."[73]

There is a softer violence which is structural rather than directly confrontational. It's a version that Clyde Woods attributes to the legacy of the plantation, a violence articulated as an epistemology to which Woods refers as "plantation bloc explanation." It exists in the narration of a federally policy-endorsed political economy that has facilitated post-slavery plantation agriculture and has had the effect of displacing Black sharecroppers in favor of a mechanized plantation capitalism in the Mississippi Delta, the locus of Woods's analysis. For the "blues bloc," which Woods poses as an oppositional Black habitus, the blues is not only an aesthetic but also an ontology and way of knowing. African American communities in the rural South (and in a state of diaspora through the post-slavery period) turned to blues epistemology to provide a "constant reestablishment of collective sensibility in the face of constant attacks by the plantation bloc and its allies" and to reaffirm "the historic commitment to social and personal investigation, description, and criticism present in the blues."[74] "Born in a new era of censorship, suppression and persecution, the blues conveyed the sorrow of the individual and collective tragedy that had befallen African Americans."[75] Unlike mainstream American history that has Black immiseration ending with emancipation, the blues is a genre of shared explanation, an "orature" that alternately laments and mocks as it both responds to continuing racially motivated barriers and assaults and participates in a "'process of communication'" [which is] a process of community."[76]

Many years after a blues aesthetic and its jazz realizations had to struggle against censorship in an early twentieth-century "culture war" – spawned by "a widespread fear of the loss of white Anglo-Protestant hegemony in American life"[77] – it has become a well-developed mode of civic expression. As Gregory Clark points out, the improvisational dynamic among players in blues and jazz ensembles is "directly relevant to the civic work of individual and group participation in a democratic society."[78] As it attunes itself to recover a repressed past, Black historiography, articulated musically as well as in other cultural genres, now faces a new era of censorship. There are widespread initiatives throughout white America to censor and suppress materials that support and elaborate on the Black Lives Matter movement and the 1619 Project begun in an August 2019 special issue of the *New York Times Magazine*. That latter initiative contains the radical counter-historical assertion that it was "not the independence declared in 1776, that marked 'the country's true birth date'"; it was the arrival in August of 1619 of the first ship carrying African slaves. "America was not yet America, but this was the moment it began."[79] To cite an exemplary instance of suppression: "On the first day of Black History month [in 2023] the College Board announced significant changes to its Advanced Placement African American studies course. The billion-dollar company made this move after widespread rightwing pushback against the inclusion of liberal, progressive and radical books by Black authors in the curriculum (they have since apologized)."[80]

THE SCARS ON THE BODY POLITIC

Returning to the scar trope with which Octavia Butler's *Kindred* concludes, a wound-figured historiography that has a notable literary history, I turn to two epic novels structured with scar allegories that challenge conventional founding narratives, Herman Melville's *Moby Dick* which precedes Butler's text by seventy-five years, and Thomas Pynchon's *Mason & Dixon* which follows *Moby Dick* twenty-plus years later. Carl Safina provides an instructive entry to that aspect of Melville's novel. Analyzing *Moby Dick*'s implied critique of the U.S.'s nineteenth-century race relations, he refers to the whale as a "white prop" and suggests that the novel's hospitality to "varied skin shades ... [and men] breathing one another's sweat in close company [while they] tended whale-boiling caldrons and looked one another in the eye" constitutes Melville's critique of "the American character's deepest congenital malignancy, then called Negrophobia."[81] It was a phobia "that lent a macabre visuality, the scars produced by the whips applied to the backs of plantation slaves, 'a kind of hieroglyphics of the flesh' as Hortense Spillers puts it."[82] Allegorizing that phobia, Melville displaces the scars on Black bodies to those on a whale by having Ismael observe "the visible surface of [a] sperm whale crossed and recrossed with numerous straight marks."[83]

In Thomas Pynchon's *Mason & Dixon*, the scar is a more pervasive trope. Showing up five times in the text, it serves as an iconic sign that structures the novel's historiography. Early in the narrative, scars are located on seemingly benign surfaces before they appear as signs of violence when the surveyors Mason and Dixon, arriving in Lancaster town, witness "'Whippings, the open'd flesh, the welling blood."[84] The seemingly innocent appearance of scars occurs early in the novel as the Reverend Cherrycoke is narrating the story of Mason and Dixon's boundary-creating survey to children in a household in

Philadelphia twenty years after the event. He's seated among scarred furniture in the living room while narrating the story from a scarred notebook he's holding. That passage is allegorical in two senses. First, the scarred furniture, "mismatch'd side benches ... some second street Chippendale ... [a] Chinese sofa ... a few odd chairs sent from England"[85] – that is, a bunch of unmatching pieces scattered about – reflects an eclectic assemblage of people. It's a living-room scene serving as an allegory for the contingencies of the national assemblage. Second, the scarred notebook references old recollections that situate the storyteller's participation in the events he's narrating: history-as-story.

Both scars set the iconoclastic mood of Pynchon's novel, which translates as a history of violence. At a moment of insight, Pynchon's fictional Mason and Dixon recognize that rather than being engaged in a mere scientific activity they are perpetrating violence; they're trespassing on "other civic entities" (the spaces inhabited by Native American Nations). Picking up the scar trope, the text figures their work as an imposition of "geometrick scars" on the landscape.[86] A few hundred pages later that scar trope is repeated. A Chinese interlocutor to whom Mason recounts the object of his survey, calling it "a boundary, nothing more," responds by suggesting an alternative cosmology:

> Boundary!... Ev'rywhere else on earth, Boundaries follow nature, – coast-lines, ridge-tops, river-banks, – so honoring the Dragon of *shan* within, from which Land-Scape ever takes its form. To mark a right Line upon the Earth is to inflict upon the Dragon's very Flesh, a sword-slash, a long perfect scar, impossible for any who live out here the year 'round to see as other than hateful assault. How can it pass unanswer'd?[87]

As the last chapter unfolds, the text applies the scar trope to immigrant bodies. Chinese sailors are described seeking refuge in Cherrycoke's sister's house in Philadelphia (not a city that lives up to the "brotherly love" its name implies) from where the novel is narrated. "They bring their Scars, their Pox-pitted Cheeks, their Burdens and Losses, their feverish Eyes, their proud fellowship in a Mobility that is to be, whose shape none inside the House may know."[88] Ultimately the novel supplies a response to a question the Chinese interlocutor raises: "How can it [the survey-as-sword-slash] go unanswer'd. It ascribes the lack of an answer to willed amnesia. The Mason and Dixon survey perpetrates a violent version of history that 'none inside the House' [as an allegory for the nation] have wanted to know."[89]

An Erasure Meets Erasure, Responding to What Many *Still* Do Not Want to Know

Amnesiac policies persist in the United States as well as elsewhere. China is especially notable for curtailing, oppressing, or incarcerating writers who seek to restore the ethno-histories of diverse peoples who have been denied forms of cultural expression. The ethnically Uyghur writer "Rahile Dawit, who recorded her people's traditions, disappeared in 2017" and has since been found to be facing a life prison sentence.[90] Willed amnesia in the United States tends to be structural – deployed, for example, in classificatory practices; "indigenous erasure" took place on the American continent to access resources and land (practices used in other settler-developed societies). While an "'inclusive taxonomy … [has been] used to classify Black Americans … for the exploitation of their labor," an exclusive taxonomy "of American Indian ethnicity facilitated greater access for settlers to land and resources."[91] The contemporary willed amnesia is historiographic rather than taxonomic. It involves the imposition of a restrictive approach to national history through censorship initiatives coming from parent groups, right-wing governors, legislators, school boards, university college trustees, and museum boards that seek to shelter (in Gospodinov's sense) America's youth from texts, exhibitions, and performances that disclose the enduring oppression of America's people of color. As Ishena Robinson summarizes the situation:

> The concerted efforts to impede racial justice in America through Orwellian measures banning, censoring, and otherwise suppressing conversations about race we see metastasizing today are the latest examples of a pattern observable throughout American history.[92]

Egregious as those initiatives are for constraining the temporal trajectories that shape civic life, allocating presences and absences, it's increasingly difficult to call sustained attention to them. As one commentary puts it,

> We are witnessing the dark side of our new technological lives, whose extractive profit models amount to the systematic fracking of human beings: pumping vast quantities of high-pressure media content into our faces to force up a spume of the vaporous and intimate stuff called attention.[93]

Nevertheless, after the murder of a young Black man, Michael Brown, by a police officer in Ferguson, Missouri was recorded and the footage went viral, the resulting Black Lives Matter movement gained substantial participation and attention, enough to result in the Justice Department's commissioning of *The Ferguson Report*, which details the racial bias of Ferguson's policing culture and specifies the reforms needed there as well as elsewhere. However, rather than elaborating on the detailed findings and calls for reform the report contains – in the current culture war carefully assembled facts make little impression on polarized thinking – I conclude the chapter with attention to a recently created "shelter" (in Jeremy Eichler's above-noted sense) whose critical effect works paradoxically through erasure.

Reacting to the report, the African American poet Nicole Sealey wrote a long poem, *The Ferguson Report: An Erasure*, in which she redacts the text by including only "600 words in the 84 pages she selects from the report."[94] Genre-wise, her text is "erasure poetry," "a discipline," as a commentator puts it, that "revolves around reading against the archive ... reading meaning into what is not said as much as what is."[95] Noting an inspiration for her critique-by-erasure, Sealey cites the artist Jean-Michel Basquiat's statement, "'I cross out words so you will see them more; the fact that they are obscured makes you want to read them' ... [and adds] In the form of poetry commonly known as erasure, a poet prunes a found body of language – often an official document or a canonical work of literature – whose ablations paradoxically lead to revelations, uncovering subtext, lyricism, lost histories, and politics barely hidden beneath the surface."[96] Among the ways Sealey figures her poetic intervention is as an attack on a building:

> I didn't come to *The Ferguson Report* with erasure in mind ... I instinctively began erasing it – not knowing what, if anything, would come of it. Striking through whole sections of the document felt physical, like ripping out drywall and taking the document down to its studs.[97]

Her architectural metaphor brings Sealey's poetic practice in line with Gordon Matta-Clark's "anarchitecture."[98] Matta-Clark attacked buildings with a chain saw, making deep cuts that changed the building into a different "vision machine" in which views from room to room as well as new scenes from the building became available.[99] Most significant for the way his creative erasures track with Sealey's, his cutting through floors and stripping away of walls and floors reveals the buildings' support structures, making available the hidden-away narrative of their construction. Demonstrating how less can show more, his modifications enable "'seeing a project from multiple positions in order to capture the narrative process of the piece being made'."[100] Like Sealey's poetic intervention – an erasure of words to call attention to a story about precarious Black lives – Matta-Clark compared his cutting away of parts of buildings to a linguistic intervention aimed at encouraging change, in his case calling attention to New York's increasingly dangerous "crumbling infrastructure." As he put it, "what I do to buildings is what some do with language ... I organize them in order to explain the need for change."[101]

The shelter effect in Sealey's intervention – restoration achieved through erasure – is also aimed at repair, in her case of "a problematic text so that something at its root might be repaired." As she states, "There was something satisfying about reconsidering *The Ferguson Report* striking through whole sections of it, as if undoing the harm that had been done."[102] Sealey's critical poetic reception of the *Ferguson Report* extends the wound-figured historiography that discloses the continuing challenges to Black civic life articulated in Octavia Butler's *Kindred*. In doing so, her textual work provides a threshold for Chapter 3's focus on automobility's implications for Black civic life. The chapter's main textual exploration is an engagement with a documentary film. Dwayne LeBlanc's *Civic*, shot entirely within a car on a route through a Los Angeles Black neighborhood, issues an alert to African Americans about their civic responsibility to negotiate living while Black, personally and interpersonally, in recognition of America's precarious racial-spatial order.

NOTES

1. Alice Zeniter, *The Art of Losing*, trans. Frank Wynne (New York: Farrar, Straus and Giroux, 2021), p. 140.
2. Richard Evans, "The Holocaust in Poland and the Erasures of the Past," *The New York Times*, July 12, 2023, at https://www.nytimes.com/2023/07/12/books/review/jews-in-the-garden-judy-rakowsky.html (last accessed August 30, 2024).
3. Michael J. Shapiro, *Methods and Nations: Cultural Governance and the Indigenous Subject* (London: Routledge, 2004).
4. On U.S. temporal governance, treated in connection with the 9/11 events, see Jenny Edkins, *Trauma and the Memory of Politics* (New York: Cambridge University Press, 2003): "On September 11, trauma time collided with the time of the state, the time of capitalism, the time of routine. States moved rapidly to reinstate their control over time" (p. 233).
5. Grossman, *Life and Fate*, p. 275.
6. Reported in *The Los Angeles Times*, August 27, 1986, at https://www.latimes.com/archives/la-xpm-1986-08-27-mn-14195-story.html (last accessed August 30, 2024).
7. Ismail Xavier, "Historical Allegory," in Toby Miller and Robert Stam (eds.), *A Companion to Film Theory* (Malden, MA: Blackwell, 1999), p. 340.
8. Jeremy Eichler, *Time's Echo: The Second World War, the Holocaust, and the Music of Remembrance* (New York: Knopf, 2023), p. 12.
9. *Ibid.*, p. 201.
10. See "The Armenian Genocide (1915–16): Overview," *The Holocaust Museum*, at https://encyclopedia.ushmm.org/content/en/article/the-armenian-genocide-1915-16-overview (last accessed August 30, 2024).
11. An interview with Atom Egoyan in *Beyond Ararat*, Disc 2 in the two-disc set by *Aspect Ratio*, released 2003.
12. Julia Kristeva, *Proust and the Sense of Time*, trans. Stephen Bann (New York: Columbia University Press, 1993), p. 4.
13. Interview with Egoyan in *Beyond Ararat*.
14. Atom Egoyan, "In Other Words: Poetic License and the Incarnation of History," *University of Toronto Quarterly* 71, no. 3 (Summer 2014): 900.

15. Marcus J. Moore, "Five Minutes That Will Make You Love Thelonious Monk," *The New York Times*, November 1, 2023, at https://www.nytimes.com/2023/11/01/arts/music/thelonious-monk-jazz-music.html (last accessed August 30, 2024).

16. See "Monk Chord Voicings," at https://www.thejazzpianosite.com/jazz-piano-lessons/jazz-chord-voicings/monk-voicings/ (last accessed August 30, 2024).

17. Gilles Deleuze, *Cinema 2: The Time Image*, trans. Hugh Tomlinson and Robert Galeta (Minneapolis: University of Minnesota Press, 1989), p. 272.

18. Nolwenn Guibert, "'Ararat' by Atom Egoyan, or the Current Influence of the Armenian Genocide," *Current Rights*, June 12, 2017, at https://creatingrights.com/2017/06/12/Ararat-atom-egoyan-current-influence-armenian-genocide/ (last accessed August 30, 2024).

19. Egoyan, "In Other Words," pp. 891–2.

20. See Cathy Caruth's analysis of the temporality of trauma in *Unclaimed Experience: Trauma, Narrative, and History* (Baltimore, MD: Johns Hopkins University Press, 2016).

21. Jill Jarvis, *Decolonizing Memory: Algeria and the Politics of Testimony* (Durham, NC: Duke University Press, 2021), p. 2.

22. *Ibid.*, p. 161.

23. Judith McCormack, *The Singing Forest* (Windsor-Ontario, Ca.: Biblioasis, 2021). The events in the novel are based on the discovery in 1988 (made public in 1989) of the bodies from mass killings in the forest of the town of Kurapaty. See Goujon Alexandra, "Kurapaty (1937–1941) NKVD Mass Killings in the Forest of the Town of Kurapaty," at https://www.sciencespo.fr/mass-violence-war-massacre-resistance/fr/document/kurapaty-1937-1941-nkvd-mass-killings-soviet-belarus.html (last accessed August 30, 2024).

24. See David Marples, "History, Memory, and the Second World War in Belarus," *Australian Journal of Politics & History* 58, no. 3 (2012): 437–48.

25. David Marples and Veranika Laputska, "Kurapaty: Belarus' Continuing Debates," *Slavic Review* 79, no. 3 (2020): 521.

26. Thornton Wilder, Letter to John Townley, "Afterword," in *The Bridge of San Luis Rey* (New York: Harper, 2014), p. 128.

27. Michael J. Shapiro, *War Crimes, Atrocity, and Justice* (Cambridge: Polity, 2015), p. 41. The inner quotations are from Shoshana Felman, *The Juridical Unconscious: Trials and Traumas of the Twentieth Century* (Cambridge, MA: Harvard University Press, 2002), p. 8.

28. Felman, *The Juridical Unconscious*, pp. 54–5.

29. Nietzsche's phrase is "my today refutes my yesterday." Friedrich Nietzsche, *Thus Spake Zarathustra*, trans. Michael Hulse (London: Notting Hill Editions, 2022), p. 35.

30. McCormack, *The Singing Forest*, p. 32.

31. *Ibid.*, p. 33.

32. *Ibid.*, p. 36.

33. *Ibid.*, p. 160.

34. *Ibid.*, p. 138.

35. *Ibid.*, p. 32.

36. *Ibid.*, p. 199.
37. *Ibid.*, p. 200.
38. The phrase echoes Julia Kristeva's analysis in *Strangers to Ourselves*, trans. Leon Roudiez (New York: Columbia University Press, 1994).
39. McCormack, *The Singing Forest*, p. 50.
40. *Ibid.*, p. 189.
41. *Ibid.*, p. 16.
42. I am borrowing the expression from the title of the Caribbean writer Wilson Harris's fictional autobiography, *The Infinite Rehearsal* (London: Faber & Faber, 1987).
43. McCormack, *The Singing Forest*, p. 16.
44. *Ibid.*, p. 228.
45. *Ibid.*, p. 41.
46. Julia Kristeva, *The Powers of Horror: An Essay on Abjection*, trans Leon Roundiez (New York: Columbia University Press, 192), p. 11.
47. McCormack, *The Singing Forest*, p. 7.
48. *Ibid.*, p. 48.
49. *Ibid.*, p. 233.
50. M. M. Bakhtin attributes that disposition to authors. See his "Author and Hero in Aesthetic Activity," in *Art and Answerability*, trans. Kenneth Brostrom and Vadim Liapunov (Austin: University of Texas Press, 1990), p.13.
51. McCormack, *The Singing Forest*, p. 50.
52. *Ibid.*, p. 41.
53. See the interview with Haruki Murakami, "Aways on the Side of the Egg," *Haaretz*, February 17, 2009, at https://www.haaretz.com/israel-news/culture/2009-02-17/ty-article/always-on-the-side-of-the-egg/0000017f-db26-d3ff-a7ff-fba694020000 (last accessed August 30, 2024).
54. Grant Rodwell, *The Power of Neo-Slave Fiction and Public History* (New York: Routledge, 2024), p. 27.
55. Kristeva, *Proust and the Sense of Time*, p. 4.
56. Walter Mosely, "Culture Zone: Black to the Future," *The New York Times Magazine*, November 1, 1998, at https://www.nytimes.com/1998/11/01/magazine/culture-zone-black-to-the-future.html (last accessed September 2, 2024).
57. John Rieder, *Speculative Epistemologies: An Eccentric Account of SF from the 1960s to the Present* (Liverpool: Liverpool University Press, 2021), p. 59.
58. Brent Hayes Edwards, "Other Afterlives," *PMLA* 138, no. 2 (2023): 234. The inner quotation is from Abdulrazak Gurnah, *Scenes of Subjection: Terror, Slavery, and Self-making in Nineteenth-Century America* (New York: W. W. Norton, 2022), p. xxxv.
59. Nadine Flagel, "'It's Almost Like Being There': Speculative Fiction, Slave Narrative, and the Crisis of Representation in Octavia Butler's *Kindred*," *Canadian Review of American Studies* 42, no. 2 (2012): 217.
60. The quotation is Ann Smock's characterization of Blanchot's view of the novel in her "Translator's Introduction to Maurice Blanchot," *The Space of Literature* (Lincoln: University of Nebraska Press, 1982), p. 3.

61. Toni Morrison, "Black Matter(s)," in *The Source of Self-Regard* (New York: Vintage, 2019), p. 143.

62. Octavia Butler, *Kindred* (Boston: Beacon Press, 2003), p. 9.

63. *Ibid.*, p. 13.

64. *Ibid.*, p. 29.

65. Flagel, "It's Almost Like Being There," p. 221.

66. *Ibid.*

67. Russell Banks, *Cloudsplitter* (New York: HarperCollins, 1998), p. 222.

68. "As reported in The Equal Justice Initiative, *Slavery in America*, it is estimated that 'more than half of all enslaved people in the Upper South were separated from a parent or child, and a third of their marriages were destroyed by forced migration.' The *Last Seen* project challenges the persistent myth of the benevolent slaveowner and sheds light on the destructive consequences of slavery for Black families." *Last Seen* at https://eji.org/news/families-torn-apart-by-slavery-sought-reunion/ (last accessed September 2, 2024).

69. Butler, *Kindred*, p. 78.

70. Lisa Yaszek, "'A Grim Fantasy': Remaking American History in Octavia Butler's *Kindred*," *Signs: Journal of Women in Culture and Society* 28, no. 41 (2003): 1060.

71. Butler, *Kindred*, p. 264.

72. Ta-Nehisi Coates, *Between the World and Me* (New York: Oneworld, 2015), p. 72.

73. *Ibid.*, pp. 8–9.

74. Clyde Woods, *Development Arrested: Race, Power, and the Blues in the Mississippi Delta* (New York: Verso, 1998), p. 28.

75. *Ibid.*, p. 17.

76. *Ibid.*, 35. The inner quotations are from Ben Sidran, *Black Talk* (New York: Holt, Rinehart & Winston, 1971), p. 11.

77. Richard A. Peterson, *Creating Country Music: Fabricating Authenticity* (Chicago: University of Chicago Press, 1997), p. 59. For an elaborate treatment of the musical contestation, see Macdonald Smith Moore, *Yankee Blues: Musical Culture and American Identity* (Bloomington: Indiana University Press, 1985).

78. Gregory Clark, *Civic Jazz* (Chicago: University of Chicago Press, 2015), p. xii.

79. Lauren Michele Jackson, "The 1619 Project and the Demands of Public History," *The New Yorker Magazine*, December 8, 2021, at https://www.newyorker.com/books/under-review/the-1619-project-and-the-demands-of-public-history (last accessed September 2, 2024).

80. Derecka Pernell, "America Has a History of Banning Black Studies. We Can Learn from That Past," *The Guardian*, February 14, 2023, at https://www.theguardian.com/commentisfree/2023/feb/14/african-american-studies-history-repression-resistance-republicans (last accessed September 2, 2024).

81. Carl Safina, "Melville's Whale Was a Warning We Failed to Heed," *The New York Times*, May 2, 2020, at https://www.nytimes.com/2020/05/02/books/review/herman-melville-moby-dick.html (last accessed September 2, 2024).

82. Michael J. Shapiro, *Writing Politics Studies in Compositional* Method (New York: Routledge, 2021), p. 82. The internal quotation is Hortense Spillers, "Mama's Baby, Papa's Maybe: An American Grammar Book," *Diacritics* 17, no. 2 (1987): 67.

83. Herman Melville, *Moby Dick: or The Whale* (Evanston, IL: Northwestern University Press, 2011), pp. 305–6.

84. Thomas Pynchon, *Mason & Dixon* (New York: Henry Holt, 1997), p. 347.

85. *Ibid.*, p. 5.

86. *Ibid.*, p. 257.

87. *Ibid.*, p. 542.

88. *Ibid.*, p. 759.

89. *Ibid.*, p. 542.

90. Tiffany May, "Star Uyghur Scholar Who Vanished Was Sentenced to Life in China," *The New York Times*, September 24, 2023, at https://www.nytimes.com/2023/09/24/world/asia/rahile-dawut-uyghur-china.html#:~:text=Rahile%20Dawut%20had%20been%20sentenced,%E2%80%9CIt's%20appalling.%E2%80%9D (last accessed September 2, 2024).

91. Raymond Orr, Katelyn Sharratt, and Muhammad Iqbal. "American Indian Erasure and the Logic of Elimination," *Journal of Ethnic and Migration Studies* 45, no. 11 (2019): 2079.

92. Ishena Robinson, "The History They Don't Want to Know," *Legal Defense Fund*, February 25, 2022, at https://www.naacpldf.org/war-on-truth-history/ (last accessed September 2, 2024).

93. D. Graham Burnett, Alyssa Loh, and Peter Schmidt, "Powerful Forces Are Fracking Our attention. We Can Fight Back," *The New York Times*, November 24, 2023, at https://www.nytimes.com/2023/11/24/opinion/attention-economy-education.html (last accessed September 2, 2024).

94. Erik Gleibermann, "Rethinking Erasure: A Q &A with Nicole Sealey," *Poets & Writers*, August 14, 2023, at https://www.pw.org/content/rethinking_erasure_a_qa_with_nicole_sealey (last accessed September 2, 2024).

95. Hugh Ryan, Review of Justin Torres's *Blackouts*, *The New York Times*, October 9, 2023, at https://www.nytimes.com/2023/10/09/books/review/blackouts-justin-torres.html (last accessed September 2, 2024).

96. Kevin Young, "The Ferguson Report: An Erasure," *The New Yorker*, July 24, 2023, at https://www.newyorker.com/magazine/2023/07/31/the-ferguson-report-an-erasure-nicole-sealey-poem (last accessed September 2, 2024).

97. "Nicole Sealey on The Ferguson Report," an interview with Sally Bliumis-Dunn, *Plume* 136 (December 2022), at https://plumepoetry.com/nicole-sealey-on-the-ferguson-report-an-erasure-an-interview-with-sally-bliumis-dunn/ (last accessed September 2, 2024).

98. For a history of the orientation, see the write-up of an exhibition at the Tate London museum: "Towards Anarchitecture: Gordon Matta-Clark and Le Corbusier," *Tate Papers* 7 (Spring 2007), at https://www.tate.org.uk/research/tate-papers/07/towards-anarchitecture-gordon-matta-clark-and-le-corbusier (last accessed September 2, 2024).

99. See my "Image Punctuations" chapter in Michael J. Shapiro, *Punctuations: How the Arts Think the Political* (Durham, NC: Duke University Press, 2019), p. 120.
100. *Ibid.* The internal quotation is from Jennifer Shields, *Collage and Architecture* (New York: Routledge, 2014), p. 153.
101. Gordon Matta-Clark, quoted in Jillian Steinhauer, "How Gordon Matta-Clark Saw the City," *The New Republic*, February 5, 2018, at https://newrepublic.com/article/146929/gordon-matta-clark-saw-city (last accessed September 2, 2024).
102. Nicole Sealey quoted in Gleibermann, "Rethinking Erasure: A Q&A with Nicole Sealey."

3. CIVIC AUTOMOBILITY: DRIVING WHITE, DRIVING BLACK

As Daniel Miller summarizes it, "The car's significance is that it reconfigures civil society involving distinct ways of dwelling, traveling and socializing in and through automobilized space."[1] Notably, however, automobility's pervasive effects on civic life have been both destructive and emancipatory. Henri Lefebvre and Ivan Illich address the former. Referring to the highways that have been a condition of possibility for automobility, Lefebvre writes, "A motorway brutalizes the countryside and the land, slicing through space."[2] And Illich, viewing automobility as an assault on conviviality, writes, "Cars are machines that call for highways, and highways pretend to be public utilities while in fact they are discriminatory devices ... They drive wedges of highways into populated areas, and then extort tolls on the bridge over the remoteness between people that was manufactured for their sake."[3]

In her L.A.-located novel *Their Dogs Came with Them*, Helena María Viramontes provides a fictional realization of Lefebvre's and Illich's observations. Focused on automobility's splintering effects on Los Angeles's Latinx assemblage, she turns LA's freeway exchange into a protagonist with which her Latina/o characters have to contend. Remarking that she "realized that the structure of the novel began to resemble the freeway intersections,"[4] Viramontes' compositional strategy has the freeway configuration – "a totalizing ecosystem engineered for its dominant organism, the car"[5] – modelling as well as affecting the fragmented interrelationships among her four human protagonists. She renders their interconnections as homologous with the structure of the East L.A. freeway exchange and shapes the novel's disjunctive narrative threads the way the freeway system fragments the city. Her characters live in a splintered urban formation that impedes convivial exchanges.[6] The historical basis for the novel is the highway system's fracturing of L.A'.s Boyle Heights Latinx neighborhood, a result of city planning that favored automobility.

As for automobility's emancipatory effects, among those that register themselves historically is the way cars provided for a Black mobility that had been stifled by racial segregation. One of the earliest observations of that effect was in Gunnar Myrdal's famous *An American Dilemma*, his mid-twentieth-century investigation of Black life in the U.S. "The coming of the cheap automobile," he noted, "has meant for Southern Negroes, who can afford one, a partial emancipation from Jim Crowism."[7] Addressing that condition more elaborately decades later, in a review of the civic consequences of Black car ownership, Paul Gilroy refers to the automobile "as a kind of *Ur*-commodity lodged at the meeting point of moral and economic relations," where the "moral" for Gilroy refers to perspectives through which lives are valued. Observing the critical interconnection between moral and political economy as it was mediated by automobile culture, he points out that once African Americans became valued consumers they were increasingly welcomed into civic participation. "The automobile," he suggests, "supplies the best tool for all attempts to understand both their behavior as consumers and their diminishing distance from citizenship."[8]

However, to wield that tool requires an extended engagement with another of Gilroy's observations: "The value of life is persistently specified along racial lines."[9] That issue is rehearsed as the main drama in E. L. Doctorow's novel *Ragtime* (covering the period 1902–12).[10] Although compositionally the novel incorporates "three groups of characters, white Anglo-Saxon protestant (WASP), Jewish immigrant and Black, that embody the cultural diversity and social turmoil of the period,"[11] the Black pianist, Coalhouse Walker Jr., is arguably the main protagonist. The way he self-confidently ignores the racial strictures of the U.S.'s pre-World War I Jim Crow period is disconcerting to segments of white America he encounters, because as he moves self-confidently through a "racially saturated field of visibility,"[12] he violates the period's dominant and degrading "Negro" imaginary. Exemplary is one white character's reaction. Perplexed by the Black musician's demeanor, "Father," the head of a family that Coalhouse visits because his estranged wife lives with them, is portrayed as if musing (in free indirect discourse) "that Coalhouse Walker Jr. didn't know he was a Negro."[13] He had sat in the family's living room having tea with "no embarrassment ... he acted as if it were the most natural thing in the world. The surroundings did not awe him nor was his manner deferential. He was courteous and correct."[14]

While Coalhouse is the novel's main protagonist, the seemingly unrelated narrative thread that locates the escape artist Harry Houdini within the same historical era provides an instructive juxtaposition. Like Coalhouse, Houdini participates eagerly in the automobile age. He has a luxuriously appointed car, a "chauffeur-driven Pope-Toledo Runabout [with] brass headlamps in front of the radiator and brass sidelamps over the fenders."[15] Similarly luxurious, Coalhouse's car, a Model T, "shone, the brightworks gleamed. There was a glass windshield and a custom pantasote top."[16] An equally enthusiastic participant in automobility, during one of his visits to Father's home Coalhouse is observed out in the street where he "dusted his car, cleaned the wheel spokes, the headlamps and the windshield."[17]

Among what distinguishes the situations of the two car owners are the perceptions of onlookers. To put it in Christina Sharpe's apropos terms, white America "annotates" and "redacts" the two car owners differently.[18] While Houdini's entrances and exits from his car attract admiring glances from onlookers, Coalhouse's attract hostility and condemnation, an unwillingness of much of early twentieth-century white America to accept Black participation in a luxurious automobility. The drama is precipitated when a segment of the city's white assemblage, the Irish firemen in the "Emerald Isle Station House," desecrate his car when he parks it in back of their building, slashing the top and placing dog feces on the front seat. Coalhouse's reactions and the consequences that ensue become the novel's main story.

Upon returning to his vandalized car, Coalhouse appeals to two traffic police officers, one of whom says to the Fire Chief, "did you or your boys do any desecratin'?" When the Chief disparages Coalhouse (using the N word) and falsely accuses him of disrupting their readiness by blocking the road in front the firehouse, making it necessary for them to move his car, the policeman comes back to Coalhouse and says, "Listen … we will push your tin lizzie back on the road and you can be on your way. There's no real damage. Scrape off the shit and be on your way."[19] In a defiant response, Coalhouse says, "I was on my way when they stopped me … They put filth in my car and tore a hole in the top. I want the car cleaned and the damage paid for."

"UNFORGIVEABLE BLACKNESS"[20]

It becomes clear that Coalhouse's "not knowing he's a Negro" implies that instead of acquiescing to Jim Crowism he asserts his agency as a civically eligible person, presuming that his licit presence and voice warrant official recognition. Living in a space in which white civic recognition is derived through a "dialectical negation of blackness,"[21] he refuses the objecthood that structures white subjectivity. The demands he utters are an instance of what Michel Foucault refers to as "fearless speech (*parrhesia*):

> a kind of verbal activity where the speaker has a specific relation to truth through frankness, a certain relationship to his own life through danger. A certain relation to himself or other people through criticism ... and a specific relation to moral law through freedom and duty ... the speaker uses his freedom and chooses frankness instead of persuasion, truth instead of falsehood or silence, the risk of death instead of life and security, criticism instead of flattery, and moral duty instead of self-interest and moral apathy.[22]

Failing to achieve legal redress, Coalhouse fearlessly risks death by turning to revolutionary activism. Along with a cadre that includes both Black activists and a white brother-in-law (an explosives expert who works in Father's fireworks business), he occupies Manhattan's Morgan Library, threatening to blow it up if his demands aren't met. The city's white officials capitulate and restore the car (it is fixed at J. P. Morgan's expense), but the resolution turns out badly for Coalhouse. Although his dignity is restored along with the restoration of his car's original condition, he remains behind to be killed by a firing squad outside the library while his followers are allowed to drive the car away.

While he was "driving Black" the fictional Coalhouse Walker Jr. exercised his self-understanding as an eligible car owner with a right to the road. In contrast with Coalhouse's dignified driving demeanor, the famous Black heavyweight boxing champion Jack Johnson, a contemporary of the fictional Coalhouse (boxing for thirty-three years, 1897–1931), was recklessly exuberant while driving Black. An enthusiastic driver who accumulated "a sizable collection of autos, including many of the leading U.S. and European makes,"[23] which he often drove at excessive speeds, he "drew hostility, harassment, and an introjected, covetous admiration from the police wherever he went."[24] Police harassment was but one kind of instance of what was widespread rivalrous rancor. Mia Bay situates Johnson's driving situation and existence in general as a target of enmity:

> JACK JOHNSON LOVED TO DRIVE. A BIG BLACK MAN WHO CARRIED himself with swaggering self-confidence, Johnson, in 1908 appalled much of the white world by becoming the first man of color to win the heavyweight championship of the world. His mastery of boxing's "sweet science" was a challenge to white masculinity, as was his penchant for consorting with white women. So was his love for cars. Far too proud and hot headed to be traveling Jim Crow, Johnson began buying automobiles as soon as they became available.[25]

Although for Johnson and since, the car has been a private space for Black drivers to move across the boundaries that defined much of Jim Crow America, long trips have required them to find services. As Black driving became more widespread, "Black motorists found it difficult to find places to stay: most roadside motels – north and south – refused to admit blacks. Diners and fine restaurants alike regularly turned away black customers. [However, as is treated in the feature film *The Green Book*, (2018)] by the 1930s ... black motorists could consult guidebooks to make their way through the country-side with as few hassles as possible."[26] As Jamila Jefferson-Jones points out, "'Driving while Black' faces a 'racialization of space' that has been part of a more general historical 'racial territorialization.' It's an adjunct of the perils of 'living while Black' and having to deal with the ongoing (and long standing) phenomenon of spatial racialization."[27] "Racial territoriality ... [the] threat of state violence through police force ... violence that includes the risk of death ... ties together 'Living While Black' and 'Driving While Black.'"[28]

The continuing perils of living while Black are visited on a wide range of generations: preteens, teenagers, and adults. They are summed up by Elizabeth Alexander under the rubric "The Trayvon generation":

> This one was shot in his grandmother's yard. This one was carrying a bag of Skittles. This one was playing with a toy gun in front of a gazebo. Black girl in bright bikini. Black boy holding cell phone. This one danced like a marionette as he was shot down in a Chicago intersection. The words, the names: Trayvon, Laquan, bikini, gazebo, loosies, Skittles, two seconds, I can't breathe, traffic stop, dashboard cam, sixteen times. His dead body lay in the street in the August heat for four hours.[29]

Rather than reviewing the cases involving the continuing perils of living and driving while Black, a situation with which many African Americans are confronted, faced as they frequently are with the racial profiling and brutal treatment at the hands of police, I want to focus on cars as moving civic spaces and on the dynamic of civic life taking place when Black drivers inhabit a car with which they can enjoy the relative freedom afforded by the open road. While residential space and the "American cultural landscapes" in general have been "hegemonically constructed as white space,"[30] Black drivers are more in control of automobilized space, "where sociability can occur"[31] in a mobile geography. Less afflicted by racialized restrictions, they are able to "dwell and socially interact via movement in and through their cars ... in a segment of the 'civil society of automobility.'"[32]

The featured text in my analysis of within-car Black civic automobility is a documentary film, Dwayne LeBlanc's 2023 *Civic*, which chronicles the car journey of a young African American, "Booker," who returns home and drives around his old Los Angeles haunts picking up passengers, two of whom are acquaintances, while we the viewers "never leave the car, even in the brief moments Booker does."[33] Deferring my reading of the documentary for later in the inquiry, I turn to an exploration of diverse aspects of within-car civic events by reviewing three texts in which the motorists are driving-while-white – a novel and two feature films in which the characters inhabit cars. In each text civic life is a series of events in which the participants involve themselves in critical exchanges. The encounters are perhaps best described as what Nathaniel Mackey calls "discrepant engagements," which "in the interest of opening closed orders of identity and signification [serve to] accent fissure, fracture, incongruity, the rickety imperfect fit between word and world."[34] To the extent that the encounters end in tentative accommodation, a temporary collective subject or in-process "we" emerges, a dynamic second person plural to which Mackey refers as a "wandering we."[35]

Richard Ford's *Be Mine*

Be Mine is the last of Ford's five Frank Bascombe novels, the character through whom he follows white bourgeois America's changing styles and preoccupations. They are all "road novels" in which Frank seems, as Dwight Garner puts it, "happiest and most himself behind the wheel, his windshield an IMAX screen through which he soaks up news about the state of his neighbors and the American experiment writ large."[36] By way of contrast, Ford's Frank Bascombe explicitly enjoys the overall civic eligibility denied to those who drive while Black. He reports, "nothing made me feel as civically invested and endorsed as public accommodation." To the extent that the feeling has attenuated, it's not from the fear of refusal that has often afflicted Black drivers but from becoming "aware of having little or no control of what's going on. In this case *Life in the Public Sphere* being not what it used to be."[37]

Ford's protagonist goes on the road in this fifth novel at age 74 to care for his son Paul, who at the outset is being treated in Minnesota at the Mayo clinic for ALS (amyotrophic lateral sclerosis). Recognizing that he has little time to overcome what has been a distant relationship with his son – it is clear that Paul is rapidly deteriorating, is increasingly unable to manage his body, and is likely to die fairly soon – Frank decides that they might bond on a road trip to Mount Rushmore:

> I have … devised as a coping strategy, for Paul and me to embark … upon a semi-epic, driving trip westward. Latter-day Lewises and latter-day Clarks, spiriting out across wintry Minnesota, and beyond to prairies South Dakota, all the way to Mount Rushmore … an impossible desti-nation, improbably embarked on in the heart of winter, but possibly one

Paul will find hilarious and capable of dousing his dread and dismays that nothing can be done for him.[38]

As the dialogue that occurs within their rental truck indicates, it's a trip that he hopes will compensate for his hitherto desultory approach to fatherhood. That commitment is a struggle for Frank who throughout the four prior novels was committed to expanding his world. Now, as he puts it, "When you're in charge of a failing son little else goes on."[39]

Nevertheless, a lot goes on. Among what is revealed is the novel's bi-temporality. At a micropolitical level Frank and Paul negotiate the congenial and uncongenial aspects of their different, generation-influenced biographies, while at a macropolitical level American political history is subjected to both commentary and witnessing as Frank reflects on iconic American leaders, those immortalized in stone at Mount Rushmore despite the politically and ethically questionable deeds for which they were responsible. Looking up at their visages, he says:

> L to R – Washington (the father), Jefferson, (the expansionist), Roosevelt # 1 (the ham, snugged in like an imposter) and stone-face Lincoln, the emancipator (though there are fresh questions surrounding that). None of these candidates could get a vote today – slavers, misogynists, homophobes, warmongers, historical slyboots, all playing with house money.[40]

As father and son (re)negotiate their relationship within the car, there are moments when the micro- and macropolitical registers converge, for example when Paul starts a conversation that connects his father's civic choices with America's controversial war history. He asks, "How do you feel about missing Vietnam?"[41] to which Frank responds after a few moments of the give and take, "I'm happy I missed Vietnam ... you wouldn't be he here if I hadn't. You could be a little Vietnamese boy."[42] Whether or not Frank is "happy" and what constitutes happiness is thematized from the very beginning of the novel. "Lately," he says, "I've begun to think more than I used to about happiness."[43] He goes on to reflect on notable alternatives, the founder of Presbyterianism, John Knox's, and Augustine's. Holding on to happiness while trying to finally achieve proper fatherhood constitutes the involvement that governs his perceptions throughout the road trip, while Paul's perceptions are structured by his own involvement: how to die with dignity. As a result, they rarely experience things the same way.

Alert to Frank's good parenting quest, Paul says, "This is your version of a do-over, isn't it?" Frank responds angrily, "Do-over what? Do you think I'm making up for lost time with you? I'm not ... I thought we could come here [to

Mount Rushmore] and experience the same thing the same way for once."[44] The situations that render them unable to experience the same thing the same way are implicitly articulated in Frank's several asides about Heidegger. Among the many times the philosopher's name appears is one in which Frank while packing for the road trip says, "I take only what is in my 'M' duffel, plus my pocket Heidegger, which puts me to sleep in five minutes, which is all I ask of it."[45] His protagonist's dismissal notwithstanding, Heidegger hovers over Ford's novel. He is thoroughly introjected in the story's discrepant engagement. Although father and son share a primary involvement in the world – they are both (in Heidegger's famous phrase) "being-toward-death" – they are on different temporal trajectories. In the plot's notable reversal, the son will predecease the father and is thus involved in the world as one who is hyper-aware that he will be leaving it "before his time." Frank's involvement is about managing an increasing loss of vitality, a premonition of a death still at a distance, which he experiences when he loses words. "Standing stock still [in a grocery store] beside a rack of under-ripe limes, I experienced an icy sensation – of captivity, of being walled off. Losing a word when you've possessed it only seconds before has about it what must be the aura of death's absorbing hollow complexity." He copes by moving through the store and reading labels to compensate for what Heidegger would call his "situation." "I had not so much located my wits as learned to get along with a smaller portion of them."[46]

Heidegger inhabits the novel's discrepancies at two levels, that between words and the world of things, and that which distinguishes the two protagonists' experiences. With respect to the former, Heidegger, favoring an expressivist position on language, asserted the need to find capable words, those that express adequately how things operate in the world, not for how they appear – "entities are much more than luminous facades"[47] – but for what they do. Thus, however automobiles may appear (for example, those that are shiny and new and attract admiring attention), to find capable words for automobility is to capture how as a mobilizing technology they alter the life world. Capability? In a lecture in which he interrogates what Nietzsche meant by "existence," Heidegger says, "waxing in confrontation with the matter itself, we must become capable of the capable word."[48] Such a capability continually eludes Ford's protagonists. Among what Frank cannot find an adequate word for is his son's "drastic intersection of life." "There should be a word for what he is, a word that can be inserted in all obituaries to help them speak truth about human existence."[49]

With respect to the latter, rejecting a frame in which the world is a perceptual field, Heidegger's philosophical grammar emphasizes the "how" of involvements rather than the Kantian "who," a subject constituted by the conditions of possibility for perception.[50] Substituting a verb for a noun, Heidegger asserts that one worlds through one's involvements; rather than merely perceiving things, one *has* a world in a particular way. Accordingly, throughout their road trip, father and son experience things differently, in part because of the difference between their longer term generational cultural attachments (Frank can barely tolerate his son's musical tastes) and in part because of the different temporal "situations" through which they world. That divide gives rise to the specifics of their different preoccupations while on the road. In an exemplary instance Paul speaks about one of his greatest fears, a "colostomy bag and permanent vegetative state,"[51] while at the same time Frank is reflecting on fatherhood and is experiencing it as "a downdrift of defeat ... the inevitable fatherly defeat of everything you do."[52] To the extent that the father and son's "wandering we," situated in a mobile civic capsule, achieves accord at a micropolitical level, it is through the admission that Frank makes: he loves his son. In contrast, there is no accord at a macropolitical level. While Paul with "eyes riveted" on the Mount Rushmore visages says, "This is great. I love this," Frank sees them as a national embarrassment. "Something's decidedly measly about them, something bally-hooed which they're not up to."[53]

Because a dialogic divisiveness and unmanageable contingencies afflict the protagonists in Ford's road story, before moving on from the text I want to evoke M. M. Bakhtin's dialogic approach to a novel's heteroglossia (its contending voices), because it captures the particularities of the characters' "sociolects." As Bakhtin puts it, "every word gives off the scent of a profession, a genre, a current ... a particular man, a generation, an era, and an hour."[54] Bakhtin also supplies the relevant genre insight. Ford's novel is shaped by what Bakhtin calls a "chronotope of the road," a spatio-temporality that is

> both a point of new departures and a place for events to find their denouement. Time, as it were, fuses together with space and flows in it (forming the road) ... the road is especially (but not exclusively) for portraying events governed by chance ... [thus] the important narrative role of the road in the history of the novel.[55]

As has been demonstrated, Bakhtin's concept of the chronotope of the road is as congenial with the film genre known as "the road movie" as it is with the novel.[56] Heeding that insight, the text to which I turn next, Ingmar Bergman's 1957 film *Wild Strawberries*, is a road movie that achieves the micropolitical potential of cinema's approach to automobility. During the elderly protagonist Isak Borg's (Victor Sjöström) driving trip from Stockholm to Lund, his car turns into a mobile civic space. Like Richard Ford's Frank Bascombe, death is on Isak Borg's mind. Life's universal journey hovers over both their road journeys. As Hélène Cixous aptly puts it, everyone has "always been on a return road [with] ... a face toward death."[57] And in particular, as is the case for Frank Bascombe, contingent encounters inside the vehicle turn Bergman's Isak

Borg toward reflections about his rigidities and inattentiveness to family life, his parenting in particular. That noted, while the 74-year-old Frank Bascombe tries to maintain a version of happiness in late life – "b-1945 – approaching my stipulated biblical allotment"[58] – Isak Borg has long given up on happiness. He's a widowed 78-year-old retired doctor with a crotchety personality, living a life devoid of social interaction. Cold and ungenerous, emotionally and otherwise, his main human contact is with his housekeeper, Agda (Jullan Kindahl), toward whom he shows little generosity. At the outset of the film, he disappoints her by deciding to head to Lund by car rather than the planned air trip on which she was to accompany him. What is common to the two characters, Frank and Isak, is the civic relevance of the road journeys in their stories.

Ingmar Bergman's *Wild Strawberries*

As the film follows Isak's journey from his home in Stockholm to Lund to receive an honorary degree from his alma mater, it features a temporal disjunction between the landscape, which is shown on the road to Lund (the film's temporal present) and a dreamscape, footage of Isak's dreams shown as flashbacks to his past unhappy life (he lost the love of his life, his intended, to his brother and ended up in a loveless marriage). Unlike Ford's Frank Bascombe, who seems to face the fact of his time running out with equanimity, Isak is haunted by the thought of it. In his first dream, which takes place when he awakes the day of his trip, he sees a driverless horse-drawn hearse from which a coffin containing a deceased Isak slides out onto the street.

Once on the road, Isak Borg has a front-seat passenger accompanying him, his daughter-in-law Marianne (Ingrid Thulin), the wife of his doctor son Evald (Gunnar Björnstrand). While we learn from a flashback of an encounter that their marriage is as unhappy as was Isak's, we see nevertheless that Marianne is along as a concerned surrogate for Evald. The trip begins with bickering between Isak and Marianne. In addition to scolding Isak about his relationship with his son, telling him that he's a selfish old man, she tries to smoke, to which Isak objects. However, as the journey progresses and hitchhikers are added to the car's ensemble, the mood becomes more convivial. And importantly, the way the road journey is shot is as much responsible for what the drama conveys as is the dialogue. Having been a theater director before becoming a filmmaker, the tendency of Bergman's camera work is to turn spaces into theaters by focalizing and framing scenes from the front. Throughout the road trip many of the shots are from in front of the car, turning the interior into a theater set and thus placing the viewer in a theater box. As the drama unfolds and people enter from off stage, the car-as-theater fills and a "wandering we" of increasing mutual recognition begins to evolve as the interactions among Isak, Marianne, and the new passengers turn the car into a mobile civic space (Figure 3.1).

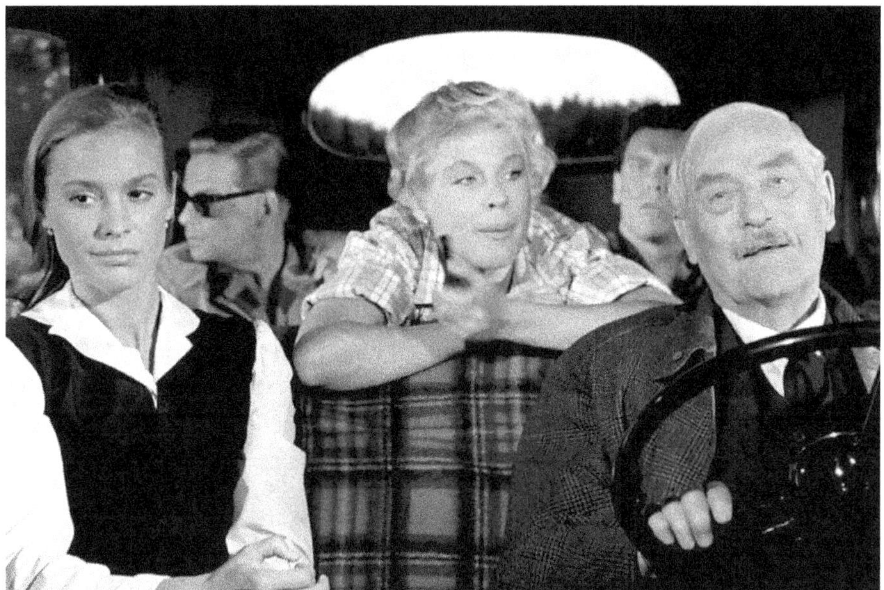

Figure 3.1 The automobile theater in Ingmar Bergman's 1957 film *Wild Strawberries*. Source: Criterion Collection, DVD, 2002.

The road trip is punctuated both by a series of civic events, theology- and ethics-implicated conversations that ensue after Isak adds the hitchhikers to the journey, and by detours when Isak stops along the way to visit places from his earlier life. During those latter intervals he is in turn visited by dreams that (re) narrate some of the unhappy moments from his past. For example, early in the drive, while he's on the road with only Marianne, he stops at his family's old summer place where he falls into a dream in which he is watching his brother Sigfrid's flirtation with his intended, Sara, a prelude to winning her affections and ultimately marrying her. The other notable dreams he has include one that is a nightmare in which he is unable to deliver his ideas successfully during a lecture and one in which he witnesses his brother enjoying the marital bliss that he was denied.

However, while on the road driving toward Lund with Marianne, as chance encounters add people to Isak's capacious automobile, the mood lightens, in part because Isak's dreams have affected him. Egil Törnqvist likens the impact of the dreams to the epiphany the apostle Paul experienced on the road to Damascus: "Like Saul's journey to Damascus ... Isak's trip turns into a penitential journey, working a conversion. Isak's Borg's career has been based on a reckless attitude to his fellow-men. Now on the threshold of death, he begins to suffer pangs of guilt."[59] As the car carrying a chastened Isak becomes a small theater that fills with actors who involve themselves in a civic encounter, a growing civility prevails and Isak, swapping his unhappy regrets for an enjoyable sociability, is swept up in the conversations. After expelling a quarreling middle-aged couple whom Isak had picked up after their road accident, because their quarreling threatens the civility of the automobile-as-traveling-civic-theater, Isak joins in the conversation's topic which has pervaded Bergman's films, the relationship between theological commitments and civic existence. As Bergman remarks, "No one is safe from religious ideas and confessional phenomena. Neither you nor I … As I see it today, any relapse is out of the question. But I can't say it's out of the question tomorrow."[60]

The other main issue pervading Bergman's films is fatherhood. In that respect, *Wild Strawberries* serves as a threshold to some of his subsequent films, especially *Though a Glass Darkly* (1961), a family drama featuring a negligent father, and *Winter Light* (1963), in which it is "God-the-Father" who is disappointing to the protagonist, a minister who has lost his faith in what he describes as an "echo God." In *Wild Strawberries* the fatherhood and theological issues are radically entangled. Sara, a young woman who is joined by two young men, plays the role of an intercessor during the civic conversation that develops after they join the ride. She's seated in between Viktor, who is a believer headed toward a career in the ministry, and Anders, an anti-theology rationalist who is planning a medical career. As the two young men argue about whether God exists and whether an acceptance of that existence enables an ethical life, she asks Isak about his point of view on the issue and whether he believes in a god. Isak's answer is enigmatic and poetic. "I see traces whenever flowers bloom."

Crucially, as the drive proceeds, Isak becomes a fatherly object of affection for the young trio. In the small automobile theater, he manages to evince the emotionally supportive version of fatherhood that he had failed to provide as a biological father. The effect he achieves is underscored when, after the ceremony in Lund, the trio serenade him outside the window of his room. Their effect on him has been so infectious that it encourages him to seek more intimacy with his housekeeper Agda, suggesting to her that they use first names (which she rebuffs), to express affection toward Marianne (for example, he allows her smoke in the car whereas earlier he had prohibited it), and to seek a reconciliation with his son Evald (offering to forgive his financial debt). As the film closes, after most of the close-ups of the dreaming Isak had shown a face in torment throughout the film's portrayal of his humiliating dreams, the last scene shows the sleeping Isak looking content.

The civic orientation of Bergman's film articulates a contentious issue located within Swedish national culture. However, doubtless at any hour the planet is filled with a wide variety of mobile civic events that automobility makes possible. Using that reality as a basis for his film *Night on Earth* (1991),

Jim Jarmusch composes a series of civic encounters in five taxicabs operating in five major metropolitan cites. The film's civic dramas, all shot mainly within the cabs with additional shots taken from outside looking in (as is the case with Bergman's *Wild Strawberries* road trip), take place in New York, Paris, Rome, Helsinki, and Los Angeles. Within each ride the viewer is mostly a virtual passenger inside the cabs with the driver and passenger, watching the encounter while occasionally seeing cities' views from the cab windows. The Los Angeles episode on which I focus is a prolonged encounter between the driver, a tough, gum-chewing working-class young woman, and an elegantly attired upper-bourgeois middle-aged woman who is a film casting agent. Once the passenger abandons the work-related interlocutors she has been speaking with on her phone and engages the cab driver in conversation, she thinks she has discovered the perfect type to cast in a film.

JIM JARMUSCH'S *NIGHT ON EARTH: LOS ANGELES*

The film opens with a shot of a scrolling global map to signal its cinema cartography, followed by a panorama of side-by-side global clocks to indicate the film's extensive temporality. As the Los Angeles segment leads off, a series of framing shots emphasize some of the city's main signatures – a palm tree-punctuated skyline, a private swimming pool – and then typical iconic urban portraits: a strip mall, telephone kiosks, a food truck, and other familiar urban landmarks. When the film finally tracks movement, we see a taxicab from the outside. It's underway as night is falling, before the camera zooms in to show the female driver seen through the cab's windshield. When she gets out to pick up her passenger, we observe an awkward choreography. The driver, Corky (Winona Ryder), begins the encounter with a demonstration of her strong professional codes. She insists on personally loading all the luggage. During the loading, her passenger, Victoria Snelling (Gena Rowlands), possessively grabs her briefcase rather than allowing it to be loaded in the trunk (signaling a similarly strong professional concern). At this stage the two are utterly anonymous to each other. Both are evincing the guarded body language of persons whose connections are formal rather than intimate. What will ultimately turn into a cross-generation, cross-class "discrepant" civic encounter, in which what begins as a commercial transaction becomes a somewhat convivial "we," is deferred until well into the ride.

Once Victoria is seated, the passenger door is closed, and Corky is behind the wheel, the anonymity surrounding a taxicab version of automobility is underscored when a recorded voice intrudes, issuing a warning that the passenger pickup zone is for loading and unloading only. It's a sign that for both Corky and her passenger the expectation is that the driver–passenger relationship will involve only loading and unloading. Victoria, whose destination is a friend's home in an upscale neighborhood, shows no interest in her driver

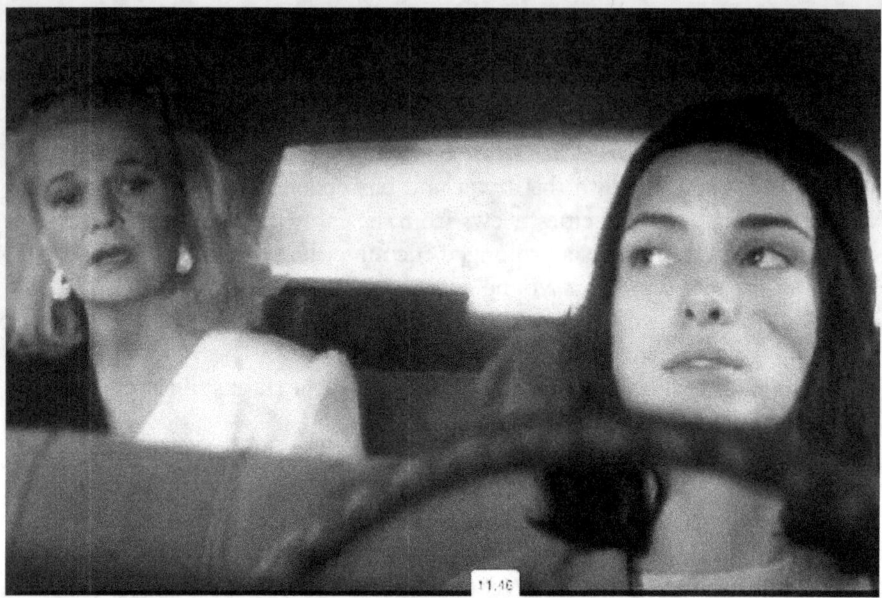

Figure 3.2 Driver–passenger anonymity in Jim Jarmusch's 1991 film *Night on Earth: Los Angeles*. Source: Criterion Collection, DVD, 2007.

at the outset. Corky shows similar lack of interest in her passenger except for moments of attention early in the ride, occasional glances in her rearview mirror with a facial expression that seems to be saying, "yeah, one of those" (Figure 3.2). While we're watching the automobile theater from the front, we hear Corky say "aw shit" as she tries to don her earphones before she utters "where to," to which Victoria's response is "Beverly Hills."

By the time the cab is underway it's dark. Outside the car is an ocean of neon while inside, as Corky takes another look in the rearview mirror, Victoria has *her* moment of frustration, uttered as a somewhat more refined curse, "damn." When Cory asks, "What's the matter," Victoria says "I left my phone book back in the suitcase with all the numbers." That statement inaugurates a reciprocity in the driver–passenger encounter, the first sign of a shared civility. In lieu of stopping to allow her passenger to retrieve her phone book, Corky hands back a local phone directory. "Why thank you, thank you," says Victoria. "No problem, just pass it back when you're done," responds Corky. Nevertheless, a social distance between the two remains at this point, seen in their physical comportments: Victoria is leaning against the back of her seat while dialing her phone, while Corky is moving to the music on her CD player as she drives. They're involved in "parallel play" rather than interaction (as one says of non-interacting children at play).

The images reinforce the dialogue in articulating the driver–passenger class divide. As she calls her friend, Victoria is wearing the kind of smile many in her class reserve for de rigueur sociability, while a relaxed Cory at the wheel is blowing a bubble gum bubble. On the phone, responding to a query from "Carol," Victoria is lamenting a casting issue, "I just spoke to him; I'm ricocheting off the walls, I don't know what to do any more. I sent him actresses who were perfect ..." and adds, "I'm supposed to have dinner with Peter and Shera tonight ... tell them I can't make it." She then says to Corky, "Miss would you turn the music off." "Sure Mom," says Cory, snidely evoking their generational divide as she complies. Still on the phone with the interfering noise off, Victoria says, "Carol, did Mr. Kincaid call?"

Hearing that, Corky suddenly charges across the generational divide and through the intimacy barrier. "Is Mr. Kincaid like your boyfriend?" Wearing a worried facial expression, Victoria responds, "Yes he is, at least I think he is." With that worried response, Victoria has invited a conversation that changes the first-person singular isolation between driver and passenger – the two I's – into a second person plural, a "we women." Corky summons that "we" with the remark, "Guys, can't live with them, can't live without them." Laughing, Victoria says, "You can say that again." Now more connected, they share observations about the ride. Victoria: "it sure gets dark fast in winter ... Driving at night doesn't seem to bother you." When Corky responds, "Why should it?" that prompts Victoria to refer to her night blindness. When Corky asks if it's because of aging, Victoria replies that she has had it "all my life." With life stories now part of the "we" agenda, Corky, using her familiar vernacular, sympathizes about Victoria's problem: "Fuckin' a man, that's fucked," she says as she lights a cigarette for the third time on the ride. Responding to the invitation to express care, Victoria turns to the language of politesse, "It isn't any of my business, but you smoke too much." That draws the same snide response, "Thanks Mom."

With conversational intimacy launched, the configuration of bodies changes. Rather than leaning back in her seat, Victoria leans forward toward the front passenger seat while she and Corky are both smoking (Figure 3.3) and starts an inquiry that will shape the rest of the encounter. "You're really happy driving this taxi, aren't you?" (something hard for Victoria to imagine, given her class's aspirational ideology). When Corky responds with "Fuck yes, I mean it's a cool job," Victoria, still unable to swallow the veracity of working-class contentment, says, "Is that your whole goal in life, driving taxicabs?" The taxi is now hosting a micropolitical actualization of a decades-long macropolitical phenomenon, an Anglo-American shift from early twentieth-century periods when working-class identification was widespread to more recent decades in which dis-identification became more common, especially among women (as Beverly Skeggs's end-of-the-century ethnography reveals).[61] As both the conversation and bodily

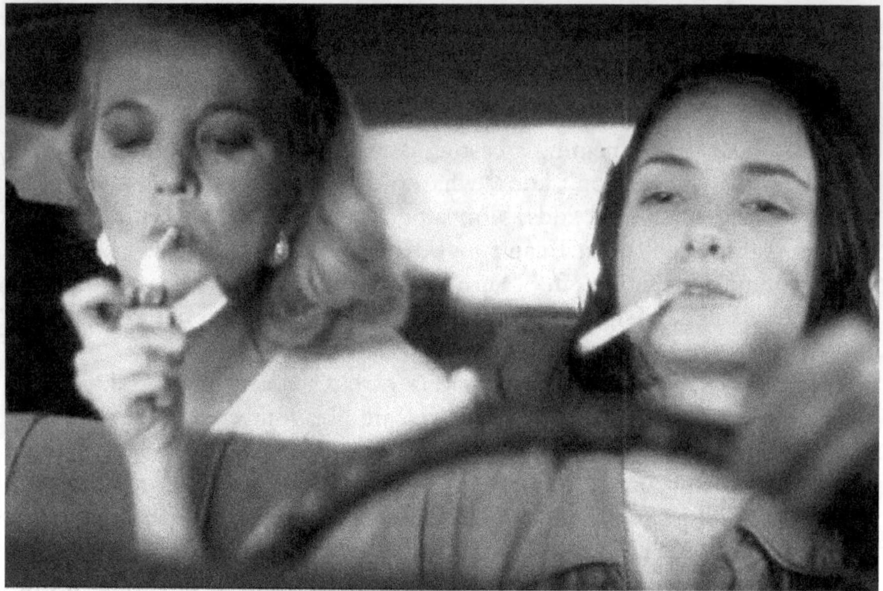

Figure 3.3 Driver–passenger conviviality Jim Jarmusch's 1991 film *Night on Earth: Los Angeles*. Source: Criterion Collection, DVD, 2007.

comportments become more congenial, Corky turns out to *be* aspirational, albeit not on the basis of the class expectations that Victoria has embraced. In her case it's an identification with brothers she admires and wants to emulate.

After Victoria utters the "is that your whole goal in life ..." question, she apologizes: "I'm sorry, I didn't mean it the way it sounded." That it was an instance of class snobbery is signaled nevertheless by a visual sequence; the camera tracks a luxury car passing the taxi through the driver side window precisely at the moment the apology is taking place. Rather than taking offense, Corky says, "Yeah well I'll tell you I don't always want to be a cab driver." When Victoria responds with "what do you really want to be?" Corky says, "A mechanic ... I already know everything there is to know about it. Both my brothers are mechanics, they're older – I'm like a girl and still younger ... it's kinda like work up to it you know."

Because the cab is now hosting an enhanced degree of shared affect and conversational rapport – the "we" is increasingly displacing the two dis-identified I's with which the ride began – Victoria, feeling entitled to prolong the interrogation, presses on. "What about marriage and family?" Indicating her strong affective identification with her older brothers, Corky responds, "definitely, want a family – boys though, lots of boys." When Victoria asks, "no girls?" Corky puts the conversation back on their initially shared terrain: "Maybe some girls; that's beside the point; the real thing is to find a good guy for the father." "Tell me about it," responds Victoria, while leaning back in her seat as Corky parks her gum and says, "I'm patient enough, at least I hope I am." "Another mechanic?" Victoria asks. "I don't care," says Corky, "as long as he loves me, takes me for who I am."

That "take me for who I am" references the agenda preoccupying Victoria, who, as she has become increasingly attentive to Corky's tough, no-nonsense persona, has been preparing to abandon her role as mere passenger and take up her vocational one as a casting agent. As the cab turns onto Beverly Court, approaching Victoria's stop, she looks at Corky and puts on the smile we saw during her first phone conversation. As the cab stops with both women in their professional modes, Corky performing her driver role asks if she can take the luggage up to the house for Victoria. When Victoria declines that gesture, Corky says, "OK, that will be 33 bucks." At that point Victoria springs the plan she has been hatching:

> Listen, can I ask you something ... now this is going to sound a little crazy to you. Uhm well, I'm a casting agent. That means I go out and find people you know, for really big movies, and I've been observing you and I honestly think you have something special. As a matter of fact, I'm casting a part that I think you'd be perfect for. This is a terrific part. You'd be a movie star.

Taken aback, Corky says, "What, like right now?" "Well yeah," is the response. Corky then dismisses the possibility: "I really wouldn't want to do that you know. I mean I have a job. I really wouldn't want to lose this job. I really wouldn't want to fuck up things right now you know. You understand, right?" Reluctant to give up, Victoria says, "Let's not be hasty. I just want you to be sure you know what I'm offering you." With what one should *know* as the main concept to which Victoria turns, Corky replies in kind. "But you *know*, I'm a cab driver. You *know* what this is what I do. As I told you, I'm going to be a mechanic." Victoria, seeking clarification, says, "Are you saying you just wouldn't be interested in being a movie star?" "Nah," says Corky. In a last try Victoria says, "You could be a mechanic later; everyone wants to be a movie star." Not so for Corky who wants to emulate her brothers and has built a strong narrative of the process that will achieve that; it's a narrative to which she clings tightly. Conceding "I might not be saying it right," she adds, "It's just that I have everything planned out for me you know. I mean everything's going right for me now." Victoria gives up, saying, "Well you can't [she can't] beat that." As she pays the fare and adds a tip, they part company. "Thanks for the tip," says Corky. "You bet," says Victoria, "take it easy." "Sure Mom," says Corky for the third time, her last reminder about the generation gap as she drives off while Victoria heads toward the house with her cell phone ringing. Victoria's "oh shut up" are the segment's last words.

EDWARD P. JONES'S "LOST IN THE CITY"

Watching Jarmusch's taxi ride through L.A. streets at night, our witnessing of the vehicle's interior shows two women each of whom is relatively comfortable (each in their own way) with their chosen paths. Although they differ in terms of what I want to call their class gnoses – each *knows* well how to negotiate her usual interpersonal milieux – they both experience the city as a hospitable place during the ride. Headed to a friend's house in an upscale neighborhood, Victoria has no doubt that L.A. is welcoming her. Similarly, driving through familiar streets while doing her usual work Corky makes clear that L.A. is congenial to her vocation, which is lodged in the midst of the life narrative she desires. To introduce a contrast, the more fraught experience of urban space for a Black taxicab passenger, I briefly review an Edward P. Jones Washington, D.C. story whose protagonist, Lydia, narrates an unwelcoming aspect of urban space for African Americans. Lydia, discomfited by her previous evening's sexual encounter with a man who didn't recall her name, upset by a phone call from a nurse informing her that her mother has died in hospital, and disoriented from some lines of cocaine she sniffs before the taxi shows up, is on her way to the hospital. Less than eager to reach her destination, she decides to plot a route that will replicate her sense of self-alienation. She tells the driver, "Just get me lost in the city."[62] At first the driver demurs: "'I'm a Capital cab driver and I ain't allowed to get lost.' 'Try,' she says, 'Try ever so hard.' She took two twenty-dollar bills from her bag, leaned forward and placed them on the seat between them."[63]

During the ride a melancholy Lydia sorts "Black memory versus state memory,"[64] as she indulges hers which arise when the cab moves through the parts of the city that her father's janitorial vocation had made familiar to her. The route articulates both the macro- and micropolitical aspects of the city, where the former includes its centers of (white) decision-making power – institutionalized state memory lodged in iconic buildings – and the latter the spaces where African Americans of her father's generation had been able to make a living. Vexed and not knowing "what else to do [the cab driver] continued driving. He passed the federal buildings along 7th, then the mall and its museums. In one of the museums white men had allowed her father to work pushing a boom, and now she was paid in one year more than her parents had earned in both their lifetimes."[65] As the drive proceeds, the city's white world continues to flood Lydia's consciousness. "At New York, he turned right, then then left on 5th street ... the further he went north, the more she knew about where they were going because the cab was nearing what the white people called the Federal Enclave."[66] Ultimately, while memory for Corky is what helps her navigate in the city, for Lydia it's about being reminded that she descends from one of the assemblages to which David Lapoujade refers as "lessor existences."[67]

CIVIC: A FRAME WITHIN A FRAME

Like Edward P. Jones's Lydia, Booker (Barrington Darius), the driver/ protagonist in Dwayne LeBlanc's documentary film *Civic* (2022), is also lost in the city. However, he is on a different kind of mission. Rather than willing to be lost, he is trying to recover a rapport both with Black Los Angeles and with himself. Having left the city years ago, what were once familiar routes in the South-Central section of L.A. where he's driving constitute a challenge to his former Black urban competence. As he proceeds along the route, his car becomes a mobile civic space in which the passengers he picks up, along with an uncle who enters the car by phone, school him about his civic responsibilities. He's enjoined to recover a place in the "we" of Black L.A.

Before he makes it to the city streets where the interpersonal encounters take place, Booker is on an L.A. freeway. As is the case in the L.A. portion of *Night on Earth*, the ride begins in the dark and is shown "daringly out of focus – seen through the windshield of a moving car, placing the action in an inner space of subjectivity."[68] From the outset, we as viewers have to contend with limited vision. Confined in the cramped space of Booker's back seat, what we see before the car exits the freeway are the back and side of Booker's head, the lights of passing cars outside the windows, and the taillights of the cars ahead. Before Booker leaves the highway, he phones his mother, "Ma did I wake you, my bad ... I was thinking about [pause] My mind's been every-where." The pause and the subsequent phrase capture's Booker's situation. He is afflicted with an ontological vertigo which he brings to the encounters he has once he leaves the highway and meets people on the streets of his former neighborhood as he takes us as viewers and auditors along on the ride. Situated within the car's mobile space we witness a series of Black intramural interactions that articulate aspects of L.A.'s Black civic life.

The L.A. street Booker revisits is in the area where LeBlanc grew up, raised by parents who emigrated from Dominica in the Caribbean. That part of his biography has entered Booker's car materially: hanging from the rearview mirror is a flag from a Caribbean country, creating a homology between the author and his protagonist. However, while LeBlanc's autobiography gives the film its locational trajectory from ancestry to the present, its form is inspired by what he learned as a student of communication and media by watching Chantal Akerman's films and others that were "part of a curriculum assembled by his screenwriting partner Nicole Otero." In particular, the composition of *Civic* is inspired by Akerman's and others' concern with identity migration and is edited to be something "his mom could watch," where his mom, according to LeBlanc, "is a metaphor for 'my community.'"[69] The way Black intramural life emerges in *Civic* is thus a realization of LeBlanc's viewer imaginary. The schooling Booker receives from his passengers is meant to be passed on to LeBlanc's community.

There is yet another structuring inspiration for the film which derives from LeBlanc's L.A. life. "Being from LA," he says, "I spend a lot of time in the car." Explicating the importance of his automobilized habitus for the film composition, he adds, "I was really interested in the frame within the frame," a microcosm of Black L.A. articulated by inhabiting a car as it travels within a section of a Black neighborhood. However, because the interpersonal connections had been historically broken, migration and reassemblage is the situation that structures engagements for the returning protagonist who is no longer comfortable in his old haunts. There are many long pauses within the conversations, especially when Booker is speaking. That filming rhythm is in accord with Michelangelo Antonioni's assertion about *his* style: "Life is also made up of pauses,"[70] he says, noting that rather than creating Hitchcockian suspense, he continually suspends the dramatic action to create ambiguity as to whose point of view dominates the scene. Bringing his own artistic version of pauses to his filming, LeBlanc figures the pattern of assertion and silence among the different voices musically as "something like a mixtape." "I wanted," he says, "to find a lot of tonality and range within Blackness."[71]

The film's first encounter begins once Booker hits the city streets. "Tee" (Maurice Powell), an old acquaintance, approaches the stopped car and in the spirit of male bonding joshes Booker about the quality of his vehicle as he climbs in (Figure 3.4): "What auction did you get this at?" The resulting conversation is emotionally disjunctive; Tee's coercive exuberance is met with Booker's reserve. Tee speaks in an upbeat Black vernacular as he attempts to re-initiate an inhibited and recalcitrant Booker in L.A.-inflected "Black talk," a "code switching"[72] that operates within a varied set of Black English sociolects in use among many African Americans. It's a practice of counter-intelligibility derived in part from an African discursive heritage and owed in part to the necessarily coded form of discourse developed among people who have been excluded from mainstream American civic expression.[73]

As their encounter proceeds, the rhythms of the shots reflect the disjunction between an estranged Booker, shown with individual close-ups, and the "we Black guys" that Tee is trying to construct, shown with shots that include the two, for example a shot from the back seat of their prolonged hug after Tee enters the car. Tee's attempt to pull Booker back into a "we" begins with an interrogation. "So, the boy's back in town, wassup?" Booker responds with a reason, which we come to understand, as the encounters proceed, is not the real reason. "I'm really just back Bro to see what's new and to check on my mom and all that." Switching from the interrogative, Tee tries to draw Booker

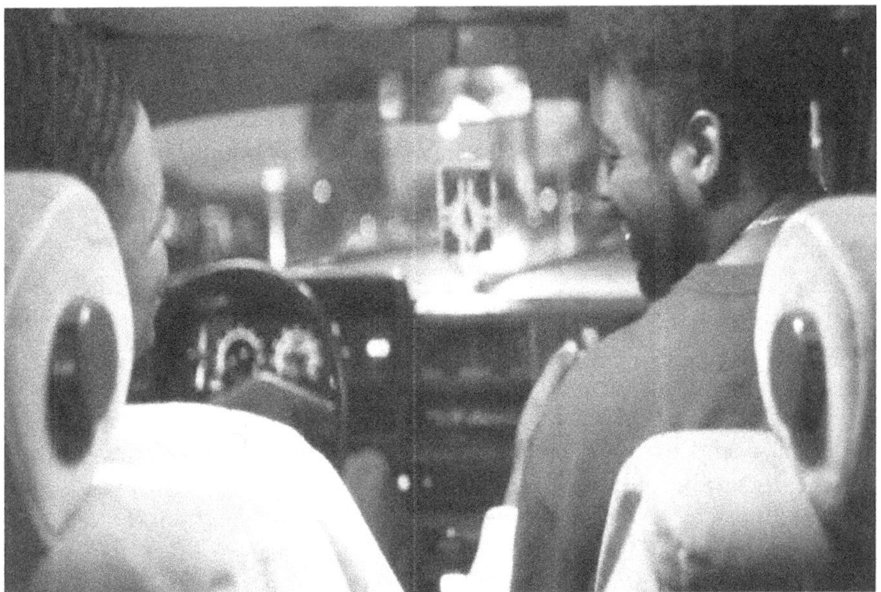

Figure 3.4 Booker and Tee in Dwayne LeBlanc's 2022 film *Civic*. Source: Criterion Collection, DVD, 2023.

into their old habits. "Let's go eat, CJ's." As they head that way, Tee chides him about his reliance on GPS. He wonders how Booker could have forgotten how to navigate in an area he once knew well. It's a telling instance of Booker' estrangement.

Once they're stopped in front of the eating establishment, civic concerns displace the issues of hunger and the recovery of an old habit that brought them to the stop. Delivering an observation that bears on local Black civic life, Tee refers to the oppressiveness of all the surveillance cameras monitoring people in their neighborhood. He recognizes that it's a current manifestation of the history of "the racial subject," which, as Achille Mbembe puts it, "would be called the Black man."[74] In response to Booker's reaction, "nothin' to do about it," Tee, in contrast with Booker's identity uncertainty, asserts his confidence in steadfastly performing who he is and what he's about. "Whatchu mean Bro; Imma do me; Imma come up always." When Booker responds, referring to the semiotics of public space, specifically the films that billboards tout, he observes that the ones he favors don't make the public displays. As the conversation has turned to the relevance to a Black assemblage of the politics of media, Tee advances a political economy explanation: "Talent don't pay the bills."

Back on the road, Tee begins another interrogation meant to identify Booker's Caribbean heritage. Complaining that Booker has gotten him up too early because he's from a different time zone, he says, "Whynt you tell me you was one of those early risers … ain't you from the islands?" At that point the resort to a second person "you" is a significant grammatical choice. It locates Booker on the periphery of the "we" toward which Tee is seeking to draw him. That grammatical mood comes up again with a different inflection in Booker's last encounter (with Harmonie, detailed below). What then happens while Tee is with him is an assembling of an augmented "we." The car stops for Tee to introduce a "homie," Josh, whom he introduces as "my [N word]," a Black talk mode of address. It's a verbal gesture of inclusion he has already used several times while conversing with Booker. Josh enters the car; there are more to come.

After Booker stops the car near a bus stop, he's approached by a middle-aged woman who, impatient because she has stood there waiting for an hour, asks him when she might expect the bus's arrival. When Booker gives her a lift, the car has begun hosting yet another local Black resident with questions for him. Looking from the back seat at the dangling flag on Booker's rearview mirror, she asks, "What's that flag about?" "This?" he says. "It's my parent's country," an indication that he has not made it a strong part of his self-identification. After she says, "That's wonderful, have you been?" Booker says in a defensive voice, "Nah not yet" and adds, "I'm really from here [pause] left a little while ago [pause] seein' what's new." "That's good to hear, Ol big shot, gone off someplace," she says implying that his ability to move has exceeded hers and others from the neighborhood who are less mobile. As she gets ready to be let out near her destination, she interrogates Booker once more, "Where is it you said you're from?" implicitly suggesting that Booker is not one of "us" (local Black people). Booker, looking straight ahead, doesn't answer, likely because he has no unambivalent answer available.

With that event over, we're watching from the back seat as Tee is jiving in place while listening to hip-hop on the car radio. Booker: "That's how you dance?" Tee urges him to join in: "Come on [N word] this is hard shit." Booker, unprepared to abide the contemporary hip-hop framing of Blackness, which has played a significant role in changing not only the Black vernacular but the English language as a whole,[75] reaches toward the radio, saying "turn this shit off [pause] it's cool I'm just sayin'…" In response Tee laughs heartily and suggests an older hip-hop that Booker might tolerate. The version to which he refers as "my shit" isn't one that Booker wants to embrace. He is outside his old neighborhood's "community of sense," the way they're currently "bound together [by sharing] … forms of visibility, and patterns of intelligibility."[76]

At that point, the car is hosting not only Tee but also three of his other friends to whom Tee explains "this [N word] left town." When they all get into a goofy conversation about fighting a duck versus fighting an ostrich as they pass a joint around, we viewers are now briefly looking from the front of the car through the windshield as the camera gives us close-ups of faces. They are shots to which Gilles Deleuze famously refers as affection images.[77] "The face," as Deleuze and Guattari point out, "gives the signifier substance; it is what fuels interpretation."[78] Booker's often dour facial expression says he's uncomfortable, contrasting with his laughing passengers who are enjoying their high with facial expressions exuding the pleasure of camaraderie. After the prolonged shot in which the film grammar is in the third person plural, a "they," we're again watching from the back seat, experiencing a grammatical shift back to the first person singular. Booker is isolated in the shot, responding to a phone call. When he takes the call, which he gets as a voice mail, his Uncle Vincent's Caribbean-accented voice fills the car's interior, imparting another civic lesson. Chiding Booker about neglecting his family obligations, he says "So you come home and not call? ... doesn't matter how long or why, you call your people." The key phrase, "your people" is stated to remind Booker about the importance of his inherited attachments.

After the call, Booker stops, gets out of his now empty car, and walks toward a store, leaving us, the viewers as virtual passengers in the back seat. As a young woman passes (played by Courtney Gabrielle Williams), he recognizes her and calls to her, "Harmonie." "I'm hearing my name – like who is this dude," she says. It's a query that transcends the problem of mere personal recollection because by now we recognize that the "dude" is unsure of who he is. After she hails him with "Yo, what are you doing here," Booker repeats one of the subterfuges he has been using: "came to town to check everything out." When Harmonie breaks in with "cross country for that, what's so urgent?" Booker demurs with "Aw nothing, just want to check on my mom." When he then asks her, "Where are you going?" Harmonie says "Home" and gets in the car. What then transpires is another transformation of his car's automobilized civic space, an intense conversation in which Booker is further re-educated about Black L.A. Intervening in Booker's duplicitous reasons – "checking everything out," "seeing what's new," "checking on my mom" – Harmonie draws him toward a more civic self-understanding, realized in his old L.A. neighborhood's participation in what Mbembe refers to as "the collection of voices, pronouncements, discourses, forms of knowledge" that constitutes "Black reason."[79]

The time with Harmonie as passenger is brief. At the outset of the encounter, while we're watching from the back seat, the film grammar articulates an initial estrangement between them. In contrast with Tee's entry into the car with a hearty embrace and playful remarks about the "boy" being back in town, the camera records Harmonie sitting close to the passenger-side door, looking straight ahead and remaining silent until she indicates where she wants to get out, "right over here." Booker, who is just a voice at that point, says, "I thought you lived at the end of the block." Harmonie, in focus from the side and seeking to leave quickly, responds, "It's cool, here's good." That's followed by a pause as Booker, not yet on camera, kills the engine and, sensing a cool distance being maintained by his former acquaintance (perhaps once a romantic relationship), says, "Yes, I know it's hard to recognize me; a lot has changed."

Booker's remark breaks the ice. Harmonie responds, "OK OK, you gained some weight," at which point, the camera switches to Booker and then back to Harmonie who, no longer looking straight ahead, has turned toward Booker saying teasingly that she recalls him always wearing a shirt that's one size too small, followed by, "I don't see anything different; you're still goofy as ever, that's for sure … you know this is Booker, right?" That reassuring remark inaugurates a dialogue whose grammatical rhythms are reinforced by shot–reverse shot camerawork (the two I-subjects in dialogue, engaging in mutual recognition with frequent resorts to the second person familiar, the "you" and "your"). Crucially as regards the conversation's civic import, it draws Booker out of his disingenuous reasons and schools him about the local version of Black reason. It's a progression that begins as a query as they sit in the car with the engine off: "what are you getting at," Harmonie asks; "you're so concerned if we can see you or recognize you? … Yes, you came back; I see you; is that better?"

As she delivers those remarks while turned toward him, the camera reverses to Booker whose face looks contemplative while his response is hesitant: "I'm not worried [pause] … wondering how I come off … I was just thinking …" (Figure 3.5). At that point Harmonie, now isolated on camera, introduces a crucial grammatical shift in which she locates herself in an "us" and "we" while hailing him as a "you." "*You* were thinking about *us*, how *we* seem?" (Figure 3.6). As the conversation proceeds from there, Harmonie, in focus with a face that shows irritability, maintains the plural identity she has introduced and says, "We're all just out here doing what we can. Shit we do what we gotta do." Booker as a voice then concedes but remains in an "I" grammar as the camera focuses on Harmonie looking skeptical. "I hear what you're saying, it's just I feel like … I'm looking for myself … looking for myself and trying to get away at the same time … so I'm here or there." Harmonie responds, "Get away, you're still Booker alright" and then continues with the first person plural, a grammatical choice that's meant to unsettle Booker's self-absorption: "Don't forget, we got a life; we out here livin' too."

Before she leaves, she chides him, ascribing his inadequate perception of his former neighborhood to a "Plato in the cave" perspective and suggests that he needs to know what it looks like "on the other side." After Booker refers dismissively to her reference to an ancient text as "AP philosophy," the camera shows him looking at her fixedly, until, after a long pause, she says with a smile on her face, "What?" Booker then, in focus, looks dour and says "nothin."

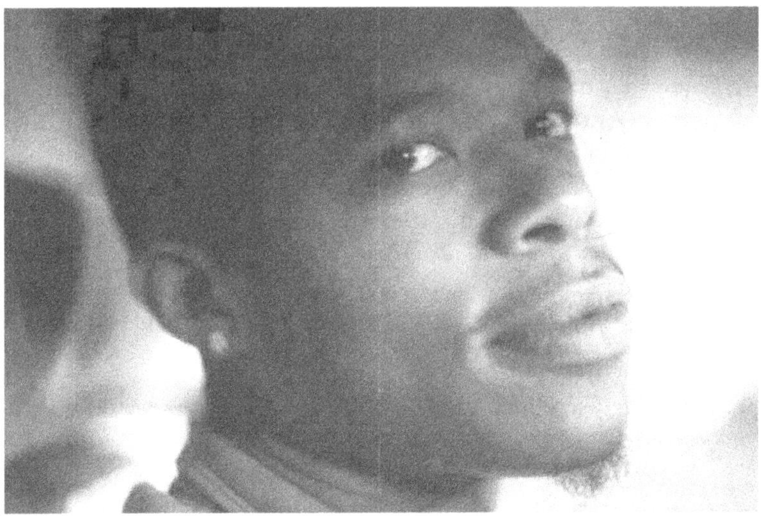

Figure 3.5 Booker looking over at Harmonie in Dwayne LeBlanc's 2022 film *Civic*. Source: Criterion Collection, DVD, 2023.

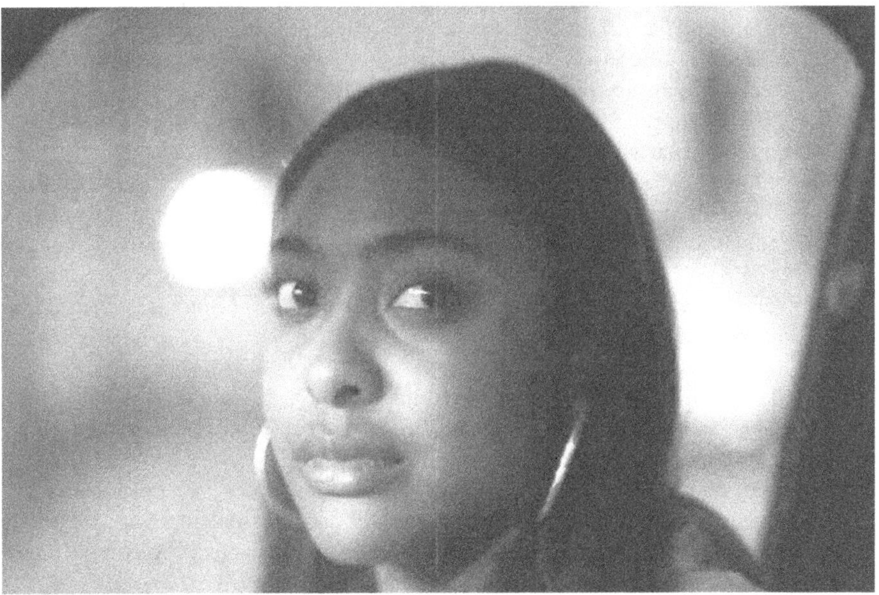

Figure 3.6 Harmonie in Dwayne LeBlanc's 2022 film *Civic*. Source: Criterion Collection, DVD, 2023.

As she leaves, she says that she has to go eat her tacos while they're still edible and adds that she has to go to work early tomorrow. The camera stays in the car with a side view of Booker looking contemplative as he rolls the driver-side window part way down so that the sounds coming from the neighborhood remind us (and Booker) about the locus of the "we" to which he has been apprised by Harmonie. All the discrepant encounters in the mobile civic space of his car have encouraged him to recover from his self-absorption and heed what Mbembe refers to as *"Black consciousness of Blackness,"*[80] a *sine qua non* of Black civic life.

NOTES

1. Daniel Miller (quoting John Urry), "Driven Societies," in Daniel Miller (ed.), *Car Cultures* (New York: Berg, 2001), p. 15.

2. Henri Lefebvre, *The Production of Space*, trans. Donald Nicholson-Smith (Cambridge, MA: Blackwell, 1991), p. 165.

3. Ivan Illich, *Tools for Conviviality* (New York: Marion Boyars, 2001), p. 58.

4. The *La Bloga* staff, "Interview with Helena María Viramontes, at https://labloga. blogspot.com/2007/04/interview-with-helena-mara-viramontes.html (last accessed September 10, 2024).

5. "Review of Ben Goldfarb's *Crossings: How Road Ecology Is Shaping the Future of the Planet*," in *The Inquisitive Biologist*, at https://inquisitivebiologist. com/2023/12/14/book-review-crossings-how-road-ecology-is-shaping-the-future-of-our-planet/ (last accessed September 10, 2024).

6. See Helena Maria Viramontes, *Their Dogs Came with Them* (New York: Washington Square Press, 2007).

7. Quoted in Thomas J. Sugrue, "Driving While Black: The Car and Race Relations in Modern America," in *The Automobile in Life and Society*, at http://autolife. umd.umich.edu/Race/R_Casestudy/R_Casestudy2.htm (last accessed September 10, 2024).

8. Paul Gilroy, *Darker Than Blue: On the Moral Economies of Black Atlantic Culture* (Cambridge, MA: Harvard University Press, 2010), p. 15.

9. *Ibid.*, p. 13.

10. E. L. Doctorow, *Ragtime* (New York: Random House, 1993).

11. Luke Spencer, "A Poetics of Engagement in E. L. Doctorow's *Ragtime*," *Language and Literature* 5, no. 1 (1996): 20.

12. The expression is Judith Butler's in her analysis of the Rodney King beating and subsequent trial of the white officers involved: "Endangered/Endangering: Schematic Racism and White Paranoia," in Robert Gooding-Williams (ed.), *Reading Rodney King: Reading Urban Uprising* (New York: Routledge, 1993), p. 15.

13. Doctorow, *Ragtime*, pp. 94–5.

14. *Ibid.*, p. 93.

15. *Ibid.*, p. 9.

16. *Ibid.*, p. 91.

17. *Ibid.*, p. 92.

18. Christina Sharpe, *In the Wake: On Blackness and Being* (Durham, NC: Duke University Press, 2016).
19. *Ibid.*, p. 104.
20. The heading is the title of Ken Burns's two-part documentary on the life and times of John Arthur "Jack" Johnson, the first Black heavyweight champion who, like the fictional Coalhouse Walker Jr., distressed the white world not only by winning the championship but also by failing to capitulate to Jim Crowism. He led a public life in which he fearlessly exercised his appetites.
21. See Biko Mandela Gray and Ryan J. Johnson, *Phenomenology of Black Spirit* (Edinburgh: Edinburgh University Press, 2023).
22. Michel Foucault, *Fearless Speech*, trans. Joseph Pearson (New York: Semiotext(e), 2001), pp. 19–20.
23. Theresa Runstedtler, *Jack Johnson, Rebel Sojourner: Boxing in the Shadow of the Color Line* (Berkeley: University of California Press, 2012), p. 12.
24. Paul Gilroy quoted in Mia Bay, *Traveling Black: A Story of Race and Resistance* (Cambridge, MA: Harvard University Press, 2023), p. 107.
25. Bay, *Traveling Black*, p. 107.
26. Sugrue, "Driving While Black."
27. Jamila Jefferson-Jones, "'Driving While Black' as 'Living While Black'," *Iowa Law Review* 106 (June 2021): 2283–4.
28. *Ibid.*, p. 2284.
29. Elizabeth Alexander, "The Trayvon Generation," *The New Yorker Magazine*, June 15, 2020, at https://www.newyorker.com/magazine/2020/06/22/the-trayvon-gener ation (last accessed September 10, 2024).
30. Euan Hague, "'The Right to Enter Every Other State' – The Supreme Court and African American Mobility in the United States," *Mobilities* 5, no. 3 (September 2010): 335.
31. John Urry, "Inhabiting the Car," *The Sociological Review* 54, no. 1 (October 2006): 27.
32. John Urry, "Travelings," in *Sociology Beyond Societies* (London: Routledge, 2000), p. 190.
33. See Blair McClendon, "Unafraid of the Dark: Dwayne LeBlanc on *Civic*," *Screen Slate*, March 31, 2023, at https://www.screenslate.com/articles/unafraid-dark-dwayne-leblanc-civic generation (last accessed September 10, 2024).
34. Nathaniel Mackey, *Discrepant Engagement: Dissonance, Cross-Culturality and Experimental Writing* (New York: Cambridge University Press, 1993), p. 19.
35. Nathaniel Mackey, *Blue Fasa* (New York: New Directions, 2015), p. xv.
36. Dwight Garner, "In Richard Ford's New Novel, One More Trip for Old Times' Sake," *The New York Times*, June 5, 2023 at https://www.nytimes.com/2023/06/05/books/review/be-mine-richard-ford.html (last accessed September 10, 2024).
37. Richard Ford, *Be Mine* (New York: Ecco, 2023), p. 320.
38. *Ibid.*, p. 25.
39. *Ibid.*, p. 192.
40. *Ibid.*, p. 321.
41. *Ibid.*, p. 29.

42. *Ibid.*, p. 31.

43. *Ibid.*, p. 1.

44. *Ibid.*, p. 306.

45. *Ibid.*, p. 192.

46. *Ibid.*, p. 286.

47. Graham Harman, *Tool-Being: Heidegger and the Metaphysics of Objects* (New York: Open Court, 2002), p. 219.

48. Martin Heidegger, *Nietzsche 2: The Eternal Recurrence of the Same,* trans. David Farrell Krell (San Francisco: Harper & Row, 1984), p. 27.

49. Ford, *Be Mine*, p. 303.

50. See Martin Heidegger, *What is a Thing*, trans. J. B. Barton Jr. and Vera Deutsch (South Bend, IN: Regnery/Gateway, 1967).

51. Ford, *Be Mine*, p. 291.

52. *Ibid.*, p. 306.

53. *Ibid.*, p. 321.

54. Tzvetan Todorov, *Mikhail Bakhtin: The Dialogic Principle*, trans. Wlad Godzich (Minneapolis: University of Minnesota Press, 1984), p. 56.

55. M. M. Bakhtin, "Forms of Time and the Chronotope in the Novel: Notes toward a Historical Poetics," in *The Dialogic Imagination*, trans. Caryl Emerson and Michael Holquist (Austin: University of Texas Press, 1981), p. 84.

56. See, for example, Alexandra Ganser and Julia Pühringer, "Bakhtin's Chronotope on the Road: Space, Time, and Place in Road Movies since the 1970s," *Facta Universitatis, Series Linguistics and Literature* 4, no.1 (2006): 1–18.

57. Hélène Cixous, "Fiction and Its Phantoms: A Reading of Freud's Das Unheimliche ('The Uncanny')," trans. Robert Dennome, *New Literary History* 7, no. 3 (Spring 1976): 544.

58. Ford, *Be Mine*, p. 1.

59. Egil Törnqvist, *Between Stage and Screen* (Amsterdam: Amsterdam University Press, 1996), p. 113.

60. *Bergman on Bergman* (interviews), trans. Paul Britten Austin (London: Secker & Warburg, 1973), p. 169.

61. Beverley Skeggs, *Formations of Class & Gender: Becoming Respectable* (Thousand Oaks, CA: Sage, 1997). See also her more recent investigation, which shows the trend increasing: "Class: Disidentification, Singular Selves and Person-Value," *Goldsmiths, Research Online*, 2016, at https://research.gold.ac.uk/id/eprint/18996/ (last accessed September 10, 2024).

62. Edward P. Jones, "Lost in the City," in *Lost in the City* (New York: Amistad, 2005), p. 148.

63. *Ibid.*

64. See Michael Hanchard, "Black Memory versus State Memory: Notes Toward a Method," *small axe* 26 (June 2008): pp. 45–62.

65. *Ibid.*

66. *Ibid.*

67. David Lapoujade, *The Lessor Existences: Étienne Souriau, an Aesthetics for the Virtual*, trans. Erik Beranek (Minneapolis: University of Minnesota Press, 2021).

68. Richard Brody, "Civic," *The New Yorker*, March 24, 2023, at https://www.newyorker.com/goings-on-about-town/movies/civic (last accessed September 10, 20224).
69. *Filmmaker Magazine* 105 (2023), at https://filmmakermagazine.com/people/dwayne-leblanc/ (last accessed September 10, 2024).
70. Antonioni quoted in Joe McElhaney, *The Death of Classical Cinema: Hitchcock, Lang, Minelli* (Albany, NY: State University of New York Press, 2006), p. 239.
71. McClendon, "Unafraid of the Dark: Dwayne LeBlanc on *Civic*."
72. John McWhorter, *Talking Back, Talking Black* (New York: Bellview Literary Press, 2017), p. 69.
73. For details of the heritage and form, see Ben Sidran, *Black Talk* (New York: Da Capo, 1971).
74. Achille Mbembe, *Critique of Black Reason*, trans. Laurent Dubois (Durham, NC: Duke University Press, 2017), p. 28.
75. See "Bringing the Black Vernacular's Vibrancy to the World," *The New York Times Magazine*, August 11, 2023, at https://www.nytimes.com/interactive/2023/08/11/magazine/hip-hop-language-dope-cake-woke.html (last accessed September 10, 2024).
76. Jacques Rancière, "Contemporary Art and the Politics of Aesthetics," in Beth Hinderliter, Vered Maimon, Jaleh Mansoor, and Seth M Cormick (eds.), *Communities of Sense: Rethinking Aesthetics and Politics* (Durham, NC: Duke University Press, 2009), p. 31.
77. See Gilles Deleuze, *Cinema 1: The Movement-Image*, trans. Hugh Tomlinson and Barbara Habberjam (Minneapolis: University of Minnesota Press, 1986).
78. Gilles Deleuze and Felix Guattari, *A Thousand Plateaus*, trans. Brian Massumi (Minneapolis: University of Minnesota Press, 1987), p. 115.
79. Mbembe, *Critique of Black Reason*, p. 27.
80. *Ibid.*, p. 30.

4. THE CIVIC LIVES OF THINGS: HATS AND GLOVES

> The Biography of the Object … not the individual person moving through a system of objects, but the object proceeding through the system of people.
>
> Sergei Tret'iakov, 1929[1]

"The Force of Things"

This inquiry in this chapter is addressed to the agency of things, specially to the civic performances of hats and gloves, attending to both their material and metaphorical presences in historical and contemporary life worlds. Ascribing agency to articles of clothing, Virginia Woolf suggests that "There is much to support the view that it is the clothes that wear us and not we them."[2] Object agency deconstructs the subject. As Fred Moten puts it, "while subjectivity is defined by the subject's possession of itself and its objects, it is troubled by a dispossessive force objects exert such that the subject seems to be possessed – infused, deformed – by the object it possesses."[3] Adding amplitude, Jane Bennett treats the agency of diverse forms of materiality, undertaking what she refers to as a "discernment of … the active powers issuing from non-subjects."[4] Focused on particular domains of what Bennett calls "the force of things,"[5] as I analyze the historical and contemporary roles of things that perform as "vestimentary signs"[6] in social and civic venues, I turn in the illustrative part of my analysis to the film and novel versions of Edith Wharton's *The Age of Innocence*, in which hats and gloves are primary vestimentary signs, and follow with extended readings of two films that are textual vehicles serving as my primary objects of analysis, the Coen brothers' *Miller's Crossing* (1990), set in an unidentified eastern city (circa 1929) in which the hat is its major iconic object, and Jane Campion's *The Power of the Dog* (2021), set in a Montana cattle town in 1925 in which gloves are the iconic presence. The visual contrast between the two films is stark. Calling for different visual vocabularies, the former's urban space features dense, enclosed scopic fields, while the latter's rural space features large, lightly populated landscape panoramas. Reserving those readings for later sections of the inquiry, I begin my analysis with a fictional moment, an exemplar of novelistic realism taking place in a prior century.

OBLIGATORY THINGS

In a seemingly insignificant scene in Leo Tolstoy's *Anna Karenina* (1877), Anna's brother, Stepan Arkadyich Oblonsky (Stiva), an aristocrat and minor government official, is reading a newspaper. It's part of a daily ritual with which he prepares himself for conversations within the aristocratic spaces he shares with his peers. "Living in a certain social set, and having a desire, such as generally develops with maturity for some kind of mental activity, he was obliged to hold views, just as he was obliged to have a hat."[7] Oblonsky's thoroughgoing complacence is similar to that of some of the novel's other characters, most notably Anna's husband Alexis Alexandrovich Karenin, who "every time he had knocked up against life itself, ... stepped out of the way."[8] Given the relatively stable class structure and lack of political instability in Oblonsky's local and national milieux, the stakes of having views are not high for an aristocrat choosing from a spectrum of political affiliations. In contrast, the situation in contemporary Russia in which its president, Vladimir Putin, is prosecuting a war in Ukraine (2014–25), which he refuses to call a war, reveals the way the arc of history offers alternative civic atmospheres. Because citizens at any social level who have used the word "war" have been threatened or punished, the safe option is what an embedded journalist refers to as an "aggressive apathy." It's a situation in which "sophistication means being in on the truth that most everything is potentially a lie."[9]

Nevertheless, although the stakes of expressing opinions in Tolstoy's nineteenth-century Russia are not high, the passage describing Oblonsky's class conformity references more than *noblesse oblige*. In particular, the hat obligation to which the passage refers has at least as much normative weight in the implicit negotiations of co-presence in civic space as that of the "views" with which Tolstoy initiates the passage. As François Ewald points out, a norm is "a way for a group to prove itself with a *common denominator*"; it is "created by the collectivity without being willed by anyone in particular."[10]

The normative obligations associated with hats, along with other aspects of clothing, have notable historical depth and a decidedly civic significance operating within the historical moment of Tolstoy's novel. An inquiry into literary representations of the nobility's clothing in nineteenth-century Russia discloses that,

> Dress was highly semiotically charged ... Clothing was a material representation of structures of power ... What a person wore depended on their status, but also partly on their inclinations. Some clothes, such as uniforms, were legally prescribed, while others, such as fashionable dress, relied on generally understood codes. Noblemen used their clothing choices to negotiate their relationship with the state and to express their political leanings.[11]

Addressing the long-term background of those prescriptions, the author adds a transnational context:

> To understand 19th-century dress culture, it is necessary to look back to the Westernizing reforms of Peter the Great (r. 1682–1725), which introduced European models into state and social structures and brought in Western clothes for the nobility. Peter's reforms were unusual in their goal of transforming society, not just reinforcing its hierarchies. Subsequent rulers continued to legislate on dress and, by the turn of the 19th century, noblemen's clothes were highly regulated, subject to both changing legislation and fashion.[12]

The Ubiquitous Bowler Hat

Socially and aesthetically akin to the way Tolstoy conveys with a single sentence an obligation structure that prescribes the way hats function within Russia's nineteenth-century civic space is another literary contribution which treats a different era's hat obligation. Delivered with a similar economy of expression, the narrator in Samuel Beckett's 1946 novella *The Expelled* recalls the day when his father prepared to take him to a hatter: "come son, we are going to buy your hat." In response, the son, reflecting on being captured within a subject position that has preceded him, muses about the biography of the hat. It's "as though it had preexisted from time immemorial in a pre-established place ... it was forbidden me, from that day forth to go out bareheaded."[13] The son's querulous aside is an indication that, like their author, Beckett's characters are anything but complacent. The bowler, a pervasive presence in Beckett's texts, is among the things that function for him as props mobilized to contest a society's normative orders. As David Lloyd suggests:

Beckett's thinking of the thing, offers the possibility of the *res publica*, of a community founded not on the sovereignty of the subject over its objects but of the insistence of the human as a thing beyond representation, suspended in its relation to the things among which it dwells.[14]

In particular, as Julie Bates points out with regard to the-hat-as-thing, Beckett "consistently undermines the patriarchal sense of continuity that is inscribed in the bowler."[15] The continuity to which Bates refers includes the bowler's artistic as well as its historical longevity:

> socially and artistically [it is] the single most significant headgear of the past hundred years ... [ranging from] the hat of the comedian (or mime or juggler), to the hat of the middle-class Western businessman ... The Bowler is the 'vestimentary sign' of both images, of comic individualist and sedate conformist.[16]

That latter observation by a historian of the bowler suggests that the social sensibilities and implicit civic obligations inherent in the hat-wearing norms articulated in the Tolstoy and Beckett texts have significance beyond what is presented in the two scenarios. Their fictional worlds call our attention to broadly distributed practices that transcend the particular scenes they compose, encouraging inquiry into what we can learn from the way a variety of textual genres treat civic obligations that are refracted through objects implicated in interpersonal exchange. By heeding Tolstoy's and Beckett's references to hat obligations we observe the way literature, with impressive concision, can provide insights into crucial aspects of civic space with attention to objects, in this case to clothing accessories that serve as props that articulate person–thing relationships for historically situated subjects.

The bowler hat, a manufactured object whose biography is revelatory with respect to changing civic milieux, has had notable attention in social, political, and literary histories. Its story begins in the mid-nineteenth century. Designed by the London hatters James and George Lock, who envisioned the hat as a protective head covering for rural gamekeepers, it was "sent ... across the Thames to the hatmakers Thomas and William Bowler for manufacture. Thereafter it underwent a spatial and class migration."[17] "Like much of England at mid-century, the bowler moved from the country to the city; and like English fashion and manners ... it moved down the social scale."[18] It also showed a capacity for migration across styles in the arts. As Peter Wollen points out, when the Belgian painter Magritte (who has men in bowler hats "more than 50 times in his work between 1926 and 1966"[19]) changed styles from "Purism" to "Surrealism," his bowler images "crossed the divide."[20]

Crucial as well to the bowler story is its role as a temporal trope. Although

> the Modern Age did not begin with the bowler hat … the bowler was one of its significant accessories, for modern life as modern dress. From precisely the middle of the nineteenth century, it floated like an emblem through the then incredible changes, a sign of the times.[21]

The film director Martin Scorsese materializes that floating. In his 1993 cinematic adaptation of Edith Wharton's Gilded Age novel *The Age of Innocence*, there's a cut to an unanticipated scene. As the protagonists Newland Archer and Ellen Olenska depart after having shared tea in one of their many desire-inhibited encounters (in an incipient affair that never happens), there's a cut to a slow-motion shot that records a large mass of bowler-hatted men marching up a Manhattan sidewalk during working hours (Figure 4.1). As they move toward the camera, the dominant part of the scene of hunched-over marching men is their bowler hats slowly bobbing up and down.

That bowler scene, which reflects a fashion development that became pervasive "during *La Belle Epoque* (1890–1910) [adopted by] tradesmen, businessmen, servants, clerical workers, artisans and some laborers,"[22] provides a telling contrast to the straw boater hats on upper-class men in leisure space

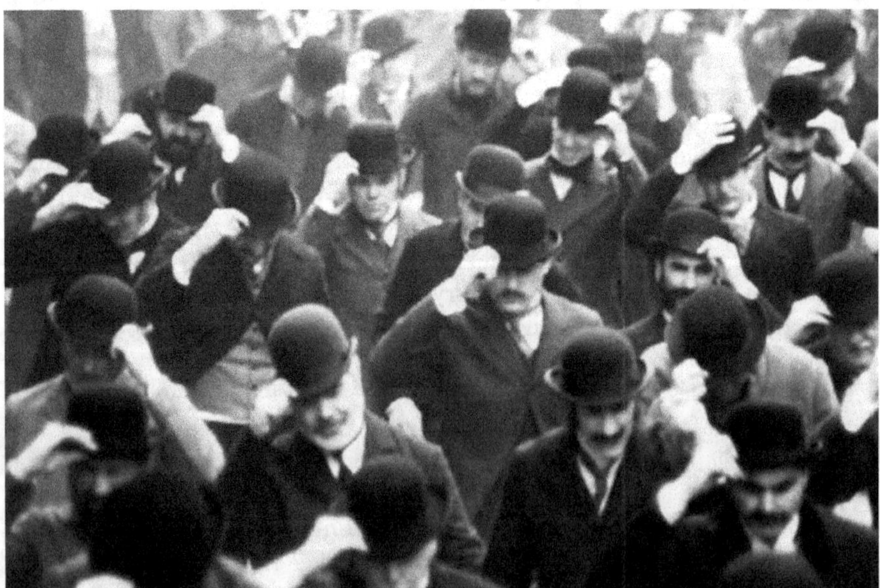

Figure 4.1 Bowler-hatted men in Martin Scorsese's 1993 film *The Age Innocence*. Source: Criterion Collection, DVD, 2018.

at a garden party in an earlier scene. It's "the first suggestion in the film of a teeming, industrious world beyond the confines of Newland and his set. Such devices boldly shake up the apparent solidity of this very materialistic world of old New York, revealing in an instant its vulnerability and evanescence."[23] As Roland Barthes points out, "Fashion" is a marker of the rapid rhythms of sociality and the vulnerability of consumers to its dictates: "[If] clothing's producers and consumers had the same consciousness, clothing would be bought (and produced) only at the very slow rate of dilapidation."[24]

The film's image-based narrative thread is concentrated continually on clothing accessories. While much of the attention is on hats, gloves are also often in focus, for example in a scene in which there is a long take of many pairs of name-labeled white silk gloves on an entry table, shed by guests on their way to the main rooms to join their hosts at a wealthy family's party (Figure 4.2). That shot registers a historical moment in the history of upper bourgeois glove wearing. "By the end of the 1800s, it was no longer deemed fashionable to wear gloves indoors."[25] Scorsese's gloves shot also emphasizes the crucial role of the scopic field that contains visible exchanges in the social and civic orders of late nineteenth-century New York. As his camera performs a tableau aesthetic with long takes that reference the social and civic salience of things, especially such iconic pieces of apparel as hats and gloves, what the

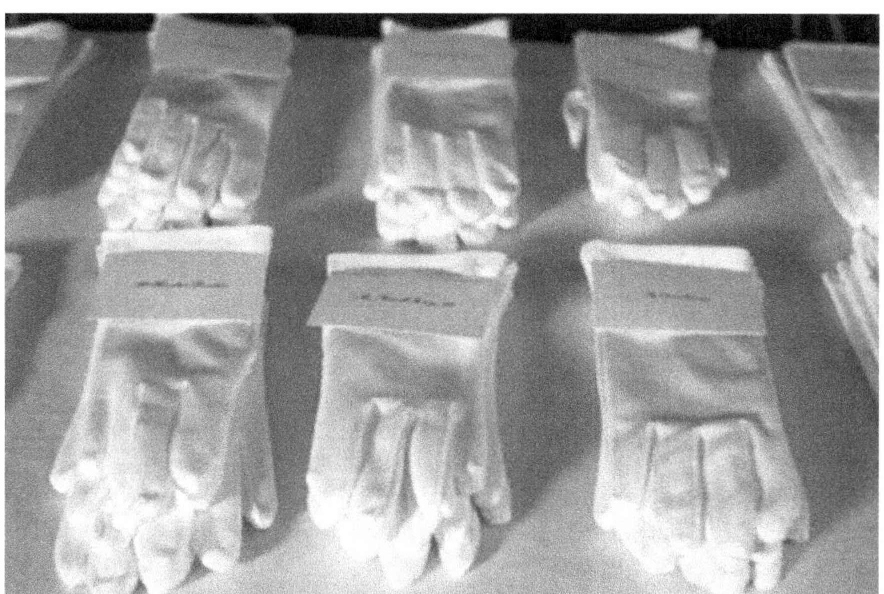

Figure 4.2 White silk gloves in Martin Scorsese's 1993 film *The Age of Innocence.*
Source: Criterion Collection, DVD, 2018.

image narrative captures is the way those things are involved in the visible sign exchanges essential to a social obligation structure.

The dense scopic field of visual exchange mapped by Scorsese's camera is also a primary focus in Edith Wharton's novels. The visual motif composed in both genres captures what Ash Amin refers to as a city's "atmospheric force." Elaborating, Amin refers to "the full weight of the ensemble of things, bodies, technologies, sounds, visual cues, buildings and more in public space [which] must be considered as an atmospheric force, working on civilities and incivilities, or indifferences and cares."[26] In a commentary on the importance of visual cues in novels, Wharton anticipates Scorsese's cinematic adaptation of hers. She refers to the "startling visibility of Dickens's characters" and suggests that they serve as "close-ups before cinema."[27] In contrast, she adds, "Trollope is ... perplexingly careless in the matter of word-painting."[28]

The social and civic privileging of visibility, which Wharton continually lends to her characters' perceptual practices, is frequently deployed on clothing-focused interpersonal exchanges. It's picked up in Scorsese's rendering of another glove-dominated scene in which the protagonist, Newland Archer, initiates his most intimate gesture: he "peels off his gloves and slowly, slowly his bare hand unbuttons Countess Olenska's caramel-colored kid glove and he kisses the inside of her wrist."[29] At that moment, Scorsese's camera is referencing a typical Wharton scene, a focus on her characters' visible accouterments in spaces that host an exchange of signs in which a given object or an ensemble of objects reflect class coherence.

Jean Baudrillard provides an instructive framing for such an object-oriented way of reading the class structure, clothing fashions among other things. He suggests that the objects are to be read in terms of their "sign function value," on what they say about the social location of those who possess them rather than their utility.[30] "Thus," he writes, "a social classification must eventually be founded upon a ... subtle semiology of the environment and of everyday practices. An analysis of interiors and of domestic spaces ... a syntax of object, which ... bring out the organizational constraints with reference to the type of habitation and the social category."[31]

Wharton's way of mapping objects in social space emphasizes a pervasive nineteenth-century constraint, the way women are treated as objects of male perception. She situates her female characters among other objects and emphasizes the consensual basis of their sign function value. Early in *The Age of Innocence* – a text in which "narration is intricately linked to visual phenomena"[32] – her protagonist, Archer, who at the outset is as complacent as the characters in Tolstoy's *Anna Karenina*, is looking around while at the opera in the novel's first major scene. Although the venue is a musical theater, looking rather than listening predominates. As is the case with key scenes in her earlier novel *The House of Mirth*, "the characters appear oblivious to the music or theatre as they relentlessly survey one another."[33] Referring to Archer's complacent mood as his perceptual activity constitutes the scene's main feature, the text states, "His contentment lies in the belief that his views are shared by all the carefully brushed, white-waistcoated, buttonhole-flowered gentlemen."[34] However, Archer's gaze, which "serves in the novel as … the center of consciousness,"[35] becomes less confident as the narrative proceeds. His "contentment" becomes increasingly fugitive as he loses control of the scopic field and is forced to recognize that he cannot control how is he situated vis-à-vis the returned gaze of two women in his life. A returned gaze is a source of unease verging on an identity crisis, as Jacques Lacan has famously theorized it.[36] In particular, Archer's self-confidence is undermined by his growing romantic obsession with Ellen Olenska who resists the subordinate female role that Archer expects to observe. Like a contemporary actor, Tilda Swinton, who in her films evinces a "self that works to subvert the standard male response to her considerable beauty … to put the watcher in the position of being watched,"[37] Madam Olenska "throws Archer's gaze of mastery and compulsion off balance, stimulating in him simultaneously feelings of alarm and compassion, contempt and protectiveness, aversion and fascination."[38] He is similarly discomfited while looking at a photograph of his betrothed, May Welland, who *Looked back at him like a stranger*, leading him to realize "that marriage was not the safe anchorage he had been taught to think, but a voyage in uncharted seas."[39]

To illustrate more elaborately the way Wharton composes the civic implications of visible exchanges, I turn briefly to two commentaries on another of her Gilded Age novels, *The House of Mirth* (one of which includes Terence Davies's film version, 2000), because they disclose crucial aspects of the force fields beneath the "atmospheric force" in urban civic life to which Amin refers. One commentary by Wharton herself pertains to the unseen underlying codes and conventions that shape New York's scopic field. The other, by Shama Rangwala, reveals the underlying political economy that shapes the structure of the city's visible levels of inequality. In her "Introduction to the House of Mirth," Wharton refers to late nineteenth-century New York as a "little hot-house of traditions and conventions [which] … were unassailed and tacitly regarded as unassailable."[40] By descending to a "certain depth" beneath the "stage-setting of manners, furniture and costume,"[41] the novel exposes the way those traditions and conventions are implicated in the destruction of the protagonist, Lily Bart. The way the novel "lifts the veil" on a part of New York's life world exemplifies Wharton's view of the novel's ability to "show what is behind it."[42]

Operating with a more explicitly political idiom, Rangwala's reading of both the novel and film adaptation conceives an economic rather than merely social structure and assigns Lily's destruction to the political economy of inequality in which an exchange system's force field selects bodies for civic inclusion and exclusion. Characterizing the novel's era as one in which "Concepts such as citizenship and civil society served as ideological smokescreens for market relations during the period of classic liberalism from the late nineteenth to the early twentieth century," she suggests that it "pulls back this screen to reveal brute inequitable market calculations."[43] Treating that effect experientially, the novel "charts the trajectory of the protagonist, Lily Bart, through a series of socio-economic positions, from a vibrant and desirable debutant to an etiolated corpse in a boarding house."[44] Within Rangwala's political economy framing, Lily's destruction follows her inability to accumulate sufficient social capital despite investing in considerable affective labor in an attempt to "completely embody the commodity form" in a society that features "patriarchal treatment of women as property."[45]

Crucially, for purposes identifying the genre effects that Rangwala contrasts, while novels typically feature a subject-centered, perception-driven framing of interpersonal exchanges, cinematic adaptations tend to privilege objects. Thus, when asked about how he translates literary form into cinematic composition, Alain Robbe-Grillet, a practitioner of both genres, refers to the role of objects:

> In my work I don't begin with a preconceived storyline. Objects give rise to thoughts, which become my novel or film. A blue shoe, a broken bottle … became the point of departure and the evolutionary force for my film *Glissiments Progessifs du Plaisir* [*Successive Slidings of Pleasure*].[46]

Rangwala's commentary on the novel versus film versions of *The House of Mirth* is in accord with that translation. She observes that while Wharton's novel "renders explicit Lily's interiority and highlights the disparities between her private labor and public image," Terence Davies's cinematic adaptation "is composed of a series of images that place the figure of Lily in particular positions, gesturing implicitly through its visible manifestations … [it] communicates obliquely through visuals and dialogue rather than explicitly rendered interiority."[47] As the film follows the story of Lily's attempt at controlling her subjectivity (the main narrative thread in both the novel and film), it focuses on "material objects [that] reflect her self-composition."[48]

Recalling Wharton's remark that Trollope is "careless in the matter of word-painting," I want to note the way paintings are main objects of attention in both Davies's and Scorsese's image narratives (*The House of Mirth* and *The Age of Innocence* respectively). In an observation that accords with the cinematic strategy of using paintings in their films, Françoise Sammarcelli refers to the role of "pictorial quotation,"[49] pointing out that in *The Age of Innocence*, "To a large extent, painting and objects help define the protagonists and convey their often-concealed feelings."[50] The "intersemiotic" social world that Sammarcelli ascribes to Scorsese's film reflects a crucial aspect of the micropolitics of civic life in general. Among the ways the social bleeds into the civic is through purposive action by persons who become qualified as civic agents by evading capture within assigned subject positions. In the words of the Holocaust survivor/writer Imre Kertész, it's about becoming qualified as "the name-giver instead of the named." In her reading of the film version of *The House of Mirth*, Rangwala treats the way naming versus the named is translated into the visual idiom with which Davies adapts Wharton's story of the destruction of Lily Bart. Pointing to Lily's inability to acquire "sufficient capital to display herself as a singular piece of art unmediated by labor or calculability but rather an expression of aestheticized embodiment," she notes that despite dressing to mimic the woman representing "Summer" in Jean-Antoine Watteau's painting *Ceres*, "she is still on display for others to calculate her value."[51]

Yet another aspect of Wharton's rendering of social and civic life deserves attention because it provides a frame for the Jane Campion film with which the chapter concludes. As is the case in Campion's *The Power of the Dog*, Wharton's *The Age of Innocence* achieves much of its coherence from a focus on hands and their episodic glove coverings. A painting that the protagonist Archer observes testifies to the iconic role of gloved hands, Emile Auguste Carolus-Duran's *La dame au Gant* (Woman with Glove). Emily Orlando's commentary points to the significance of the intertextuality between painting and novel in that scene. The painting in which "Carolus-Duran's lady playfully tugs at her gloved hand … acts as a tease for the male spectator: she seems to dare him to retrieve her fallen glove." That image calls attention to the novel's characters: "Archer," she notes, "seems determined to align Ellen with the woman in the painting," and, she adds, "Wharton also uses [the painting] to play with the iconic significance of hands," specifically "Archer's constant fetishizing of Ellen's."[52] Reserving analysis of the contrasting roles of hands and gloves between Wharton's novel and Campion's film for later in the inquiry, I return to the bowler hat story to emphasize its critical role in contemporary texts whose characters resist the complacency and conformity of those in the nineteenth-century novels I've analyzed.

CRITICAL INTERVENTIONS: THE BOWLER HAT IN DIVERSE GENRES

The primary aspect of civic analysis in Wharton's *The Age of Innocence* consists in a narration of the process in which Newland Archer's "privileged viewpoint" loses its confidence. His mind, pre-populated with rigid gender protocols, has him continually misperceiving "the cultural text of social interaction."[53] Characteristically, literature abounds in perception narratives. The disenabling effect of Archer's initial confidence in his perceptual acuity, which progressively attenuates, contrasts markedly with a character in Alfred Döblin's urban novel *Berlin Alexanderplatz* (1929). *His* protagonist, Hans Biberkopf, undergoes the opposite perceptual experience:

> As our story begins, Franz Biberkopf leaves Tegel Penitentiary where a previous foolish life had taken him. He has difficulty initially adjusting to Berlin [during the ride into the city Biberkopf is assaulted with images he cannot decipher], but finally to his relief, he succeeds and vows to stick to the straight and narrow from now on.[54]

It is through Archer's misreading from which, unlike Biberkopf, he fails to recover that Wharton mounts a critique of a world of forms in which the Gilded Age society has incarcerated itself (well illustrated in Scorsese's film adaptation with a tableau aesthetic focused on social rituals and clothing accessories). In contrast, the critical treatment of the contexts of those accessories in the contemporary textual genres to which I turn, involve object-oriented rather than perception-based critique. Through the critical use of repetition, they locate forms and objects in multiple reoccurring contexts. In particular, the bowler hat, which Scorsese seized on as a significant critical object, appears repeatedly in the novels of Samuel Beckett and Milan Kundera, the paintings of René Magritte, and the film antics of Charlie Chaplin and Stan Laurel and Oliver Hardy. In their different ways, those texts provide commentary on the stultifying effects of social and civic conformity. In each case the critical functions of their texts turn on a concept that evokes a persistent aspect of bourgeois historicity.

Referring to Beckett's frequent use of bowlers, Julie Bates identifies the relevant Beckett concept: "While they may be vaunted in middle class society, the values and practices embedded in the bowler are identified by Beckett's narrators or characters as insidious, largely because they are habitual."[55] Habit is precisely what Beckett disparages; he does so elaborately in his treatment of Proust's unease with his society's stasis. "Habit," Beckett writes in his Proust study, "is the generic term for the countless treaties concluded between the countless subjects that constitute the individual and their countless correlative objects." Inspired by Proust's habit aversion, Beckett uses a habit-breaking mixed metaphor: "Habit is the ballast that chains the dog to his vomit."[56] Although Milan Kundera exhibits a similar unease with entrenched social forms, there is a more urgent geopolitical historicity associated with his unease. His novel *The Unbearable Lightness of Being*, situated during the Russian invasion of Czechoslovakia that crushed the "Prague Spring" underway in 1968 under Alexander Dubček, turns on the concept of kitsch, particularly as it manifests itself within totalitarian governance. As he puts it, "whenever a single political movement corners power, we find ourselves in the realm of totalitarian kitsch … what I mean is that everything that infringes on kitsch must be banished for life: every display of individualism … every doubt … all irony."[57] While Kundera's kitsch attention is initiated with a focus on what he calls "Communist kitsch," he ultimately contends that kitsch "is the aesthetic ideal of all politicians and all political parties and movements."[58]

There are two persistent aspects of Kundera's kitsch-resistant compositional strategy in his novels. He along with his characters are what Deleuze and Guattari refer to as "conceptual personae"; they serve as vehicles for the "author's concepts" (articulated through the novel's essayistic commentary that accompanies its plot).[59] Most notable as regards his contribution to my focus on object-oriented narration, Kundera lends a subversive agency to objects (as well as unreliable, misreading-prone words) which participate along with his contrarian subjects in the disruption of social and civic orders. For example, in a passage on "An Old Church in Amsterdam," he ascribes disruptive agency to interior objects, the seating accommodations provided for "wealthy burghers … The chairs and stalls seem to have been placed there without the slightest concern for the shape of the walls or position of the columns, as if wishing to express their indifference to or disdain for Gothic architecture."[60]

The disdain on which I want to focus is the main attribute of his character Sabina, one of "a quartet of characters who perform the intricate set of variations that make up what there is of action in the book."[61] In addition to the painter Sabina, the novel's protagonists include Tomas, a surgeon, Tereza his wife, and Franz, a lecturer, all of whom have their lives destabilized by the 1968 Russian invasion. Sabina has a disdain for masculine dominance: "A man who wanted to master her? How long would she put up with him? Not five minutes! From which it follows that no man was right for her. Strong or weak."[62] She toys with accepting versus rejecting masculine control by wearing a bowler hat as a prelude to sex with Tomas as well as in other scenes (Figure 4.3 shows her in Philip Kaufman's film of 1988). Kundera fashions her bowler hat-wearing with a musical metaphor:

> The bowler hat was a motif in the musical composition that was Sabina's life. It returned again and again, and all the meanings flowed through the bowler hat like water through a riverbed … each time the same object would give rise to a new meaning, though all former meanings would resonate (like an echo, like a parade of echoes) together with the new one. Each new experience would resound each time enriching the harmony.[63]

The bowler makes several appearances in the novel. With a nod to Nietzsche's concept of "eternal return," Kundera refers to its five kinds of appearance, repetitions in which "things appear other than we know them"[64]:

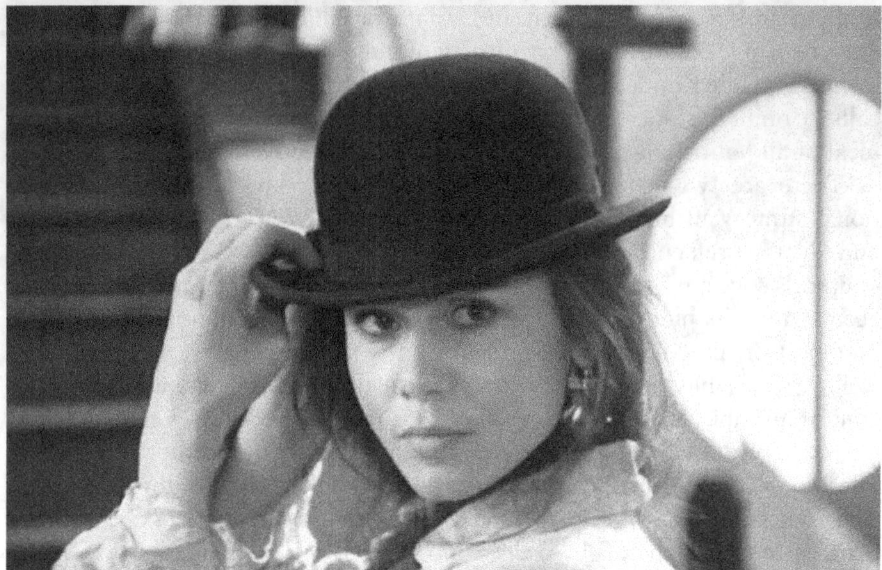

Figure 4.3 Sabina in Philip Kaufman's 1988 film *The Unbearable Lightness of Being.*
Source: Warner Brothers, DVD, 2006.

> First, it was a vague reminder of a forgotten grandfather, the mayor of
> a small Bohemian town … Second, it was a memento of her father …
> Third, it was a prop for her love games with Tomas … Fourth, it was
> a sign of her originality, which she consciously cultivated … Fifth …
> now that she was abroad, the hat was a sentimental object. When she
> went to visit Tomas in Zurich, she took it along and had it on her head
> when he opened the hotel-room door. But then something she had not
> reckoned with happened: the hat, no longer jaunty or sexy, turned into
> a monument to time past.[65]

The proliferation of bowler contexts, as the hat returns repeatedly, each time
with a different significance, constitutes its role as an anti-kitsch statement.
Noting that "totalitarian kitsch" resists "every display of individualism …
every doubt (because anyone who starts doubting details will end by doubting life itself); all irony (because in the realm of kitsch everything must be
taken quite seriously)," Kundera counters with a celebration of individualism,
doubt, irony, and the "unintentional," where the last-mentioned is a feature
he ascribes to New York, "a place where things are 'unintentional.'" His
repeated objects "sparkle with "a sudden wondrous poetry."[66]

The bowler hat is as pervasive an image on the canvases of the artist
Magritte as it is in Kundera's novel. In photographs and films Magritte himself

has been shot wearing a bowler hat, and it has been his primary icon since its appearance in "his first major work, *The Musings of a Solitary Walker*."[67] Most significantly for the purposes of my focus on the agency of objects, Magritte is notable for "choosing to ally himself with things rather than 'knowers.'"[68] Stamos Metzidakis summarizes the Magritte aesthetic appropriately as

> a transformation of man in general as a unique being having control over his environment, to just another object living in a pictoro-poetic universe. [For example] His famous painting that depicts a crowd of identical men wearing bowler hats, falling out of the sky, like so many drops of rain. (*Golconde*, 1953).[69]

As Magritte characterized his object-centered interventions in the fifty plus times he included bowlers on his canvases, he like Kundera sought a "subversive effect" through repetition. He had the bowlers "exist again with the appearance they have in reality."[70] As Fred Miller Robinson summarizes the effect, what Magritte reproduces and effectively renders comical is "the man 'of the masses,' the 'standardized' man, the 'suburbanite,' the 'commuter' [in order] to exaggerate his stereotypicality ... Their very uniformity implies an alienation that the environments they are placed in exaggerate."[71]

The role of the bowlers worn by Charlie Chaplin and by Laurel and Hardy in many of their films is also comedic, in their cases because the hat references hopeless aspiration, a reach toward a faux respectability contradicted by the low prestige of the occupational levels in which they are ensconced in their films. Here I want to elaborate on one particularly dark comedy, Chaplin's *The Great Dictator* (1940) in which he plays two characters, a nameless bowler-hatted Jewish barber, and Adenoid Hynkel (Hitler), Dictator of Tomania (for ptomain poison). Although much of the subversive effect of the comedy is rhetorical – Chaplin "fatally pricks and deflates Nazi rhetoric [with] guttural gibberish [which] rapidly descends into mere coughs and splutters"[72] – the bowler Chaplin wears as the Jewish barber (Figure 4.4) is crucial to the way it evokes a history of persecution and violence. "In Germany in the thirties, the bowler had become exclusively identified with Jews ... a Nazi epithet for the bowler was *Judenstahlhelm* ('steel helmet of the Jews')."[73]

Historically, the Jewish hat has been a marker of a different variety of anti-semitism. As an investigation discloses, "The quantity and complexity of anti-Jewish iconography featuring hatted Jews [began] in the twelfth century."[74] A horned hat (*pileus corulus*) was a Jewish style during the later Middle Ages ("it was brought ... to Poland and France by way of Germany") before being and abandoned as they starting dressing like their host Christian populations. However, in 1267 the Breslau synod, comprised of Christian churchmen, "prescribed that 'the Jews' should resume wearing the horned hat."[75] Since

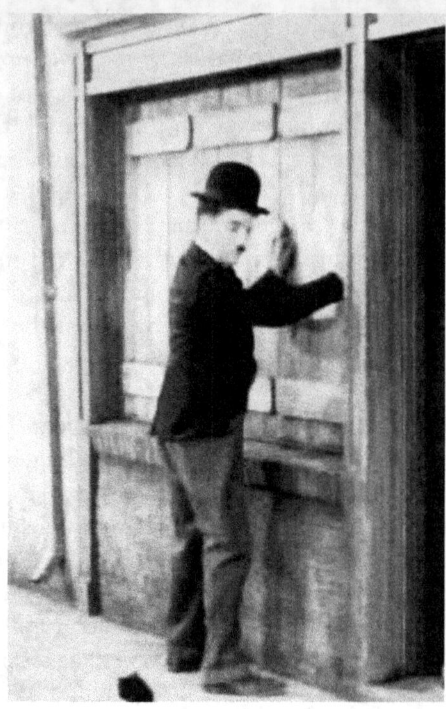

Figure 4.4 Charlie Chaplin as a Jewish barber in his 1940 film *The Great Dictator*.
Source: Criterion Collection, DVD, 2011.

then, there has been a historical dialectic of identity difference afflicting Jews. For example, in 1416 a Jewish woman "was arrested in Ferrara, Italy, for not wearing earrings ... In an era when superfluous adornment was condemned as a sign of sin, Jews were required by law to wear conspicuous jewelry."[76] If we recognize that, as Roland Barthes suggests, fashion is non-verbal communication, a mandate for the "compulsory visibility"[77] of a clothing fashion constitutes coerced speech.[78]

Fast forward to contemporary France in which an assimilationist ethos implemented by legislative, juridical, and policing agencies prevails, reversing cultural identity policies that have prescribed compulsory clothing at diverse historical moments in a variety of national venues. Exemplary is the famous 1989 *affaire du foulard* (the headscarf affair). As I noted in an earlier inquiry,

> When three young Muslim women entered a middle school in Ceil
> wearing them, they were expelled, and the expulsion was officially vali-
> dated when the highest judicial body in France ruled that the girls were

in violation of the *Laïcite* (secularism) law. Rather than being mere religious insignia, the wearing of the headscarves was deemed by the court to be an act of proselytizing.[79]

In this case, to proscribe a cultural fashion statement was to impose silence. While head covering issues persist in various places, hats, which have been more or less liberated from theological and state forms of coercive authority, are now materially mainly a commodity and symbolically a persistent status-oriented metaphor.

Jamaica Kincaid's account of her father's attachment to an English hat while living in the Caribbean colony of Antigua testifies to the latter:

> My father ... a carpenter and cabinet maker ... wore [a] brown felt hat. Felt was not the proper material from which a hat that was expected to provide shade from the hot sun should be made, but my father must have seen and admired a picture of an Englishman wearing such a hat in England, and this picture that he saw must have been so compelling that it caused him to wear the wrong hat for a hot climate most of his long life.[80]

With respect to the former, the "Jack Kennedy effect" has achieved significant notice. Because he was thought to be "the first U. S. president to appear hatless at his inauguration" – and "routinely went hatless before and after the election" – it was speculated that "JFK single-handedly killed the hat industry" (even though he was merely following a trend that had preceded his presidency).[81] Whether or not the Kennedy effect weighed against the hat as a commodity, hats persist as a social and civic metaphor, based on a long historical trajectory in which they have participated in several aspects of life worlds. The hat's iconic role in the Coen brothers' film *Miller's Crossing*, to which I now turn, testifies to that persistence.

MILLER'S CROSSING

Some reviewers of the Coen brothers' *Miller's Crossing* expressed dissatisfaction with the slow pace of the plot, expecting rapidly unfolding action from what on the surface is a noirish gangland drama. Well attuned to the brothers' cinematic aesthetic, in his book-length treatment of their films Jeffrey Adams recognizes what they were doing: "With careful attention to production design and period accuracy, the story unfolds in a fictional gangland milieu, where style is paramount and fashion, especially in men's apparel, takes precedence over the violent action of a generic gangland movie."[82] The hat, the major iconic presence throughout the film, appears before the credits are run. A framing shot shows it sitting on the ground in the forest (which we subsequently learn is known as Miller's Crossing) before a gust of wind blows it away as the camera records its tumbling disappearance into the distance.

A relatively simple gangland plot serves as the pretext for the film's apparel-oriented visual narrative. The main protagonist, Tom Reagan (Gabriel Byrne), is the consigliere for Leo O'Bannon (Albert Finney), an Irish mob boss who runs the city. O'Bannon controls the police department and mayor's office (both the police chief and mayor make no decisions without consulting him) and runs the fixes through which he and his associates profit from gambling on prize fighting. The drama begins when Leo offers his protection to his girlfriend Verna's (Marsha Gay Harden) brother Bernie Bernbaum (John Turturro), a bookie who skims off the bet on the matches and has violated a code, failing to follow through on a fix that was to yield winnings for the Italian mob boss Johnny Casper (Jon Polito). That sets off the film's first scene in which Casper is in Leo's office asking Leo's permission to kill Bernie, paradoxically saying it's a matter of "ethics." "I'm talking about ethics ... It you can't trust a fix, what can you trust?" he says. The scene initiates both the status situation and power dynamic. While Casper is speaking the camera does a frontal close-up of his uncouth-looking flapping lips, while it shows Leo from a side shot in an oblique conversational posture, turned aside from Casper to show his detachment from the request (which he refuses to grant).

The other situation driving the drama is Tom Reagan's vulnerability because he's having a secret love affair with Verna, which ultimately estranges him from Leo. Actually and metaphorically, hearts are as implicated as hats throughout the narrative. It is through several references to Tom's heart – for example, twice when he's about to shoot Bernie who tells him to "look into his heart," and a moment when Verna points out that his jealousy of her relationship with Leo "means you've got a heart" – that much of the film is a quotation of the crime stories and novels of Raymond Chandler and Dashiell Hammett, especially the latter. The detective Sam Spade's heartlessness is a main feature of Hammett's most famous noir novel *The Maltese Falcon*. Early in the plot, after Spade has taken on Brigid O'Shaughnessy as a client, his secretary receptionist Effie says, "Sam, if that girl is in trouble and you let her down or take advantage of her, I'll never forgive you."[83] By the end of the novel Effie learns from reading the paper that Sam has solved the case by implicating Brigid as the murderer. When Sam appears at the office, he drops his hat on the desk, "sits down" and says to Effie, "So much for your woman's intuition." Upset, Effie says, "You did that, Sam, to her ... I know you're right, you're right [but] ... don't touch me now."[84]

Just as a hat is a feature of Hammett's last scene, hats figure prominently in the opening scene of *Miller's Crossing*, both materially and metaphorically. Leo, who holds the loftiest subject position, is hatless throughout the scene, while Casper shows up and leaves in a bowler, suggesting his proletarian status. Metaphorically, he is in front of Leo with hat in hand. His thug assistant Eddie Dane remains in the background wearing a more sophisticated hat, a fedora, which is also the kind Tom Reagan wears (which he's holding during the scene before putting it on as he leaves). Thereafter, at various moments in the film Tom pulls the fedora down, as a visual quotation of moments in noir detective films. He's copying the gestures of hardboiled detective dramas, film versions of Raymond Chandler's Philip Marlowe and Dashiell Hammett's Sam Spade both of whom pull down their fedoras so that their eyes are barely visible beneath the brims.

Before the conversation in Leo's office is over, hats achieve their main metaphorical status. Feeling wronged by Leo's refusal, Casper becomes increasingly vociferous about the "anarchy" he is charging Leo with tolerating and complains that he is being "high-hatted." Donning his bowler to leave, he grouses about being treated "just like some snook who likes to get slapped around." Leo's response is to tell him to leave and take his "flunky" with him (Figure 4.5). Leo's ethnically tinged contempt for the Italian mobster is matched by Casper's for the Jewish bookie. Throughout his appeal to Leo to let him kill Bernie who cheated him by selling the fix to others, he uses a derogatory vestimentary metaphor, referring to Bernie Bernbaum as "the *schmatte*," a Yiddish word for a rag or a low status or worthless piece of clothing in manifestly poor shape.

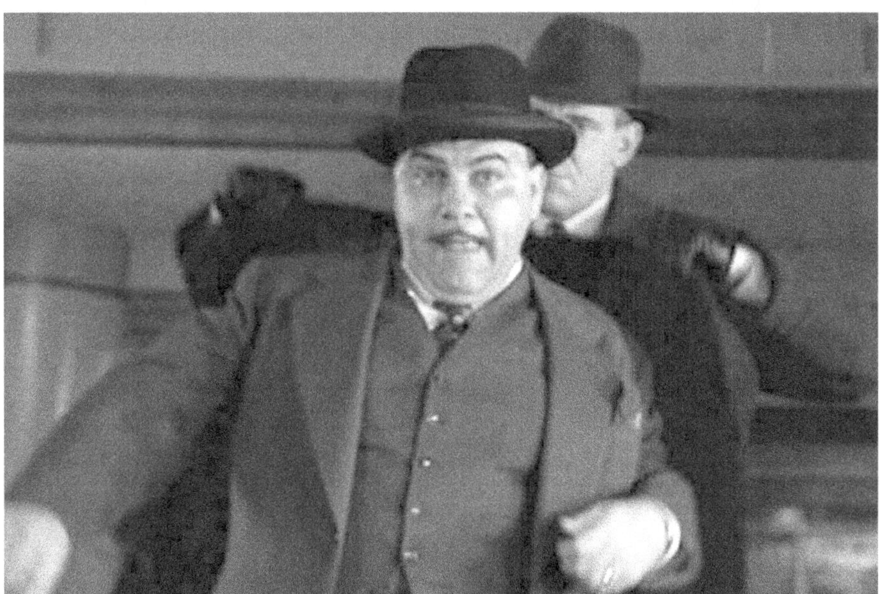

Figure 4.5 Johnny Casper and his "flunky" in the Coen brothers' 1990 film *Miller's Crossing*. Source: Twentieth Century Fox, DVD, 2003.

After Casper leaves, the credits are run and the hat on the ground in the middle of Miller's Crossing appears again, flopping down at the center of the scene before it blows away. Its animated movement reminds us that the film allocates agency to things, hats especially, as well as persons. As the next scene opens, the hat that appeared in opening scenes as a disconnected icon is displaced by a hat that appears both materially and metaphorically related to a character. Cutting away from the credits, we see Tom waking up with a hangover on a couch in Leo's nightclub, asking the barman about the whereabouts of his hat (where the hat to which he refers is not only the material fedora but also a metaphorical marker of where his loyalties lie). Once we are apprised of the plot, the metaphorical significance of Tom's question becomes evident.

As complicated emotional entanglements proceed throughout the plot, trust is a featured concept. Tom continually articulates the Hammett ontology that no one is ultimately trustworthy because "nobody knows anybody well" (which he says to Verna and Casper on different occasions) and that no one even knows themselves (in the last scene he asks Leo if he always knows what he's up to). However, rather than following the shifting emotional rhythms of the plot, and the various vulnerabilities characters' habits create (for example, Tom's gambling addiction and Leo's penchant for "bad plays," as Tom puts it), I want to heed the Coen brothers' insistence that the film is mainly about men in hats and note some additional moments in the hats' actual and metaphorical appearances, which follow their appearances as signs in the opening scenes. To re-invoke Virginia Woolf's suggestion about clothes wearing us, the narrative dominance of hats implies that they wear their subjects. Specifically, the film adopts a narrative in which a historical era in the biography of hats constitutes a story of the economic and emotional entanglements of the subjects they wear.

To pick up on the metaphorical significance of Tom's question to the barman: while as Tom says to Leo that he has made a bad play upsetting Casper, Tom makes a good one. Rather than following Leo's unsubtle order to "jump on the guinea with both feet," he pretends to switch sides, metaphorically hanging his hat with the Casper mob, during which he destroys Casper with bad advice. At the point at which Casper allows Tom to hang his hat on his side, accepting his loyalty, he remarks, "The last time we jawed, you gave me the high hat." Thereafter the hat continues its complicated itinerary, turning out to be as ambivalent as it is duplicitous and unreliable. When Tom visits the character Drop, who helps fix fights, he picks up a hat from a table and puts it on Drop's head. Referring to it both materially and metaphorically, he says, "It's too small for such a fat head," adding that Drop has outgrown it (implying that he's no longer a reliable fight fixer).

The hat is just as unstable in Tom's preferred relationship. Although he tells Verna that his relationship with Leo is over – he won't be hanging around

Leo's office – metaphorically his hat has remained hanging there. The good play he makes to destroy Casper (setting him up to be shot by Bernie) turns out to have been for Leo's benefit. In the last scene, Leo says he was fooled as well, "I thought you'd gone over." Tom cautions Leo with his oft-said observation that no one knows for sure what they're up to. Hats are pervasive markers throughout that last scene, which takes place at Bernie's funeral in a cemetery. In attendance with Verna, Leo is wearing a Jewish skullcap, a yarmulke, which he doesn't remove until he's about to leave. Tom's hat is no longer in Verna's vicinity, as it was during one of their lovemaking scenes, which was preceded by his tossing it on a nearby chair. His heart has been worn on his hat rather than his sleeve, but it has had an erratic trajectory, represented in Verna's dream in which a gust of wind blows it off Tom's head while he's walking in the woods. As the last scene ends, Verna has walked away telling Tom to "drop dead" (in their last conversation she had called him a "no-heart sonofabitch"). Leo also walks away, finally donning his regular hat once he's well in the distance, after Tom has told him he won't be working with him any longer. The last view of Tom has him with his fedora in place as the film ends with a quotation of the cinematic versions of Chandler's and Hammett's noir plots. Tom pulls it down so that his eyes are showing just under the brim, once again imitating Chandler's Philip Marlowe and Hammett's Sam Spade (Figure 4.6).

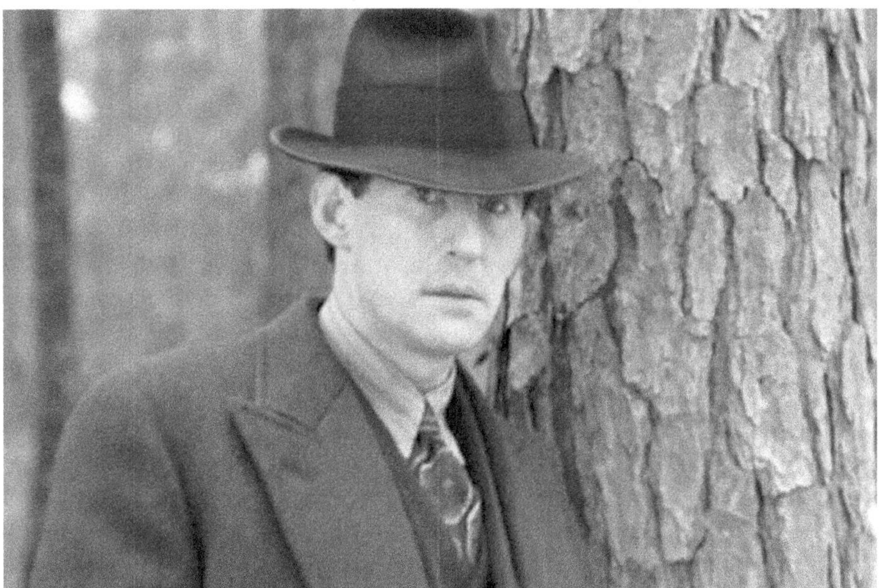

Figure 4.6 Tom Reagan in pulled-down hat in the Coen brothers' 1990 film *Miller's Crossing*. Source: Twentieth Century Fox, DVD, 2003.

From Cityscape to Landscape: Gloves

Set in rural Montana in 1925, Jane Campion's film is an adaptation of Thomas Savage's novel *The Power of the Dog*, a product of "the Golden age of American landscape fiction [in which] ... landscape is used not just as decorative background, but to drive the story and control the characters' lives."[85] As the film opens with "Montana 1925" on screen we see a moving body. In contrast with the portrait-like filming of the Coen brothers' *Miller's Crossing* in which interiors dominate, here we see a man in motion, walking onto the landscape where a house sits with openness all around it. We are then suddenly brought inside what looks like a Gothic manor. The ranch, we learn as the film narrative proceeds, is the legacy of a rich ranching family. However, its family genealogy is a story that the main protagonist, Phil Burbank (Benedict Cumberbatch), strives to displace with an alternative account. A clash of narratives is therefore a main feature of the film.

The film's opening panorama is followed by a panning shot of many things in motion: moving cows and the running bodies of cowhands, with the landscape's horizon in the distance. Peter Høeg's novel *Smilla's Sense of Snow*, located in Copenhagen and Greenland, provides a way to appreciate what we can discern by watching Campion's film after watching the Coen brothers' film because it rehearses the kind of stark difference between the many enclosures in the urban space of the eastern city in *Miller's Crossing* and the vast openness of rural Montana in *The Power of the Dog*. Although Høeg's novel is a crime story on the surface – the protagonist, Smilla, while in Copenhagen recognizes that a boy's footprints in the snow of a roof imply that the fall to his death resulted from being chased – the novel's main contribution is its milieux contrasts. Its narrative is broken up into three parts, the city, the ocean, and the ice. In part 1 while in Copenhagen, Smilla has to navigate the urban life world of enclosures, moving from room to room, for example an archive in "a low-ceilinged room with countless wooden shelves."[86] In parts 2 and 3 she has to manage a seascape and snowscape respectively, where the former is a "uniform abyss of water,"[87] and the latter is a "wasteland ... of packs of ice."[88] For the reader, the distinctiveness of city space as a space of enclosures becomes evident when Smilla moves on to the vast open spaces of parts 2 and 3. Similarly, watching the spatial panorama throughout *The Power of the Dog*'s cinematic narrative, one becomes aware of "the tighter confines of the East,"[89] the extent to which – except during the scenes in the forest at Miller's Crossing – the protagonists are mainly in enclosures: rooms, hallways, staircases, and automobiles, all of which shape the interactions taking place (in the meetings, hiding places, drive-by shootings, and other violent encounters) that determine who survives.

The open spaces of a rural Montana ranching town call for a different visual vocabulary than what we witness in the Coen's brothers' city film, well described in Brandon Taylor's commentary in which he points out that Campion's film features "Shots of cattle flowing across hills and into the great plains ... Sequences of men at play and at work. Light striking bare flesh, muscles rippling as they pull ropes and goad their horses." It's a visual vocabulary *The Power of the Dog* shares with a film version of an Annie Proulx Wyoming story, *Brokeback Mountain*.[90] However, while the landscape "encompasses" the characters (a feature Gilles Deleuze ascribes to John Ford's western films[91]), a different aspect of Campion's visual vocabulary has greater thematic significance. As is the case with *The Age of Innocence* (in both Wharton's novel and Scorsese's film adaption), the presence and absence of gloves, which punctuate the film narrative in several places, testify to what Campion's aesthetic and thematic shares with Wharton's, the social and civic significance of hands.

Although the filming proceeds with long takes of several of the characters' points of view, in shot–reverse shot sequences that move back and forth between eyes and what they're observing, the point of view that receives primary attention belongs to Phil Burbank whose gaze, like Wharton's and Scorsese's Newland Archer's, serves as the novel's center of consciousness. However, while as noted Archer's contentment becomes increasingly fugitive because he loses control of the scopic field, Phil's is a casualty of something else. He becomes increasingly agitated because he loses control over his brother George Burbank (Jesse Plemons), a phlegmatic and reticent contrast to Phil's aggressive self-assertion. While sharing ownership of the ranch with George, Phil depends on him not merely for his management ability but also to affirm the narrative he ascribes to their ranch's success. Savage's cinema-ready description of Phil's watchfulness and tactile sensitivity in the novel provides the basis for Campion's character, for which the blue-eyed, high-strung Cumberbatch is an ideal casting.

"Phil's eyes were day-blue, expressionless? ... But they were sharp, very sharp eyes, and the iris was no less sensitive that the cornea; so the subtlest change in light or shadow alerted Phil. Just as his hands sense the hidden rot at the heart of the wood ... So Phil lived ... watching, noting, figuring – as the rest of us see and forget."[92] Phil's impatient vigilance reflects two aspects of his insecurity, both of which are connected with his mythic and erotic attachment to the late Bronco Henry, an older rancher to whom he had a secret sexual attraction. He publicly exposes only the mythic part, telling stories in which he valorizes Bronco Henry's heroic masculinity, dwelling in particular on his extraordinary horsemanship while insisting that he rather than his parents initiated the ranch's legacy for which he and George are custodians. Phil's investment in the story that their successful management of the ranch was learned from the hyper-masculine heroics of Bronco Henry requires continual affirmation from George. His demands on George to affirm that narrative are accompanied by constant disparagements. He addresses him as "fatso" to assert his own (alleged) hard-tempered masculinity.

Phil's homosocial relationship with his brother requires proximity; he needs George close by both for verbal affirmation of the story he wants to maintain and for the contrasting character he wants to represent. After outside panning shots initiate the film and take the viewer inside the house, we observe Phil walking into their shared bedroom, saying, "have you figured it out yet fatso." George is in a bathtub just off the bedroom while Phil has started a discussion that he is to repeat later, noting that it is now many years since they had taken over the ranch "from the Old Lady." He is still on George's case the following morning. Riding next to him among the men herding cows, he suggests that they go camping "the way Bronco Henry taught us," cooking elk liver on a campfire. The remark conjures Phil's libidinal investment in his former and much-missed love object and mentor, who for Phil is (paradoxically) an icon of manliness.

The next scene is a cut to a sequence showing a strikingly unmanly-looking protagonist, the frail effeminate-appearing Peter Gordon (Kodi Smit-McPhee), who along with his mother Rose Gordon (Kirsten Dunst) lives as a pariah because their father/husband, a doctor, had died by suicide. Peter walks out onto the prairie where he looks dwarfed by the landscape. Like Phil, he is involved with a legacy, that of his late father on whose grave he is placing some paper flowers he has made. In contrast with Phil's desire to emulate Bronco Henry's toughness, is Peter's desire is to honor his father's work life by acquiring a medical degree. He studies medical books and dissects small animals with a scalpel while wearing gloves (an implement and hand covering that are to show up later in a very different context). In this scene, Peter's frail inept body, which seems barely able to negotiate the rigors of moving about on the prairie, is juxtaposed to a group of cowhands walking briskly in a line after dismounting from their herding. After a frontal shot of the sturdy-looking men, the camera looks back at Peter who is standing still and fussing with his hair. Nevertheless, manhood is as much on Peter's mind as it is on Phil's. Before the opening credits are shown, Peter in a voiceover says, "What kind of man would I be if I didn't help my mother?"

While a manhood issue is the primary homology between Peter and Phil, it is particularly vexed in Phil's case. His visible, aggressively maintained homosocial relationship with his brother contrasts with his hidden, closeted homosexual connection with Bronco Henry. What results from his maintenance of a personal economy of revealing and concealing is "the villain we see on both the page and the film."[93] It renders him continually contemptuous and outspokenly critical of everyone, hyperalert to what is going on around him, and especially needful of George as an ally in the story with which he masks the erotic basis of his deep sense of loss. Until George undertakes a courtship and marriage, they sleep in twin beds separated only by a small night table, and he is loath to start gatherings, for example common meals with the other cowhands assembled, until George has shown up. In an early scene in a bar/bordello where the men hang out before they head to the restaurant to eat, we see an agitated Phil impatient because George is late. When George finally appears, Phil shouts "dinner time boys," and as soon as they are seated in Rose's Red Mill restaurant, George's presence provides Phil's agenda. It begins with his usual invidious comparison. Phil says, "fatso couldn't get through college" and follows that with a demand for George to lend support to his cherished story; "who taught us to succeed at ranching?" he asks. George accepts the cue: "Bronco Henry," he says.

As the meal begins, Phil acquires a new whipping boy, which subsequently seals his fate. Mocking the paper roses in a vase on the table he says, "well ain't them purdy, I wonder what little lady made these." Peter who has walked in to serve dinner says, "Actually I did sir. My mother was a florist so I made them to look like the ones in her garden." As Peter exits, Phil launches into another Bronco Henry story. By the time Peter returns Phil is setting the paper roses on fire and using them to light his cigarette. What follows sets the tone for the combination of abjection and intimacy that marks the trajectory of Phil's and Peter's relationship. Composing yet another homology between the two, a montage sequence shows Peter and Phil performing similar gestures through which they express their agitation. In response to being humiliated by Phil, Peter rushes out of the restaurant and once outside angrily twirls a hula hoop, his most extravagant physical gesture thus far in the film. Before he leaves the restaurant, Phil, upset because George lingers after entering the kitchen to settle the bill rather than accompanying him homeward, angrily twirls one of the dining room chairs. In addition to providing a hint that Phil and Peter will ultimately evince similar traits, that sequence is an early indication that George is becoming increasingly independent, absenting himself from the daily rhythms he has shared with Phil. They had habitually moved through the day together in virtual lockstep, George absorbing Phil's taunts with seeming equanimity.

What ultimately brings out Phil's extravagant acts of cruelty is George's radical intervention in the household's libidinal economy, which had hitherto been exhausted by manifest brotherly intimacy and hidden erotic longing. George's marriage to Rose Gordon after a brief courtship adds a disjunctive page to the family story to which Phil has been clinging. Bringing his new wife into the home for the first time, George says guilelessly, "Phil, you remember Rose." As soon as he and Rose are alone in the living room and Rose attempts a friendly conversation, "Well brother Phil," Phil becomes agitated and hostile, responding with, "I'm not your brother, you're a cheap schemer." Thereafter,

Phil begins a campaign of harassment and humiliation of Rose and Peter, driving Rose to drink (literally) and Peter to hatching a plan to "protect his mother."

The intra-family struggle proceeds within the household soundscape. Upset at having lost his brother to a love relationship, Phil is afflicted by new sounds: Rose in the bathroom brushing her teeth and a squeaking bed in the next room as she and George are having sex. At one point, on hearing the squeaking bed and the lovers' moans, an agitated Phil leaves the house and enters the barn where he has a shrine to Bronco Henry consisting mainly of his old saddle. There's a long take of him lovingly oiling and caressing it, one of several gestures in which his grieving is manifest in attempts at restoring Bronco Henry's presence with tactile performances. In a later scene, Phil reposes by his secret swimming hole with an unlaundered piece of clothing with a BH for Bronco Henry monogram. After extracting it from inside his pants, he places it over his face. Returning to the house, Phil's campaign against Rose within the home's soundscape begins. When she tries practicing the piano he obstreperously strums on his banjo, while at other times he marks his presence by whistling.

Phil's campaign of humiliation against Peter takes place outside the house. In one scene while he's gathered with his cowhands one of them points to Peter, who is standing near the house, asking who it is. Phil responds by referring to Peter contemptuously as "Miss Nancy" and "Little Lord Fauntleroy." Subsequently, while Peter is in the yard near the horse corral playing a running game with the Burbanks' dog, Phil whistles to summon the dog. Having left Peter exposed and vulnerable, he then sends the cowhands to circle their horses around him in close proximity, intimidating him to a point where he's spooked and runs toward the ranch's front steps for security. However, something changes Phil's posture toward Peter, seemingly the need for a new interlocutor to listen to his Bronco Henry stories because George is no longer consistently available. What inaugurates the change is a different kind of horse mediation. Phil puts Bronco Henry's saddle on a tall horse and changes from an antagonist to a mentor. He summons Peter and begins to teach him to ride. Although the riding goes badly at the outset – Peter falls off the horse during one of his initial attempts – he eventually becomes competent enough to ride off toward the mountains on his own. It's a competence that becomes part of the narrative thread in which gloved and ungloved hands are involved.

THE DENOUEMENT: HANDS AND GLOVES

In her "intimate history" of gloves, Anne Green reviews the persistence of gloves as hand coverings whose fashion existence is shaped by norms and rituals of revealing and concealing, and notes as well their metaphorical existence: "Just how deeply embedded in our culture they have become is evident from the way they have seeped into everyday language. We 'throw down the gauntlet' or take it up to issue (or accept) a challenge; we know that a 'velvet glove may hide an iron fist'; we 'handle someone with kid gloves' … Garments 'fit like a glove.'"[94] However, while the gloves featured in the novelistic and cinematic versions of *The Age of Innocence* are caught up in fashion norms that govern covering versus uncovering hands and in rituals of interpersonal intimacy, the hand and glove narrative in *The Power of the Dog* is focused on non-fashion-related but nevertheless norm-regulated practices, all of which distinguish differences among the film's protagonists.

Phil's distinctive resistance to wearing gloves is a central feature of the plot. While it appears in an early scene in the novel in which Phil is castrating steers without wearing gloves, Campion reserves it for the middle of the film, an inspired placement because by then seeing the aggressive uninhibited way he grasps a steer's testes and cuts, wrenches, and tosses them aside, reminds us about his emasculating treatment of his brother George. It is also in accord with the tactile way he approaches his erotic feelings, resonating with the scene in which his recollection of his deceased lover Bronco Henry is expressed by an elaborate oiling and caressing of his saddle with his bare hands. The Phil one hears, with his angry demeaning remarks, and sees, observing his offputting severe facial expression, is disjunctive with the Phil articulated through the hands with which he recollects the erotic memory of his deceased lover.

With respect to his work life the hands speak differently, articulating instead the hypermasculine Phil. His bare-handed approach to steer castration is distinctive enough to elicit reactions from his cowhands. One of them says, "how come you don't wear gloves," to which Phil responds, "how 'bout because they're not needed." It's a remark belied by an accident. He nicks his thumb at the very end of the steer castrating process. Lamenting that as he walks over toward George with a piece of cloth wrapped around his cut, he says, "What a bitch! Castrate fifteen hundred head, then nick your thumb on the last one." Phil's insistent resistance to wearing gloves results in frequent cuts. In many scenes his dirt encrusted hands show signs of bleeding: for example, in the scene in which he's holding Peter's paper flowers, the palm of one of his gnarled, dirty hands is bloody from a small cut.

In its hand and glove narrative the film does close-ups of several other hands as well, for example George's and Rose's, which contrast markedly. Highlighting the singularity of Phil's work-callused hands is a pre-courtship scene with George reacting very differently to the paper flowers. He "traces his finger along the flower stems on the oilcloth [and] … glances at Rose's hands and likes how busy and soft they are."[95] Most significantly as regards the hand and glove narrative is the Phil–Peter contrast. While Phil's hands are continually exposed, Peter's are often obscured. When he first deliberately closes the distance between Phil and himself – walking toward him to make an inquiry (a step in the process of a deceptive courtship) – his hands are

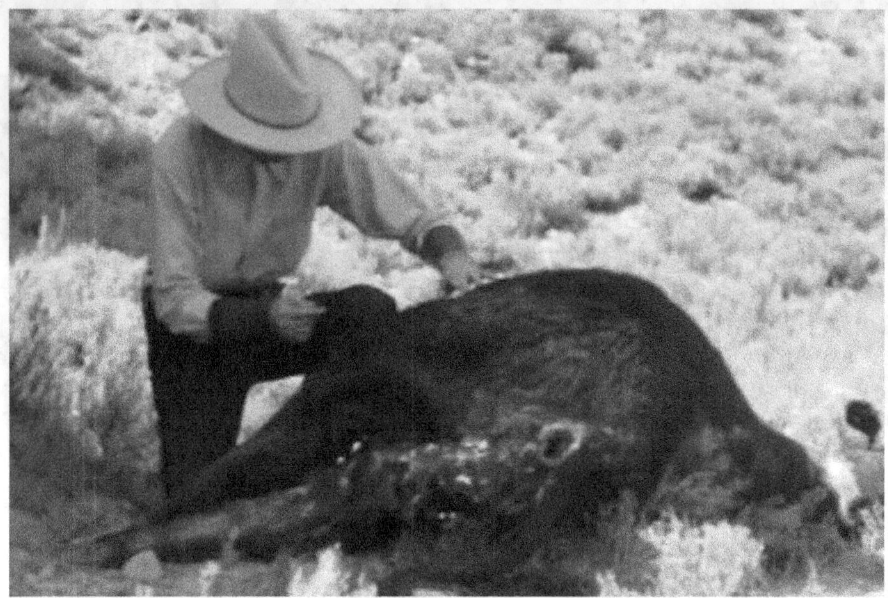

Figure 4.7 Peter Gordon preparing a gift of death in Jane Campion's 2021 film *The Power of the Dog*. Source: Criterion Collection, DVD, 2022.

jammed in his pockets. And in two of the key scenes he wears surgical gloves, first to dissect a rabbit (part of his preparation for medical training) and then to strip cowhide from a steer that has died of anthrax, as he initiates his plan to rescue his mother by collecting diseased rawhide strips to be gifted to her antagonist (Figure 4.7). It's a gift of death that gives the bare-handed Phil, whose hands have vulnerable points of entry because of their open cuts, the deadly disease.

Having drawn closer to Peter emotionally, Phil is vulnerable to Peter's deception. With George distracted and less available to hearing his Bronco Henry stories, Phil turns to Peter and shares what is in effect the primal scene of his erotic attachment to his former love object. He tells Peter that Bronco Henry's heroism saved his life. The most intimate of his Bronco Henry stories, which he narrates during what he thinks is a convivial moment with Peter, involves an erotic body-to-body encounter with his lover. His characterization of Bronco Henry's sleeping on top of him in a shared sleeping bag as merely an act of life-saving heroism, keeping him from freezing on a cold night's outdoor camping, is a textbook example for psychoanalysis, the fraught substitution of "'a mind in flight,' fleeing its own pain and obscuring its meanings …"[96]

Phil's desperation for an imitate interlocutor for his love story, combined with two events, one purposive and the other coincidental, seals his fate.

Thinking he has successfully secured a protégé, he decides to make a rawhide rope as a gift for Peter. Among what attracts him to a young man he had once thought to be unmanly is a scene in which they come upon a rabbit in a trap, which Peter kills with a quick and competent twisting of its head. It's yet another moment that speaks to film's development of a homology between the two. Peter's father had anticipated that aspect of his son's character. In Peter's opening voiceover at the beginning of the film he refers to his father's view of him as one who (like Phil) is "too strong and unkind." That revelatory rabbit-killing moment draws Phil closer to Peter, who sees his opportunity to make the anthrax-tainted rawhide strip gift that ultimately kills Phil when he bare-handedly reciprocates fashioning the rawhide rope gift for Peter.

The purposive event is Peter's journey on horseback into the nearby mountains where the scalpel he used to dissect a rabbit is in his gloved hand yet again as he extracts strips from the skin of a steer that died from anthrax disease. The other necessary condition for the rope-making event is coincidental. Phil ultimately makes use of Peter's anthrax-tainted cowhide strips because Rose has given Phil's stash of cowhide to a Shoshone father, Edward Nappo (Adam Beach), and his son (Mason Stone Skuggedal) whom she hails when she sees them passing the ranch. That episode, a crucial part of the film's glove narrative, is part of an allegory with which the film adds historical depth (a feature to which I turn as I conclude).

Rose learns from "Mrs. Lewis" (Genevieve Lemon), the household manager, that Phil burns the hides he collects. "Phil doesn't want anyone else to have them. He waits till there's a pile and burns the lot," she tells Rose. Phil's main reason for their destruction is to withhold them from members of the Shoshone nation from a nearby reservation, who use steer hides to make gloves, among other things. After Edward Nappo and his son pass the house, Rose pursues them, establishes her fiduciary identity – "My husband owns the ranch," she tells them – and offers them the collected hides that Phil has yet to dispose of. In return, Edward directs his son to hand Rose a box with a pair of leather gloves he has made (Figure 4.8).

Rose's timing turns out to be prophetic. Just at the point at which Phil returns to the ranch to look for his hides to use for the planned rope and has a tantrum about Rose giving them away, Peter turns up with the anthrax-infested strips soaking in a bucket. Expressing his appreciation for the gift, Phil thanks Peter and proceeds with the bare-handed rope making that gives him a fatal disease. While Peter has been triumphant, having finally protected Rose from her nemesis, Rose also triumphs. The final glove scene is one in which she has overcome the family's ambivalence about her marriage to George. It's a scene in which bare hands perform a ritual of welcome rather than violence, as the "Old Lady" (Frances Conroy), Phil and George's mother who has returned to

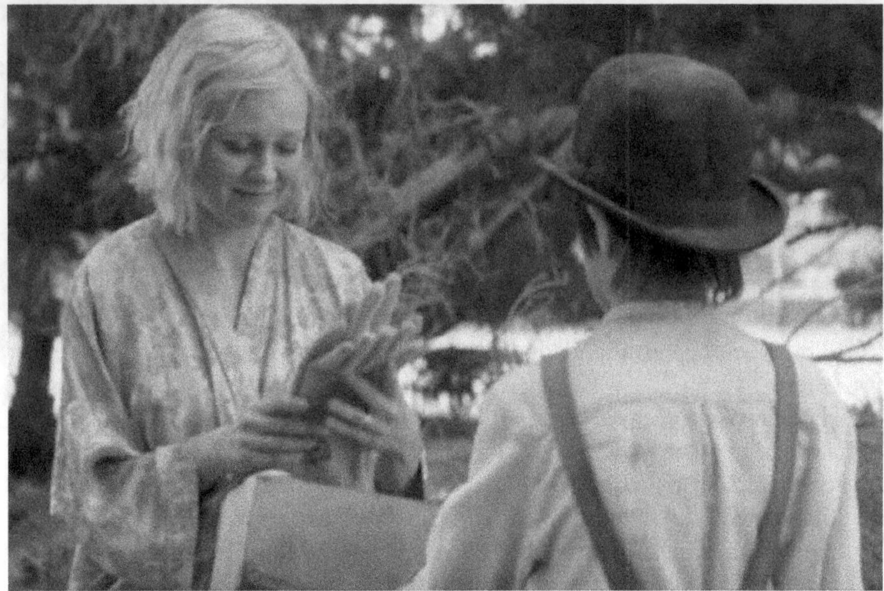

Figure 4.8 Rose Gordon in a gift exchange in Jane Campion's 2021 film *The Power of the Dog*. Source: Criterion Collection, DVD, 2022.

the ranch for Phil's funeral, warmly welcomes Rose into the family. In a close-up shot of hands, she takes Rose's hand into hers, removes her own rings and puts them in Rose's hands.

CODA: THE FILM'S "ALLEGORICAL INTENTION"

In his analysis of the critical value of allegory, Walter Benjamin points out that in the operation of a text's allegorical intention, "all the things which are used to signify derive, from the very fact of their pointing to something else, a power which makes them appear no longer commensurable with profane things, which raise them to a higher plane."[97] I want to make the case that Phil's refusal of hospitality toward the "Indians" who pass by his ranch points to "something else," the historical dispossession of Native American nations whose survivors were displaced from the spaces of their long-term tenancy on western lands. Savage's novel records the effect of the displacement. "When the last of the Indians were herded off their lands and sent packing to a reservation, the government no longer even pretended to believe in treaties."[98] The legacy of that displacement is articulated as Phil's inhospitable reaction to those remnants of Native Americans that pass through his ranch and occasionally seek to stop and camp. In the novel version, after Phil sees a group of Indians camping on ranch property, he angrily questions George, "What in the good holy hell are them Indians doing out back," to which George replies, "Take it easy, I told them they could camp for a few days."[99]

William Cronon, George Miles, and Jay Gitlin describe the changing spatial practices involved in the historical process of the Native American dispossession that Phil's remark acknowledges and supports. They note that at the outset of the Native American–Euro-American encounter in the West, it took place on a "frontier," which, before strict lines of demarcation had been installed, was a zone of negotiation between assemblages with different cultural perspectives on how to share a life world. Once Euro-American domination was institutionalized, the landscape was configured by regional boundaries; Native American voices lost their civic purchase as "zones of fluid ongoing conflict and opportunity gave way to the stabler, more coherent area we know today as the regions of North America."[100] In Campion's film version, Phil confronts "them Indians" directly and asserts the strictures of his property's boundaries. While out riding he comes upon Edward Nappo and his son camping on the ranch property and says, "What the hell do you think you're doing here?" When Edward says "my boy and are camping a little," adds, pointing toward the surrounding mountains, "my grandfather is buried up there," and states as well, "my father was the chief," Phil angrily states his lack of interest in Edward's family's history and says, "nothing doing." Edward then pulls out some gloves he's made, which he says are worth five dollars, and proposes a trade, the gloves for two days of camping. Dismissing the gesture as a "bribe," Phil orders him and his son off the property.

When later in their encounter with Rose while passing by the ranch, Edward and his son give her a pair of gloves, it is a mutual acknowledgment of a gift exchange rather than an attempted bribe. In thanking Rose for giving them the accumulated hides by offering the gloves, they are turning back the historical clock to a period before the money form had displaced the exchanges involved in Native American–Euro-American reciprocity. That encounter turns our attention to a period in which gift exchanges, as Marcel Mauss famously points out, involved the creation of symbolic capital. Less important than the materials exchanged were the intersubjective relations they established.[101] And crucially, it illustrates *The Power of the Dog*'s allegorical intention. That aspect of the gloves' participation in the narrative takes the story beyond a family drama and restores a repressed history.

NOTES

1. Sergei Tret'iakov, "The Biography of the Object," *October* 118 (2006): 62 [translated from a 1929 Russian version].
2. Virginia Woolf, *Orlando: A Biography* (New York: Harcourt, 1956/1928), p. 187.

3. Fred Moten, *In the Break: The Aesthetics of the Black Radical Tradition* (Minneapolis: University of Minnesota Press, 2003), p. 1.

4. Jane Bennett, *Vibrant Matter: A Political Ecology of Things* (Durham, NC: Duke University Press, 2010), p. ix.

5. *Ibid.*, pp. 1–19.

6. The expression plays a key role in Roland Barthes, *The Fashion System*, trans. Matthew Ward and Richard Howard (London: Jonathan Cape, 1985).

7. Leo Tolstoy, *Anna Karenina*, trans. Louise and Aylmer Maude (New York: Dover, 2004), p. 327.

8. *Ibid.*, p. 2683.

9. See Bret Stephens, "Prigozhin's Mutiny Against Putin's Reign of Lies," *The New York Times*, June 27, 2023, at https://www.nytimes.com/2023/06/27/opinion/russia-putin-prigozhin-ukraine.html (last accessed September 11, 2024).

10. François Ewald, "Norms, Discipline, and the Law," trans. Marjorie Beale, *Representations* 30 (Spring 1990): 154–5.

11. Daniel Green, "Noble Dress in 19th-Century Russia," March 22, 2023, at https://doi.org/10.1093/acrefore/9780190201098.013.1239.

12. *Ibid.*

13. Samuel Beckett, *The Expelled*, in *Samuel Beckett: The Complete Short Prose, 1929–1989*, ed. S. E. Gontarski (New York: Grove Press, 2007), p. 46.

14. David Lloyd, *Beckett's Thing: Painting and Theater* (Edinburgh: Edinburgh University Press, 2018), p. 22.

15. Julie Bates, *Beckett's Art of Salvage: Writing and the Material Imagination, 1932–1987* (New York: Cambridge University Press, 2017), p. 35.

16. Fred Miller Robinson, "The History and Significance of the Bowler Hat: Chaplin, Laurel and Hardy, Beckett, Magritte and Kundera," *TriQuarterly* 66 (Spring 1986): 173.

17. Fred Miller Robinson, *The Man in the Bowler Hat: His History and Iconography* (Chapel Hill: University of North Carolina Press, 1993), p. 16.

18. *Ibid.*, p. 17.

19. "Why Magritte Was Fascinated with Bowler Hats," *Artsy News*, at https://www.tumblr.com/caveartfair/172864140462/why-magritte-was-fascinated-with-bowler-hats (last accessed September 11, 2024).

20. Peter Wollen, "Magritte and the Bowler Hat," *New Left Review* 1 (January/February, 2000): 113.

21. Miller Robinson, *The Man in the Bowler Hat*, p. ix.

22. Miller Robinson, "The History and Significance of the Bowler Hat," p. 175.

23. Geoffrey O'Brien, "*The Age of Innocence*: Savage Civility," *The Criterion Collection Reviews*, March 12, 2018, at https://www.criterion.com/current/posts/5460-the-age-of-innocence-savage-civility (last accessed September 11, 2024).

24. Barthes, *The Fashion System*, p. xi. The consciousness to which Barthes refers developed rapidly in Paris in the nineteenth century, where, for example, "Hundreds of publications were dedicated to discussing the virtues and vices of [voluminous crinolines], and of women's fashion in general." Anne Higonnet, *Liberty, Equality, Fashion* (New York: W. W. Norton, 2024), p. 2.

25. "Gloves: Fashion and Meaning," a publication of The Leeds Museums & Galleries, at https://museumsandgalleries.leeds.gov.uk/featured/gloves-fashion-and-meaning/ (last accessed September 11, 2024).

26. Ash Amin, *Land of Strangers* (Malden, MA: Polity, 2012), p. 71.

27. Edith Wharton, "Visibility in Fiction," in Frederick Wegener (ed.), *Edith Wharton: The Uncollected Critical Writings* (Princeton, NJ: Princeton University Press, 1996), p. 165.

28. *Ibid.*, p. 167.

29. Carrie Rickey, "Haunting, Powerful, Passionate: Martin Scorsese's *The Age of Innocence*," *The Moviegoer*, February 10, 2016, at https://www.loa.org/news-and-views/1119-haunting-powerful-passionate-martin-scorsese8217s-the-age-of-innocence/ (last accessed September 11, 2024).

30. Jean Baudrillard, "Sign Function and Class Logic," in *For a Critique of the Political Economy of the Sign*, trans. Charles Levin (St. Louis, MO: Telos Press, 1981), p. 35.

31. *Ibid.*, pp. 34–5.

32. Theodora Tsimpouki, "Realism, Narrative Visuality and the Hieroglyphic World of Newland Archer," *Brno Studies in English* 34 (2008): 127.

33. Julianne Pidduck, *Contemporary Costume Film* (London: BFI, 2004), p. 46.

34. Edith Wharton, *The Age of Innocence* (New York: Penguin, 1996), p. 11.

35. Tsimpouki, "Realism, Narrative Visuality," p. 129.

36. See Jacques Lacan, "The Split Between the Eye and the Gaze," in *The Seminar of Jacques Lacan: The Four Fundamental Concepts of Psychoanalysis*, trans. Jacques-Alain Miller et al. (New York: W. W. Norton, 1998), pp. 67–104.

37. Hilton Als, "Tilda Moments," *The New Yorker Magazine*, March 18, 2002, at https://www.newyorker.com/magazine/2002/03/18/tilda-swinton-profile-hilton-als (last accessed September 11, 2024).

38. Wharton, *The Age of Innocence*, quoted in Tsimpouki, "Realism, Narrative Visuality," p. 131.

39. *Ibid.*

40. Edith Wharton, "Introduction to the House of Mirth," in *ibid.*, pp. 265–6.

41. *Ibid.*, p. 266.

42. Edith Wharton, "The Art of Henry James," in *The Uncollected Critical Writings*, p. 310.

43. Shama Rangwala, "Visibilities of Exchange Across Forms," *Public* 28, no. 55 (June 2017): 72.

44. *Ibid.*

45. *Ibid.*, p. 74.

46. Godelieve Mercken Spaas, "An Interview with Alain Robbe-Grillet and Lillian Dumant," *The French Review* 50, no. 4 (March 1977): 653.

47. Rangwala, "Visibilities of Exchange Across Forms," p. 75.

48. *Ibid.*, p. 80.

49. Françoise Sammarcelli, "Of Art, Codes, and Transcoding," *Edith Wharton Review* 36, no. 2 (2020): 134.

50. *Ibid.*, p. 137.

51. Rangwala, "Visibilities of Exchange Across Forms," p. 77.
52. Emily Orlando, "We'll Look Not at Visions, but at Realities," in *Edith Wharton and the Visual Arts* (Mobile: University of Alabama Press, 2009), p. 179.
53. Tsimpouki, "Realism, Narrative Visuality," p. 127.
54. Alfred Döblin, *Berlin Alexanderplatz*, trans. Michael Hoffman (New York: NYRB, 2018), p. 4.
55. Bates, *Beckett's Art of Salvage*, p. 27.
56. Samuel Beckett, *Proust* (New York: Grove Press, 1957), p. 8.
57. Milan Kundera, *The Unbearable Lightness of Being*, trans. Michael Henry Heim (New York: Harper & Row, 1984), p. 132.
58. *Ibid.*
59. Gilles Deleuze and Felix Guattari, *What is Philosophy?* trans. Hugh Tomlinson and Graham Burchell (New York: Columbia University Press, 1994), p. 63.
60. Kundera, *The Unbearable Lightness of Being*, p. 109.
61. John Banville, "Light but Sound: John Banville Rereads *The Unbearable Lightness of Being*," *The Guardian*, May 1, 2004, at https://www.theguardian.com/books/2004/may/01/fiction.johnbanville (last accessed September 11, 2024).
62. Kundera, *The Unbearable Lightness of Being*, p. 58.
63. *Ibid.*, p. 44.
64. *Ibid.*, p. 1.
65. *Ibid.*, pp. 43–4.
66. *Ibid.*, pp. 51–2.
67. For a comprehensive review of Magritte's bowler images, see Peter Wollen, "Magritte and the Bowler Hat," *New Left Review* 1 (January/February, 2000): 104–21.
68. Stamos Metzidakis, "Semiotic Intersections in Baudelaire and Magritte," *L'Esprit Créateur* 39, no. 1 (Spring 1999).
69. *Ibid.*
70. Magritte, quoted in Susan Gablik, *Magritte*, trans. Susan Gablik (New York: Thames & Hudson, 1985), p. 184.
71. Miller Robinson, "The History and Significance of the Bowler Hat," p. 192.
72. Julian Petley, "Laughs and Sneezes," *Index on Censorship* 6 (2007): 156.
73. Miller Robinson, "The History and Significance of the Bowler Hat," p. 180.
74. Naomi Lubich, "The Wandering Hat: Iterations of the Medieval Jewish Pointed Cap," *Jewish History* 29 (2015): 224.
75. Raphael Straus, "The 'Jewish Hat' as an Aspect of Social History," *Jewish Social Studies* 4, no. 1 (January 1942): 60.
76. Richard Thompson Ford, *Dress Codes: How the Laws of Fashion Made History* (New York: Simon & Schuster, 2021).
77. The expression is borrowed from Joseph Pugliese, "Compulsory Visibility and the Intralegality of Racial Phantasmata," *Social Semiotics* 19, no. 1 (March 2009): 9–30.
78. Barthes, *The Fashion System*.
79. Michael J. Shapiro, *Aesthetics of Equality* (New York: Oxford University Press, 2023), p. 97.

80. Jamaica Kincaid, "On Seeing England for the First Time," *Transition* 51 (1991): 33.
81. Andrew Snavely, "Did JFK Kill the Men's Hat at His Inauguration 60 years Ago?" *Primer Magazine*, at https://www.primermagazine.com/2021/learn/jfk-mens-hat (last accessed September 11, 2024).
82. Jeffrey Adams, *The Cinema of the Coen Brothers* (New York: Columbia University Press, 2015), p. 51.
83. Dashiell Hammett, *The Maltese Falcon*, 1929 reprint (New York: Vintage, 1989), p. 42.
84. *Ibid.*, pp. 216–17.
85. Annie Proulx, "Afterword," in Thomas Savage, *The Power of the Dog* (New York: Little, Brown, 1967), p. 281.
86. Peter Høeg, *Smilla's Sense of Snow*, trans. Tiina Nunnally (New York: Dell, 1993), p. 82.
87. *Ibid.*, p. 296.
88. *Ibid.*, p. 417.
89. Proulx, "Afterword," p. 281.
90. Brandon Taylor, "Jane Campion's Gothic Vision of Rural Queerness in 'The 'Power of the Dog,'" *The New Yorker*, November 19, 2021, at https://www.new yorker.com/culture/culture-desk/jane-campions-gothic-vision-of-rural-queerness-in-the-power-of-the-dog (last accessed September 12, 2024).
91. Gilles Deleuze, *Cinema 1: The Movement Image*, trans. Hugh Tomlinson and Barbara Habberjam (Minneapolis: University of Minnesota Press, 1992), p. 146.
92. Savage, *The Power of the Dog*, pp. 66–7.
93. Aaron Kushner, "'The Power of the Dog' Messages the Urgent Need for Civic Education," *Popmatters*, March 30, 2022, at https://www.popmatters.com/pow er-of-dog-civic-education (last accessed September 12, 2024).
94. Anne Green *Gloves: An Intimate History* (London: Reaktion Books, 2021), p. 10.
95. Quoting from the screenplay, at https://deadline.com/wp-content/uploads/2022/ 01/The-Power-Of-The-Dog-Read-The-Screenplay.pdf (last accessed September 12, 2024).
96. The phrase is from Parul Sehgal (inner quotes from Jacqueline Rose, her interviewee), "Presence of Mind: How the Critic Jacqueline Rose Learned to Read the World," *The New Yorker Magazine*, August 21, 2023, p. 13.
97. Walter Benjamin, *The Origin of German Tragic Drama*, trans. John Osborne (New York: Verso, 1998), p. 175.
98. Savage, *The Power of the Dog*, p. 17.
99. *Ibid.*, p. 196.
100. William Cronon, George Miles, and Jay Gitlin, "Becoming West," in *Under an Open Sky* (New York: W. W. Norton, 1992), p. 7.
101. See Marcel Mauss, *The Gift: The Form and Reason for Exchange in Archaic Societies* (New York: W. W. Norton, 2000).

5. THE CIVIC LIVES OF GENDER: DISRUPTIVE AND ENABLING "MONSTROSITIES"

In an analysis that has implications for understanding reactions to a wide variety of fear-arousing disruptions to normative orders, Georges Canguilhem begins his approach to what he calls the disconcerting phenomenon of monstrosity with these observations: "The monstrous ... disconcerts":[1]

> The existence of monsters calls into question the capacity of life to teach us order. This calling into question is immediate – so comprehensive was our prior confidence, so firmly accustomed had we been to seeing wild roses blooming on rose bushes, tadpoles turning into frogs, mares suckling foals, and, in general the same engender the same. A breach in this confidence, a morphological divergence, an appearance unequivocal as to its species is enough for us to be gripped by radical fear.[2]

Doubtless the intensity of the radical fear to which Canguilhem refers varies with the degree of investment that attends normative orders at particular historical moments. As Deirdre (formerly Donald) McCloskey notes in her memoir about her crossing experience, "monsters [her example is Anthony Perkins in *Psycho*] are detested by those who value order over freedom."[3] Simply put, "The Monster undoes our understanding of the way things are and violates our sense of how they are supposed to be."[4] Historically, among the notably revealing monstrosity effects was the gender dysmorphia of the hermaphrodite Herculine Barbin whose mid-nineteenth-century memoir of her/his tribulations gained contemporary critical attention through Michel Foucault's accompanying commentary in the English version. In light of the prevailing mentality of the period the case was a radical disturbance to the nineteenth-century gender order. As Jessica Webb suggests, "Herculine's battle with her own gender exposes a worrying dangerous threat of monstrous criminality."[5]

In his remarks on Herculine's memoir and fate Michel Foucault refers to how the threat exposed the era's gender-related normative order, and raises the question, "Do we *truly* need a *true sex*?" His question illuminates a case in which "she" ("called Alexina by her familiars") was destroyed by a "will to truth," which through a combination of "biological" and "juridical conceptions of the individual," combined with "forms of administrative control," had "led little by little to rejection of the idea of a mixture of two sexes in the same body."[6] In subsequent commentary on gender dysmorphia Foucault evokes monstrosity, treating it as an ascription applied to "someone with two sexes who one didn't know whether to treat as a boy or girl." What makes such a body a monster, he suggests, is the perspectives of official warranting agencies. A two-sexed body "is a monster only because it is also a legal labyrinth, a violation of and an obstacle to the law."[7] Before I return to Foucault's elaboration on the discursive aspects of the power/knowledge-driven truth effect on Barbin's brief life, I want to provide a more elaborate framing by looking at the historical contexts of other order-disrupting sex and gender-implicated events.

SEX/GENDER DRAMAS

The attention to sexuality and gender differences in the contemporary era of what Judith Butler has famously called "gender trouble" is being played out (among other ways) in the politics of location.[8] Attracting intense scrutiny and conflict are the spaces within which transvestite and transgender people participate in civic life as well as in ordinary daily life, the former in special events (drag queen performances and LGBTQ rallies and parades) and the latter in everyday spaces that are now drawing extraordinary attention, most notably public bathrooms. In his revisionary approach to Freudian psychoanalysis, Jacques Lacan imparts relevant instruction on some implications of that everyday space. Impugning the accepted naturalization of sexual identity, Lacan argues that it is "not based on biological gender, or any other innate factor, but is learned through the dynamics of identification and language."[9] To illustrate that position he evokes a scenario in which a brother and sister spy the separate bathrooms at a train station platform:

> A train arrives at a station. A little boy and a little girl, brother and sister, are seated in a compartment face to face next to the window through

which the buildings along the station planform can be seen passing as the train pulls to a stop. "Look," says the brother, "we're at 'Ladies'; Idiot! Replies his sister, "Can't you see we're at Gentlemen."[10]

Lacan proceeds to figure the gender binary that the scenario articulates with a geopolitical metaphor:

> For these children, Ladies and gentlemen will be henceforth two countries towards which each of their souls will strive on divergent wings, and between which a truce will be the more impossible since they are actually the same country and neither can compromise on its own superiority without detracting from the glory of the other.[11]

The impossibility of a truce to which Lacan refers is especially evident of late. German Lopez identifies the main locus of the contemporary anti-transgender drama as "Bathrooms," which "have become a huge political battleground in America."[12] Among the anti-trans positions of those involved in this particular culture war is that letting "trans people use the bathroom that corresponds with their gender identity" would encourage "men [to] disguise themselves as trans women to sneak into bathrooms and sexually assault women."[13] Lopez suggests that the fears expressed by those supporting legislation that would disallow bathroom use on the basis of one's gender identity disguise a more fundamental one, a fear that the gender-related normative order to which they are accustomed is undergoing change, challenging their habitual reception of society's peoplescape. When familiar identity spaces are in discomfiting flux, norms prescribing access to civic space become contestable. As one trans person victimized by a new prohibition in his state recognizes, "This wasn't just about bathrooms. It was about the right to exist in public spaces for trans people."[14] Attributing the denial of civic status to trans bodies to the desire for identity continuity, Valo Vähäpassi summarizes the civic implications of the contestation thus: "America is threatened by granting civil rights to these non-linear bodies."[15]

In sum, the threat of an increasingly visible civic existence for trans people is fueled by a loss of certitude, analyzed by Canguilhem as investment in life's lessons and by Foucault as the will to truth. Trans people destabilize the gender order on which people depend to shape their self-understandings of the truth of what and who they are. It's a motivated "truth" assembled from the beginning of the life cycle. In Lacan's words:

> Identity is built up as a composite of images and effects … taken in from the outside world from the start of life, which are developed in relation

to the desire for recognition and the ... social requirements for submission to an arbitrary law.[16]

An encounter described in *The Green Hat*, an early twentieth-century novel, captures the unease people experience when their self-affirming representational system fails its mission. The narrator, having just met the sister of his acquaintance "Gerald," who is living in an apartment above his, says:

> We have all of us a crude desire to "place" our fellows in this or that category or class: we like to know more or less what they are, so that, maybe, we may know more or less what we shall be to them. But, even with the knowledge that she was Gerald's sister ... I couldn't, "place" Mrs. Storm. You had a conviction, a rather despairing one, that she didn't fit in anywhere, to any class, nay, to any nationality ... she wasn't any of the ghastly things called "society," "county," upper, middle, and lower class. She was, you can see, some invention, ghastly or not, of her own.[17]

To elaborate on the context of extravagant fears that result from alterations in the system of recognition attached to sexuality and gender orders, I turn to an instructive episode, a gender drama that took place in the eighteenth century during a change to which Thomas Laqueur refers as the ontology of "sex making." In an inquiry that borrows Foucault's insights into the politics of epistemology and the intimacy between "talk about sexuality" and "the social order,"[18] Laqueur historicizes an event that affected perspectives on the bio-sociality of sex. The eighteenth-century drama to which he refers involves a disruption in which men were disconcerted on finding themselves having to adjust to a change in the ontology of sexual difference. It was a moment in which "the understanding of the female body was undergoing a marked conceptual alteration."[19] Locating that disruption within the temporality of the relationship between sex and gender, Laqueur writes, "*sex*, or the body, must be understood as the epiphenomenon, while *gender*, what we would take to be a cultural category, was primary or 'real' [and adds] ... Gender – man and woman – mattered a great deal and was part of the order of things [and was] ... what we call a 'one-sex model' explicitly bound up in a circle of meanings" for which there was no conceptual means for "escape."[20]

The shift from what Laqueur calls a "a one-sex/flesh model to a two-sex flesh model" (to one in which female organs are no longer seen as alternative versions of male organs) had extensive implications for understandings, at a biological level, of the female anatomy and at the social level, of sexual pleasure and male versus female roles in it. What followed were disruptive aftereffects, disturbances resonating within the identity matrix within which self and other recognitions were contained. Released into civic life was heightened attention to "difference and sameness" and contention over "which ones count and for what ends." It was a situation in which any resolution had to be negotiated "outside the bounds of empirical investigation."[21] That noted, there are modes of "empirical investigation" that are not truth-seeking in the ordinary discovery sense that shapes inquiry in the physical and social sciences. Among those who have provided cogent alternatives is Louis Althusser.

The Contingency of Facticity and the Truth Effect

In one of his late essays Althusser constructs a version of empiricism with political implications that are anathema to those who cling to identity-affirming necessity. Althusser's empiricism, based on what he calls "the materialism of the encounter,"[22] embraces "the transcendental contingency of the world." Rejecting a philosophy based on "the Reason and Order of things," Althusser crafts one based on "a theory of their contingency and a recognition of the *fact*, [which is] the fact of contingency, the fact of the subordination of necessity to contingency, and the fact of the forms which 'give form' to the effect of encounter."[23] It's a philosophy that envisions the condition of possibility for a politics that "does not take anything for granted. It is in the political *void* that the encounter must come about."[24] For purposes of my focus on gender contention, it's also a political philosophy that warrants political thinking resistant to the mode of facticity from which sexuality and gender essentialisms achieve support. Facts for Althusser are accomplishments rather than markers of necessity. As he puts it, "One reasons not in terms of the Necessity of the accomplished fact, but in terms of the contingency of the fact to be accomplished [and] … nothing guarantees that the reality of the accomplished fact is the guarantee of its durability."[25]

Althusser's treatment of facts as accomplishments tracks with Harold Garfinkel's ethnomethodological investigations in which facts are accomplished through "artful practices of everyday life."[26] Knowledge production in Garfinkel's inquiries occurs not through the conceptual and empirical work of the social analyst but through the activity of his epistemological subjects who are involved in accomplishing the varying kinds of facticity on which his investigations have focused. Among his studies are a group with the task of identifying suicides, the staff of a Los Angeles Suicide Prevention Center for whom the fact of suicide emerges through their coding practices; while another, which I want to review, is his study of "Agnes," a transsexual whose accomplishment of gender, the "fact" of her being a woman, emerges through her years-long efforts (with medical assistance) to manage the change. Although Garfinkel avoids political language in his Agnes ethnography, what it mainly reveals is the micropolitics of gender management.

AGNES'S STRUGGLE

To summarize the circumstances briefly: After showing up at "the gender identity clinic at the university of California, Los Angeles," Agnes was observed by the clinical staff as "a physically and socially feminine woman with male genitals." Because they were unaware that Agnes had been "taking synthetic female hormones," they inferred that she had a "rare intersex condition known as testicular feminization syndrome" and decided to fulfill her desire for "a genital transformation" by arranging for an operation that would give her a vagina. Alerted to the case, "Garfinkel saw an opportunity to investigate Agnes's situation as an example of how the patient and the doctors collaboratively participated in upholding their shared sense of what properly constituted 'woman.'" Once his inquiry was underway his focus was on what he called "the managed achievement" of Agnes's gender choice, the way she along with her medical collaborators accomplished her identity as a woman.[27]

It turned out that the operation was just a first step in the transformation. Among what Agnes had to manage was not only what she had to achieve but also what she had to hide. As regards the achievement, Garfinkel states that "The natural normal female was for Agnes an ascribed object ... [it] was the object that Agnes sought to achieve for herself." He adds, "Two meanings of 'achievement' are meant in speaking of Agnes' having achieved her status as a female:"

> (1) Having become female represented for her a status of up-grading from that of a male which was for her was of lesser value than the status of a female. For her being female made her a more desirable object ... (2) The second sense of achievement refers to the tasks of securing and guaranteeing for herself the ascribed rights and obligations of an adult female by acquisition of the use of skills, capacities, the efficacious display of female appearances and performance, and the mobilizing of appropriate feelings and purposes.[28]

As for hiding, among what emerges from her conversations with Garfinkel is her need to hide her biography, both from herself (she referred to the genitals with which she was born as an abnormal growth) and from everyone else unfamiliar with her past. Her tactics included keeping a distance from others who showed gender ambiguity lest she be associated with them. From the point of view of the conceptual contribution of the story of Agnes's transsexual achievement, Garfinkel's account illuminates the phenomenological aspect of a sex change, the extraordinary work on the self that distinguishes a transsexual person from those who have occupied the same gender continuously without having to worry about social or official recognition.

HERCULINE'S "ABNORMALITY"

What distinguishes the analysis of Herculine Barbin's case from Agnes's is that although "Alexina's" memoir also articulates her/his experience from a subjective perspective, Foucault's account historicizes the case, giving it significance within a genealogical rather than phenomenological analytic. Although Foucault's account heeds Herculine's narrative, his emphasis is on a notable disjuncture between the personal account of the experience and the historically situated medical accounts that insisted on assigning a single sex to an ambiguously sexed body. What counts for Foucault with regard to situating the issue of blurred gender boundaries was the contested discursive spaces within which the issue was negotiated outside of Herculine's control by those in professional circles as well as in the public sphere. Reviewing the discursive controls that attend such cases in a lecture on abnormality, Foucault says:

> The whole field of notions of perversity converted into their puerile vocabulary, enables medical notions to function in the field of juridical power and, conversely juridical notions to function in medicine's sphere of competence ... This set of notions functions, then, as a switch point ... and the weaker it is epistemologically the better it functions.[29]

To return to his opening question in his Herculine Barbin commentary, "Do we *truly* need a *true* sex," no definitive answers are available. What Foucault enjoins is not evidence but an alternative to the will to truth. "They," those imposing a single sex on Herculine, "have obstinately brought into play this question of a 'true sex' in an order of things where one might have imagined that all that counted was the reality of the body and the intensity of its pleasures."[30]

The truth issue Foucault brings to the case is one he treats elaborately in his inaugural lecture at the Collège de France. Outlining his future investigations, he refers to his plan to undertake a genealogy of the will to truth and its power-knowledge effects on the policing of sexuality. Following up on that promise in a subsequent lecture, Foucault refers to "the game of truth," which exists in a network of constraints and dominations; "the system of truth and falsity," he states, "will have revealed the face it turned away from us for so long ... its violence."[31] With the violence he discerned in the "game of truth" in focus, Foucault found Herculine Barbin's victimization exemplary. As he has noted, when he pursues answers to historical questions – in this case the implementation of the will to truth – he looks for "'a concrete example' to 'serve as a testing ground for analysis.'"[32] Putting the case in context, he notes that by the eighteenth century, "As the modern state reinforced its ruling power medicine biology, juridical institutions, and administrative mechanisms functioned together to deny her freedom to choose one's social sex."[33] Thereafter, "everyone was to have one and only one sex. Everybody was to have his or her primary, profound, determined, and determining sexual identity."[34] Herculine's case fitted well with Foucault's plan to treat a practice of exclusion that began at the beginning of the nineteenth century, "taboos which affect the discourse of sexuality ... the sets of discourses – literary, religious or ethical, biological or medical, juridical too – where sexuality is discussed, and where it is named, described, metaphorized, explained, judged."[35]

In the century that followed Herculine Barbin's misfortune of becoming an object of scrutiny in "a game of truth," new players came on the scene. In 1966 Dr John Money established a Gender Identity Disorder Clinic as a follow-up to his research in the prior decade on "intersex, trans, and gender non-conforming persons," where much of the research and treatment was focused on sex assignments for cases of "hermaphroditism."[36] Re-establishing a version of the nineteenth-century will to truth to which Herculine Barbin was subjected, Money and his associates invented a new truth game, which, like the prior one, operated in the service of the normalization of gender, albeit with a conceptual innovation. Their truth game relied on a "variable" they called "'Gender role and orientation, established while growing up,'"[37] a concept for which evidence gathering requires observations of a patient's "comportment," to serve as a guide to the truth of a patient's sexual orientation. What was invented was a truth-pursuing sexology that would disclose a person's "gendered inclinations," which would then allow for a definitive gender assignment, a reinscription of "the logic of heteronormativity and corporeal dimorphism as standard in the lives and collectivities of trans and gender-nonconforming folks."[38]

What, then, is the appropriate response to the repressive practices articulated as a pursuit of truth, whatever are the scientific pretenses involved in the normalizations for which truth games are implemented? For Foucault it is critique, to which he refers as an "art of voluntary insubordination, that of reflected intractability. Critique would essentially insure the desubjugation of the subject in the context of what we would call ... the politics of truth."[39] Here I want to summon monstrosity again, heeding insights from a collection of writings on "Monsters and Methodologies" in which the concern is an epistemological one about what the monster "offers to our thinking" insofar as it "highlights the supposed divisions between the acceptable and conventional and their opposites, drawing attention to the production of knowledge."[40] The collection's authors' main point as regards their view of the role of monstrosity in critical political thinking is their suggestion about the disposition one needs to open a space "where voices are multiple, speaking with/to each other, and yet still maintaining the semblance of individual thought and being." It's a type of knowledge, they assert, which "has the power to make us monstrous to ourselves, and ensures that there is no easy, one-way look at the monster as object … [or at] the Other as a subject."[41]

If we also heed Foucault's position that subject-making and -constraining discourses are events, which are "fragile, temporary" and subject to possible reversals which would release those subjugated, we are encouraged to ask what would constitute counter-events.[42] Because Foucault's critique manifesto leaves open the question of the vehicles of expression (media genres) with which the insubordination to which he refers can manifest as counter-event, I want to engage Pedro Almodóvar's cinematic gender constructions because both thematically and formally his films, spanning the twentieth and twenty-first centuries, are a critique of Spain's strict twentieth-century, officially authorized and enforced sexuality and gender order as well as its less restrictive one in the twenty-first century. While his camera's gaze ambiguates his subjects' genders within the film dramas, there are also implicit glances backward at the repression that took place toward gender ambiguity and activism in Spain under Franco. "An essential axis of meaning in much of his film work," as Marvin D'Lugo puts it, "lies precisely in the ways the ideas and icons of Francoist cinema – those related to religion, the family, and sexual repression – are set up as foils to stimulate the audience to embrace a new post-Franco cultural aesthetic."[43]

Spain's gender-restricting normative order within which Almodóvar has composed his films has not been singular. With regard to the European scene in general, "most histories benefit from critical engagement with how states govern biopolitical, epistemological and ontological systems."[44] The state-sponsored medical gaze to which Herculine Barbin was subjected in the nineteenth century has persisted in many national venues into the twentieth and twenty-first. It's a gaze that the above noted sexologist Robert Money tried to correct with a new sexological empiricism, "the age-old practice of inferring on the basis of a single glance" the correct sexual assignment for ambiguous bodies.[45] By dint of cinematic form, Almodóvar's films contest medicine's perfunctorily implemented scopic regime by offering a more complex and durational gaze which consists of multiple prolonged looks rather than fleeting glances. Because the oblique historical references in his films take Almodóvar's cinematic thinking beyond a narrow medically informed biopolitics to the wider problem of state-initiated cultural governance, I want, before turning to his films and the Spanish historical context to which they are a response, to revert to Weimar Berlin where an exemplary and instructive parallel dynamic was taking place.

Once Hitler came to power, a fascism-initiated culture war was underway between the artistic expression of multiple gender representations and sexualities and Nazi repression. There is perhaps no better modeling of that encounter than in the opening scene in Bob Fosse's film *Cabaret* (1972), based in part on Christopher Isherwood's Berlin stories (written while he lived there in the 1930s). At one point, as Isherwood observes, "Berlin was in a state of war, hate exploded suddenly, without warning, out of nowhere, at street corners, in restaurants, cinemas, dance halls, swimming baths, at midnight, after breakfast, in the middle of the afternoon."[46] Picking up on that condition at the outset of *Cabaret*'s film narrative, while a gender-bending performance is taking place onstage at a Berlin cabaret theater Nazi thugs are beating the theater director in an alley outside, their blows delivered with the same cadence as the musically assisted choreography of the performance.

Weimar in the 1930s

The name Magnus Hirschfeld looms large in the story of Germany's twentieth-century gender politics. He invented the term "transvestism," which he applied to "people whose gender identity and preferred clothing did not align with the sex to which they are assigned at birth."[47] Going beyond mere discursive invention Hirschfeld created the "Institute of Sexology" dedicated to incorporating trans people into the social order by promoting a policy (accepted by the governing authorities) in which members of the Institute could apply for transvestite certificates that would allow them to move about within the civic sphere, dressed as they wished without fear of arrest. When the Nazi Party came to power, "Hirschfeld's Institute of Sexology [was] one of its first targets."[48] There were many others: "Within months of Hitler's appointment as Chancellor, the Nazis shut down many of the gay, lesbian, and transvestite clubs. Queer magazines were shuttered and queer titles removed from bookstores as part of the Nazis' 'Campaign for a Clean Reich.'"[49] The nightmare that Berlin had become under Nazi control was akin to a "horror film," where, as Barbara Creed renders that genre effect, they "constructed a border between ... 'the clean and proper body' and ... the abject body, or the body which has lost its form and integrity."[50]

Much like other fascist nationalists, what the Nazis and those who shared their mentality hated was Berlin's culture of enjoyment which thrived on gender-crossing and other boundary transgressions. It's a mentality well elaborated in Gilles Deleuze's gloss on Spinoza where he refers to a "portrait of the resentful man" for whom "all happiness is an offense."[51] Such resentments, which actualize as vilification of others' lifestyles, often disguise a more ontological level of resentment, what William Connolly calls "resentment against finitude ... [an inability] to live without projecting a fundamental unfairness into being and resenting it."[52] Writing in the late 1930s, Svend Ranulf offered a similar but more historically situated reading of that resentment-fueled hatred. Noting the "resentment of pious, thrifty, debt-ridden peasants at urban creditors, bankers, atheists, and liberals" among others, he infers that they envy those who did not submit to the constraints under which they had suffered.[53] Engaging Ranulf's analysis elsewhere, I posed the question, "What was there to envy?" My suggested answer is "enjoyment ... the exuberant acting out within Weimar's Cabaret Culture, which flourished in an open and tolerant cosmopolitan Berlin in which gender bending and a wide variety of other identity improvisations were featured."

> Reinforced by an artistic environment – the theatrical events of the period, e.g., the Brecht/Weil *Three Penny Opera*, *avant-garde* film, and clubs – in the gatherings in Cabaret clubs, androgynous and wildly decorated bodies were works of art, canvasses upon which alternative dispositions were being scripted. Cabaret Culture thrived on a "Berlinisch attitude of ironic bemusement and a slightly curled lip"[54] until the Nazis came to power to give that attitude a fat lip – shutting clubs and theaters, burning books and engaging in a "fierce campaigns against feminism, jazz, modern architecture and much else."[55]

Recent archival work has recovered the draconian Nazi measures that particularly targeted trans people along with their other violent actions against the gender-bending and unconventional sexualities that were part of Weimar popular culture. Trans women who failed to escape the Nazi crackdown and whose stories had been unknown by the German public ended up being sent to concentration camps where they were murdered.[56]

Spain Under Franco: In Almodóvar's Rearview Mirror

The name that looms large in Francoist gender policies is that of Judge Antonio Sabater, *Juez de Vagos y Maleanes* (Judge of Vagrants and Thugs), whose "psycho-medical constructions of homosexuals" was the basis for "the codification of homosexuals as transgressing gender roles and posing as a threat to the heterosexual family" (a perspective foundational to the Franco regime).[57] The violent crackdown on alternative sexualities and gender crossing in the period of Franco's rule, which emulated the Nazi policies, remained in force under the provision of "Spain's so-called 'Social Danger Laws,'" passed in 1970 and not abolished until 1978.[58] The harsh penalties under that law included torture and shock therapy along with imprisonment in "re-education" camps organized mainly by medical professionals but in one case "in Fuerteventura in the Canary Islands, ... by priests." One "law used by Franco's regime to control and torture, was repealed only in 1996."[59]

To create a threshold for Almodóvar's intervention in the politics of sexuality and gender, I want to re-evoke Althusser's insights into the effects of alternative attachments to necessity versus contingency by attending to two entangled temporalities: historical time and subjectivity duration. Subjectivity time involves the phenomenology of subjective self-fashioning, while historical time is marked by a series of events that change the conditions within which subjective self-fashioning strives. In subjectivity time subjects strive to manage the changing demands they must confront as the stages of the life cycle unfold. Their management of their world (expressed in German as their *umwelt*) faces complications when either events or developing social alterations destabilize the intersubjective terrain in which they reside – for example, publicly recognized increases in non-binary gender practices which scramble the subject positions that had formerly conformed to their notion of the order. My suggestion is that those who engage the world within an ontology that embraces contingency and uncertainty are prone to having a hospitable reception of anomalies or monstrosities, while those with a strong will to truth are prone to being inhospitable to them. I want to add, in accord with what Mary Ann Doane points out, that cinema is especially suitable as a vehicle to rehearse the tensions between determinism and contingency because, as she puts it, "Cinema, born in a period when the battle over contingency, determinism, and meaning was strong, embodies both epistemologies."[60]

From his very first cinematic endeavor, *Pepi, Luci, Bom and Other Girls Like Mom* (1980), Almodóvar's cinematic hospitality to alternative sexualities and gender ambiguity has been an intervention in and rehearsal of a fraught political scene, one characterized by an official and popular lack of hospitality to proliferating non-binary gender choices by those who resist gender essentialisms. With cinematic compositions that feature anomaly and monstrosity, Almodóvar peoples his films with transgender types (in *All About My Mother* [1999] and *Bad Education* [2004]), transvestites (in many), and generally with ambiguous gender comportments both within and between characters. Among his challenges to the disconcerting effect of transgender people is his character Juan Agrado (Antonia San) (Figure 5.1) whose improvised standup comedy routine in front of a theater audience in *All About My Mother* turns their disappointment about a cancelled Barcelona theatrical performance of Tennessee Williams's *A Streetcar Named Desire* into a moment of shared jouissance. When she (a former he) emerges onstage to announce the cancellation, she promises to offer substitute entertainment for those who want to stay. While a few leave immediately, most stay, initially out of curiosity, as Agrado (Spanish for pleasing or liking) launches into a tongue-in-cheek routine about how much she has paid for each body modification.

Beginning with reference to her name, she says, "They call me La Agrado because throughout my entire life I've tried to make life pleasant for everyone else." As she continues, her humble hospitality toward herself becomes infectious. Referring to her accomplishment after having selected her multiple surgeries, she says, "In addition to being *agradable* (nice), I am also very authentic." Like Garfinkel's "Agnes," she has accomplished becoming a woman, but unlike Agnes she feels that he has nothing to hide. She (doubtless

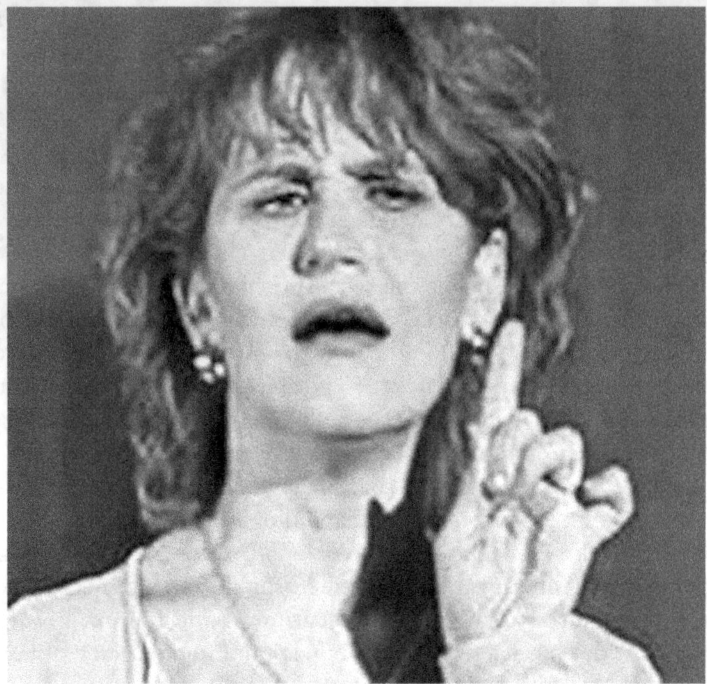

Figure 5.1 Juan Agrado in Pedro Almodóvar's 1999 film *All About My Mother*. Source: Criterion Collection, DVD, 2002.

Almodóvar as well) wants to make her gender transition a case for the social inclusiveness of the process as well as the result. Continuing with, "Look at my body, all made to measure," Agrado justifies the expense of all the modifications with a parody of commitments to the authenticity of gender roles: "It costs a lot to be authentic but one can't be stingy with these things." Propitiously for purposes of my analysis, Agrado also plays with the concept of monstrosity. Treating monstrosity parodically she says, "Tits, two because I am no monster, 70,000 each." What ultimately "brings the house down" with a burst of laughter and applause by the entire audience are her remarks about the depilation one has to undergo to achieve feminine authenticity, "two to four sessions depending on how hairy you are. But if you're a flamenco diva, you'll need more." As for where Almodóvar stands with respect to the gender issues his film rehearses, his dedications as the credits are run include the line, "to all people who want to be mothers." Motherhood, he is suggesting, has no gender requirements.

Almodóvar's gesture of recognizing all people as potential mothers fits with his general attitude toward transgender persons, treating them as legitimate civic subjects. As he states in his review of gender crossers in his film work,

"I wasn't talking about their problems, or The Transgender Problem – I was saying they exist, and their lives are as legitimate as any other."[61]

However, what I particularly want to explore about what Almodóvar's films do in mobilizing themes that challenge officially authorized sexual and gender arrangements is *how* they do what they do. Through camera angles, striking colors (for example intense moods achieved with abundant use of the color red), light and sound effects, and the intermixing of a wide variety of artistic genres – the Bette Davis film *All About Eve* and the Tennessee Williams play, *Streetcar Named Desire*, among other artistic intertexts, shape much of *All About My Mother* – he composes a series of non-linear fragments that challenge the enduring myths on which social norms are based. In that regard I was struck by the wealth of intertextual reference in the first of his films I watched shortly after its release, *Women on the Verge of a Nervous Breakdown* (1988), which draws on Hitchcock film imagery, Spanish telenovelas, Pina Bausch dance choreography, soap operas, melodrama, film noir, and a Cocteau play, *The Human Voice*. Although it also has a strong theme – women who, reacting to the suffering they experience from men, struggle to manage their destiny without them – what stands out are fragments within which the viewer is confronted with a wealth of details.

With that aesthetic in mind, I want to illustrate the effect as it operates within *Women on the Verge of a Nervous Breakdown*. Pepa (Carmen Maura), one of the film's protagonists, takes several rides in a taxi whose driver expresses typical macho clichés about women needing men to manage their lives. Although the interior of the taxi, which is decorated with scores of multi-colored cultural items, may seem oblique to the action and dialogue, the decorative items constitute a significant statement. The camera's exploration of the many cultural clichés on display in the cab's interior, which are more prolix than the driver's voice, tells the viewer that just as the driver is a passive consumer of the cultural clichés arrayed in his cab's interior, he is also one who passively accepts and passes on conventional gender protocols.

The panning shot of the taxi's interior is typical of Almodóvar's compositional approach in which fragments carry more of his films' ideational contribution than does the overall film narrative. Noting the way the fragment dominates Almodóvar's cinematic aesthetic, Julián Daniel Gutiérrez-Albilla points out that critical interpretive work on Almodóvar films has to be "teased out from a close reading of selective scenes (or fragments)."[62] That cinematic aesthetic compares with Flaubert's cinema-compatible novelistic style, which fragments reality into discrete scenes, a style that is "an anticipation of cinema ... *avant la lettre*."[63] To add to an appreciation of such a compositional strategy I refer as well to Theodor Adorno's evocation of an aesthetic of fragmentation, "the tendency of artworks," he states, "to wrest themselves free of the internal unity of their own construction, to introduce caesuras that no longer permit the totality of the appearance."[64] The importance of fragments within Almodóvar's film corpus is again on display in a scene in one of his films eight years later, *Volver* (2006). Thematically, it is another film in which women confront and overcome male dominance, in this case more decisively. After Paula (Yohana Cobo) murders her father to avoid being raped, she and her mother Raimunda (Penélope Cruz) hide the corpse in a freezer (for later burial). In her explication of the film's theme, Leora Lev refers to *Volver*'s "creative female spirit,"[65] a spirit captured in one of the film's metaphorical fragments. After an overhead shot shows Raimunda washing away the blood on the knife with which Paula had murdered her father, a neighbor who shows up asks about a bloodstain on Raimunda's neck. Rather than reveal the specific acts – the murder and stowing of the body – from which the stain comes, Raimunda utters a double entendre, referring to it as "women's trouble." Women's trouble is constantly thematized in Almodóvar's films, which at the same time blur the boundaries of gender while giving it durational variability. However, rather than review the corpus as a whole, which is rich in such telling fragments, I want to engage his *Habla con Ella (Talk to Her)* (2002; hereafter *Habla*), because it stands out for the way it lends a complex temporality to the civic lives of gender by inventing characters whose gender comportments shift episodically.

In accord with Foucault's lament about what is lost by the policing of sexuality – "one might have imagined that all that counted was the reality of the body and the intensity of its pleasures" – Almodóvar's films react to the way sexuality and gender have been experienced under the constraints within the Spanish historical context and also imagine what they could be by drawing on artistic genres that resist social constraints by giving bodies a freer range of self-definition and movement. Providing a threshold to his *Habla*, one fragment in his *All About My Mother* testifies to that intention. As Almodóvar puts it,

> In *Todo sobre my madre* ... there was a poster of Pina [Bausch] in Café Müller (it was hanging on the wall in Celia Roth's son's room). I didn't know then that that piece would be the prologue to my next film ... I only wanted to pay homage to the German choreographer.[66]

Talk to Her: Gender as Choreography

Although *Habla* thinks with an impressive array of artistic and media genres – not least of which is a main character, Benigno, modeled on one in Patricia Highsmith's novel *This Sweet Sickness* – I want to stress the dance performances with which the film begins and ends. In the opening scene two men who are unknown to each other and have different capacities for being affected are sitting side by side watching the Pina Bausch's *Tanztheater* performance of

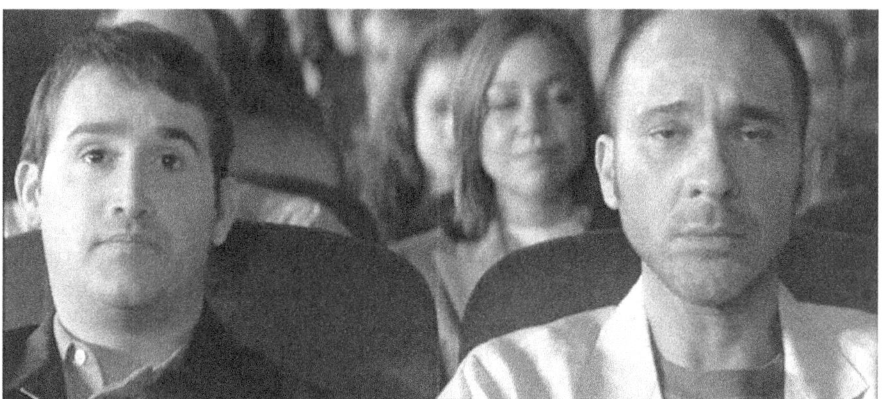

Figure 5.2 Benigno and Marco in Pedro Almodóvar's 2002 film *Talk to Her.*
Source: Sony Pictures, DVD, 2003.

"Café Müller" with Bausch herself and a protagonist, Alicia (Leonor Watling), among the dancers. One of the men, Benigno Martin (Javier Cámara) is looking on, seemingly emotionless, while the other, Marco Zuluaga (Dario Grandinetti), is moved to tears (Figure 5.2).

Before providing a brief sketch of the plot that follows that opening (Benigno and Marco ultimately meet and become close friends), I want to note the instructive reaction of another filmmaker, Wim Wenders, to a Bausch *Tanztheater* performance, because his commentary on the experience adduces the emotion-arousing effects of the performances as well as their particular appeal to filmmakers:

> It was ... just human beings performing there who moved in a different way from anything I had seen before, which in turn moved *me* in a way I had never experienced ... after a few moments of incredulous bewilderment I just gave free reign to my feelings and began to weep without restraint.[67]

He adds that although as one who directs "motion pictures" he is supposed to be an expert on motion, he found that he had something to learn about motion. Bausch, "without necessarily wanting to be," he says, "is a great teacher for all those who think they are well versed in the field of motion."[68]

Referring to his own experience of the Bausch *Tanztheater* dance aesthetic in which bodies are a theater of expressivity, Almodóvar states that after watching "Café Müller," he "looked at Pina's face again, with her eyes closed, and at how she was dressed in a flimsy slip, her arms and hands outstretched, surrounded by obstacles ... I had no doubt that it was the image which best represented the limbo in which my story's protagonists lived."[69] Elaborating on that limbo cinematically, what Almodóvar's camera tells us about his protagonists is that they are durational. Their faces and bodily movements testify to an instability in their gender identities; they are serially involved in interpersonal encounters that affect their gender comportments. Their "sexed subjectivity," which Almodóvar rearticulates within his film narrative as a whole, articulates gender orientation as something that is "not ... located within the body, but rather something that happens between bodies."[70] In Donna Haraway's terms, Bausch's dancers and Almodóvar's characters are involved in "articulation" rather than "representation."[71]

While the scenes involving the dance routines with which *Habla* begins and ends – "Café Müller" and "Masurca Fogo" respectively – track the changes in one protagonist, Marco, an appreciation of the role of the Bausch choreographies requires heeding another choreography in the midst of the film, the staging of Lydia Gonzales' (Rosario Flores) preparation for and performance of her role as a matador. In a scene where she is about to face a bull in Madrid's Plaza del Toros there is an extended process during which an aide is helping secure her matador costume. Cinched to be tight fitting, once it has been secured she looks as if she has donned a suit of armor that immobilizes much of her body. There and in all the shots that show her in the bullring, a place of ritualized macho masculinity, we are looking at what appears to be a man, hair tucked into the cap and facial features looking hard and masculine (Figure 5.3). Until she is gored during the second of her bull fight scenes, ending up in a coma, the choreography of her bull fighting shows a historically prescribed, ritualized set of movements that are purposively aimed at exhausting and killing the animal.

The Pina Bausch *Tanztheater* performances also provide a semiotics of constraint but within a more complexly gendered, trans-person staging. Combining theatrical drama with dance routines that feature improvisational encounters between male and female dancers, the Bausch staging of "Café Müller" with which *Habla* opens features moments of "isolation, despair and mental illness" in a setting figured as social by the presence of "tables and chairs on stage."[72] While Lydia's bull fighting is a space of masculinity, Bausch's "Café Müller" is a transgressive space of male–female encounter in which the dance gestures transgress gender boundaries ("dancing across borders," as Johannes Birringer puts it[73]), while at the same time shifting back and forth between supportive and violent inter- and intra-gender episodes of normative constraint. Among what a "Bausch [dance performance] reveals [is] how individuals feel physically compelled to participate in the games people play – seeking recognition, affection, and social acceptance."[74] The fluctuating episodic aesthetic with which she composes gender encounters between and within subjects comports with Almodóvar's constructions of inter- and

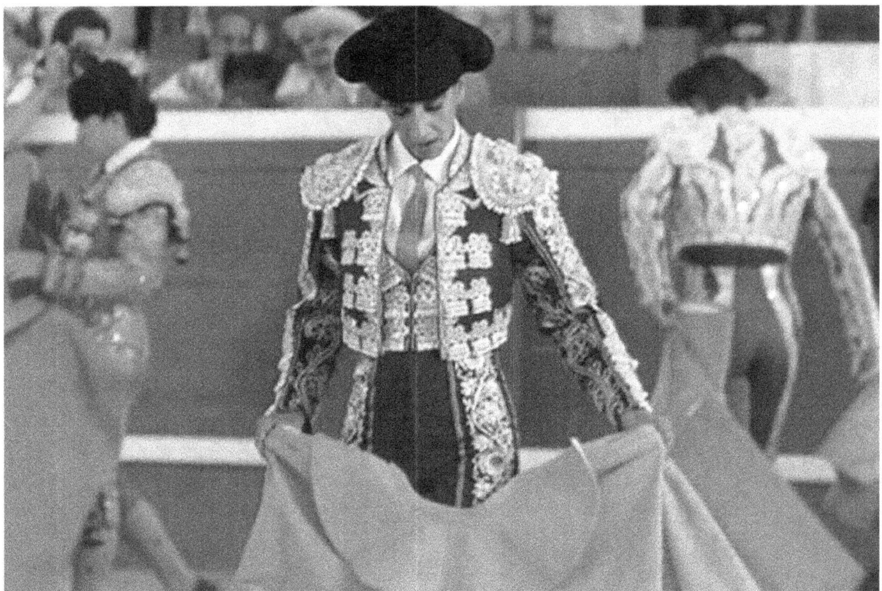

Figure 5.3 Lydia as a matador in Pedro Almodóvar's 2002 film *Talk to Her*.
Source: Sony Pictures, DVD, 2003.

trans-subjectivity. In *Habla*, as in his other films, gender comportments change from one encounter to the next. Lydia's changes are exemplary in that respect: when encountering a bull (with hair hidden and body tightly encased in a rigid suit), she draws on masculine subjectivity, while when involved amorously with Marco (with her hair down and flowing and with seductive bodily gestures) she is femininized (Figure 5.4).

Bracha Ettinger's concept of matrixial trans-subjectivity effectively captures the Bausch/Almodóvar approach to sexuality and gender temporality as episodes of encounter. Bausch's *Tanztheater* performances and Almodóvar's films compose what Ettinger calls matrixial border spaces, "spheres of encounter-events where intensities and vibrations as well as their imprints and memory traces are exchanged and experienced by fragmented partial-subjects who are reattuning their affective frequencies."[75] They are spaces that "concern shareability yet evade collective community and organized society ... [and involve] a particular mode of difference – an originary feminine difference that evades the dichotomy between masculinity and femininity."[76] The concept of matrixial trans-subjectivity articulates well with the identity temporality that Almodóvar constructs. His approach to cinematic composition "hosts moments of co-emergence-in-differentiation." In sum, for Almodóvar, identity is always in flux, dependent on events of encounter; it's an "unstable ... evanescent byproduct

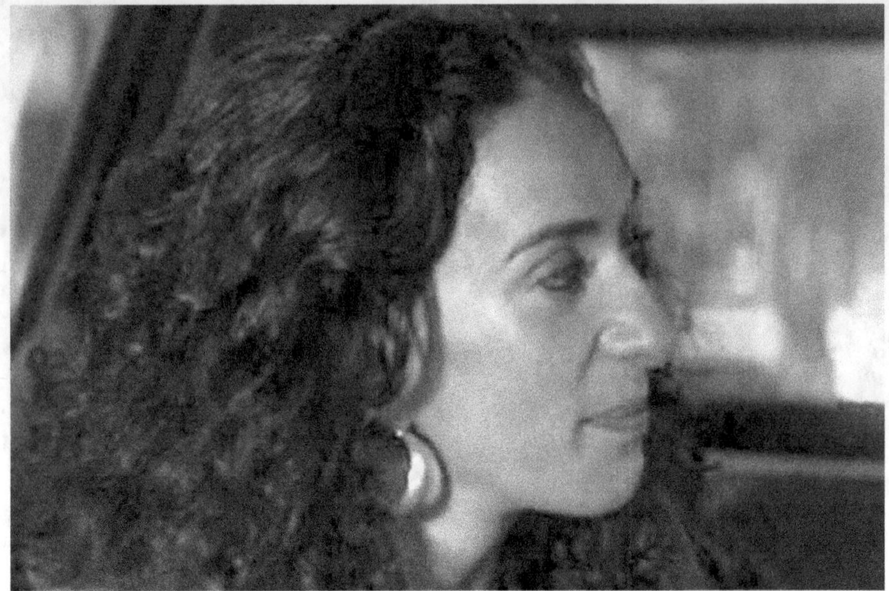

Figure 5.4 Lydia feminized in Pedro Almodóvar's 2002 film *Talk to Her*.
Source: Sony Pictures, DVD, 2003.

of an ever-flowing but ever-present difference [in which] ... difference as such provides no *terra firma*."[77]

THE CHARACTERS

Ettinger's concept of "encounter-events" fits the shifting identity effects in *Habla*, which are evident not only in the changing appearances of Lydia between facing a bull versus a lover but also in Marco's comportment after he is befriended and affected by Benigno. Scrolling back to the beginning of the film while heeding Ettinger's concept of trans-subjectivity, I return to Benigno and Marco, whom we first see in attendance at the Pina Bausch "Café Müller" performance. The dynamic of identity/difference that the Benigno–Marco encounters articulate is the primary interpersonal dynamic within the film's changing identity comportments.

Once we see later encounters, the reason for the difference between the dry-eyed, seemingly unmoved Benigno and the tearful Marco at the "Café Müller" performance becomes evident. Benigno has had no amorous experiences, traumatic or otherwise; "a child unprepared for adult love,"[78] he has been living with his mother, while we learn from one of Marco's conversations with Lydia that Marco has had a painful marriage breakup from which he says he has never recovered. While the dance performance triggers Marco's reservoir of grief, Benigno, who lacks a personal archive of traumatic interpersonal experiences, is unmoved by unhappy recollections. He is moved only by the sight of the dancer, Alicia, whom he subsequently endeavors to meet. Almodóvar's camera continually explores the differences in the bodily comportments of the two friends. Benigno, who as a nurse occupies what is historically a mainly feminine caring vocation, is soft looking and moves with a woman's typical feminine body language. Observing Almodóvar's construction of Benigno, Adriana Novoa writes, "Almodóvar has subverted the meaning of Benigno's masculinity ... he has made Benigno the best mother in the film."[79] Although she suggests that it's a "twist" on his usual character constructions, the dedication at the end of his *All About My Mother* suggests continuity. Given that (as noted) he dedicates the film "to all *people* who are mothers," that earlier film anticipates the way he composes Benigno's motherly feminine comportment in his nursing of the comatose Alicia.

The film's main identity/difference narrative thread casts a virile-looking Marco, who in contrast with Benigno has a more typically masculine position as a journalist and tones his body by working out on an exercise machine. His masculine bodily comportment achieves recognition during one of the conversations among female nurses in the break room at the hospital where Benigno works and Marco visits. One of them says to the others that she imagines that Marco is "well-hung." If we heed the fairy tale genre that characterizes Benigno's and Marco's relationships with their love objects (both of whom, Alicia and Lydia respectively, are in comas – until Alicia awakes and Lydia dies – rendering them as "sleeping beauties"), we have to attend to another stark difference between the two men: their different relationship to talking. As Novoa suggests, "the contrast between Marco's literary vocation and the orality with which Benigno practices his vocation locates them differently within 'the fairy tale context.'"[80]

Talking, Benigno's primary mode of addressing his world, occurs immediately after the scene where he is sitting next to the weeping Marco at the Pina Bausch performance. A cut to a hospital room shows him caring for the "sleeping beauty," Alicia, while describing the choreography of the Bausch performance he watched. In that monologue he fluently conveys what he saw, showing that he's quite able to turn receptive, experiential moments into words. However, to appreciate the role of talk in the film we have to heed discursive variations which become available in a flashback to an earlier set of scenes that begin with Benigno watching Alicia from his apartment where prior to the accident that put her in a coma she is rehearsing in the dance studio across the street.

Having evinced a desire for contact with her he decides to attempt a face-to-face encounter by pretending to have a psychological problem so he can visit her psychiatrist father, Dr. Vega (Roberto Alvarez), whose office is within the family's living space. The contrasting forms of talk within the psychiatric office rooms are revelatory. On the one hand, there is banal everyday talk, which Almodóvar illustrates with a humorous phone call the receptionist is having with an acquaintance. We hear her saying, "this morning I had an elephant sized dump." As for more serious professional conversation, once he is ushered in to see the psychiatrist Benigno is at a loss for words.

To borrow a concept from the Dutch sociologist/psychoanalyst Abram de Swaan, Benigno, who has been an isolated homebody with little experience of modernity's discursive practices, is not "proto-professionalized" with regard to psychiatric counseling. As de Swaan points out, to identify yourself as one having a need for psychiatric counseling you have to be already familiar with psychiatric discourse, at least at rudimentary level, so that you can express a psychiatry-relevant problem.[81] When the doctor asks Benigno why he has come, Benigno is silent for some time as he grasps for relevant words. All he can come up with eventually is something he experiences; he refers to being lonely. Before he leaves the office complex, he wanders surreptitiously through the apartment looking for Alicia. When he bumps into her in one of the rooms, he is as much at a loss for words as he was with her father. All he is able to utter is "I'm harmless." In contrast with the continuous monologue he later accomplishes while she is in a coma, at this point he lacks *savoir faire* for romantic talk and is unable to say anything but the reassuring "I'm harmless" expression before he departs.

Marco has a different kind of disability. His journalistic vocation impairs his ability to focus on the present. His initial encounter with the matador Lydia, the woman with whom he later falls in love, is as a journalist seeking an interview. Because at that moment he is already imagining a future in which he will be writing up the exchange, he cannot then, nor in subsequent more intimate moments, achieve an adequate focus on Lydia's life struggle. Lacking a tendency toward intimate conversation, once Lydia becomes the film's second "sleeping beauty," resulting from her injury in the bullring, Marco is unable to emulate Benigno's ability to talk to his beloved despite Benigno enjoining him to do so. He ends up losing her to her estranged husband who returns to her bedside. Marco's self-imposed, vocation-related distraction becomes ironic when in another scene his new friend Benigno confides that he wants to marry Alicia. In response Marco has a tantrum in which he denies that Benigno has an actual relationship with Alicia. "You're involved with someone who is effectively dead," he says; "your so-called relationship is a monologue." Benigno's response at that point is to utter a truism: "we get along better than most married couples." Although Benigno is a sociopath who lacks the words to reflect on his own delusional condition, he is insightful about typical marriages within which couples are unable to evince the kind of elaborate caring he shows for his "princess," massaging her muscles, giving her sponge baths and talking to her tenderly.

After the fraught conversation between Benigno and Marco takes place, a central focus of the film becomes evident, well summarized by Carla Marcantonio:

> *Talk to Her* is a story about the friendship between two men, about loneliness and the long convalescence of the wounds provoked by passion. It is also about the incommunication between couples, and about … how monologues before a silent person can be an effective form of dialogue. About silence as 'eloquence of the body', about film as an ideal vehicle in relationships between people … It is also a film about madness so close to tenderness and common sense that it does not diverge from normality.[82]

The "madness" to which Marcantonio refers references an act that seals Benigno's fate. When an examination reveals that the comatose Alicia has become pregnant, a meeting of the hospital board is called during which those assembled learn that because of a scheduling issue, Benigno has been with Alicia unsupervised and has committed a rape. After Marco returns from a trip abroad – exercising the cosmopolitanism that distinguishes him from Benigno who remains tied to his Madrid neighborhood – he learns that Benigno is no longer employed at the hospital because he has been prosecuted and imprisoned for the rape. On hearing the news Marco hastens to Segovia to visit the imprisoned Benigno, who appears morphologically changed from the way he looked while working as a nurse. His formerly feminized body now looks more masculine (Figure 5.5): he's grown facial hair, looks leaner, and is more resolute and assertive in the way he converses. In contrast with the scolding with which he had reacted earlier to Benigno's desire to marry Alicia, rather than being censorious about Benigno's crime, Marco, having shed his rigid masculinity, has become affectionate and sympathetic. What follows moves beyond mere sympathy to identification. Marco takes over his lodging and his gaze. He moves into Benigno's apartment and, just as Benigno had, looks through the apartment window at the dance studio across the street, where we see an alive Alicia visiting her former work venue. Visiting a law office and learning that Alicia had awaked from her coma and had given birth to a boy that was stillborn, he agrees with the lawyer that the truth would be too disturbing for Benigno. When he travels back to visit the prison, he finds a tearful Benigno who, having heard from the lawyer that he is unlikely to ever be released, says he is consoled only by knowing that Alicia is unaware of his situation.

As the two men sit, separated by a glass partition that prevents physical contact between prisoner and visitor, the scene hints at the movement from difference to identity between Benigno and Marco. The shot–reverse shot sequence during the scene creates the impression that each of them is

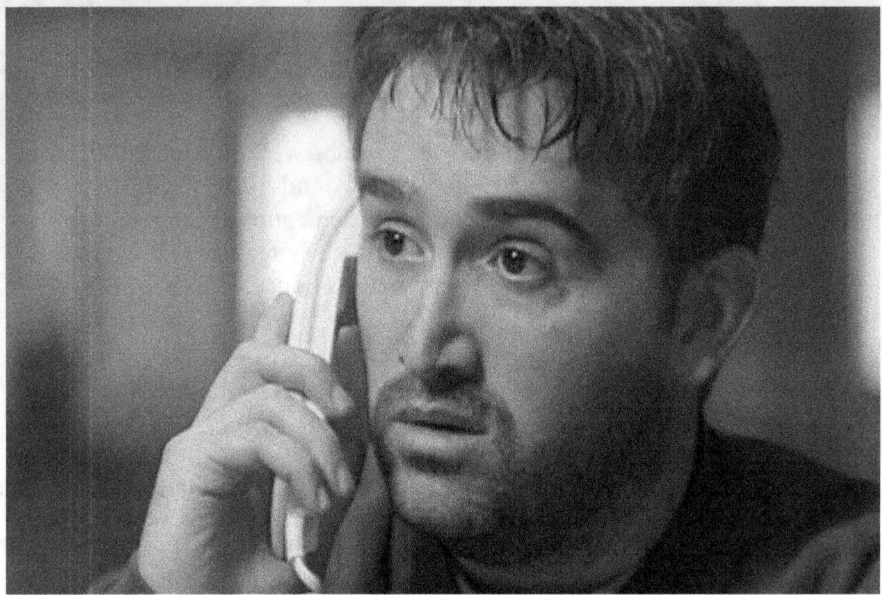

Figure 5.5 Benigno masculinized in Pedro Almódovar's 2002 film *Talk to Her.*
Source: Sony Pictures, DVD, 2003.

looking in a mirror. The ensuing conversation adds to the identity convergence. Benigno asks Marco if it bothers him that some at his jail think Marco is his boyfriend, and adds that he wishes he could hug him (while saying as well that he has hugged very few people in his life). Marco responds that he's not at all bothered by the assumption. He puts his hand on the glass between them and kisses it. The homosociality and movement from difference to identity that has developed between them takes on a special intensity when Marco, having taken over Benigno's apartment, finds and fondles a souvenir, a hairclip Benigno had taken from Alicia's apartment, and then proceeds to inhabit his gaze more thoroughly. Marco, who had looked at Lydia for the first time when watching her on a television broadcast while he was on an exercise machine, is now seeing with a Benigno-like comportment as his gaze on an alive Alicia is from the very same vantage point that Benigno in an earlier scene had watched her from, looking toward the dance studio across the street.

By the end of the film, Marco is once again attending a Bausch dance performance, this time smiling rather than tearful as he watches Alicia in a performance of "Masurca Fogo," a dance whose mood is quite different from the "Café Müller" performance he had watched while sitting next to Benigno. In contrast with the film's "Café Müller" opening, a dance to which Almodóvar (as noted) refers as a "perfect way of communicating the limbo in which the story's protagonists lived, the limbo between life and death,"[83] "Masurca Fogo" has what Almodóvar sees as vitality and optimism ... unexpected images of painful beauty." He has turned to it for his conclusion, he says, because it "begins with the sadness of the absent Benigno ... and [has then] united the surviving couple (Marco and Alicia) through shared bucolic emotion."[84]

What can we say about the monster, Benigno, that Almodóvar invents? In Foucault's terms, inasmuch as he "broke the moral law," his act was "a monstrosity of conduct rather than a monstrosity of nature."[85] While the Spanish legal system criminalizes his conduct, it's evident that Almodóvar, like his character Marco, is solicitous rather than censorious about Benigno's rape. As he states, *Talk to Her* is both "a film about the joy of narration and about words as a weapon against solitude, disease and death [and] ... also about madness, about a type of madness so close to tenderness and common sense that it does not diverge from normality."[86] Although the Benigno that Almodóvar locates within his sleeping beauty scenario is the fairy tale persona known as an ogre, he's one who has "the virtues of a fairy tale ogre ... an ogre [who] possesses the power to change reality."[87] Benigno's monstrousness thus suits Almodóvar's cinematic critique of normalizing gender positions because, like many monsters, he "reveals the unpredictability of categories, bodies, narratives and lives."[88] "[A]t the very simplest level, the monster," as Margrit Shildrick suggests, "is something beyond the normative, that resists the values associated with what we choose to call normality, and that is instead a focus of normative anxiety."[89]

Marco's non-judgmental acceptance of Benigno as a friend in spite of his monstrous act therefore stands in for Almodóvar's affective connection with his transgressive character. Noting that he (Almodóvar) "made a real effort not to judge the character" – "I treat the character Benigno as a friend. I see him neither from the point of view of normality nor abnormality, only in terms of his near fanatical romanticism" – he invents a film, *The Shrinking Lover*, within *Habla* "in order to cover up what Benigno has done."[90] The film, which Benigno watches and then describes to the comatose Alicia, combines an Almodóvar homage to the era of silent films and a model of a complex tension between masculine desire and fear. Featuring a lover, Amparo, shrunk by a potion his wife administers and is unable to reverse its effect (having lost the antidote), the film is an allegory of the entangled desire and intimidation activated in Benigno's penetration of the sleeping Alicia. In the film's shocking scene, a tiny Amparo crawls over his wife's sleeping body and disappears into her vagina, performing the plan that Benigno follows, to have hidden, non-consensual sex with his sleeping beloved.

Apart from the playful attitude of Almodóvar's construction of the delusional, norm-transgressing Benigno, whose habitus – apartment and ultimately the beloved – Marco takes over, is the question of what the film does politically. With its assemblage of multiple gender tonalities in a montage of media genres, *Habla* counters the gender-normalizing "monotone of the state." That noted, I want to conclude by situating the film within a contrast between a nationalistic, state-supported medicalization of gender, where medicalization supports an imperative of the state – a reified gender binary that is part of its management of its population – and national allegiance-resistant nomadism. As Hil Malatino puts it, the state "privileges the fixed over the metamorphic" and "fetishizes the eternal and stable … fixed, immutable and essential understandings of being."[91] Typically wary of the contingencies involved in national consolidations, those steering nation-states seek to impose essences on historically contingent individual and collective identities. Nevertheless, there are exorbitant resistances in non-binary fluid, anti-essentialist gender identity practices perhaps best characterized as what Deleuze and Guattari refer to as a "nomadism" that challenges "state science."[92] Heeding Deleuze and Guattari's "conceptual nomadism," central to their narrative of "state critique," I want to close the chapter with a textual illustration that dramatizes two aspects of nomadism to challenge a state-medicalization *dispositif* that normalizes gender identity.[93]

SPACES OF NON-BINARY GENDER EXPERIENCE: URBAN, RURAL, AND NOMADIC

Malatino supplies an apropos preface to the text, Stephan Elliott's film *The Adventures of Priscilla Queen of the Desert* (1994) to which I turn to conclude the chapter:

> What we need today to resist the violences entailed by late modern disavowals of corporeal difference, is a coalition of monsters – those beings that embrace corporeal nonnormativity, hybridity and mixity as a source of strength and resilience capable of challenging understandings of extraordinary bodies as pathological, aberrant, and undesirable.[94]

To appreciate the relevance of the film, which features three drag queens who leave their accepting city performance venue to perform in Australia's more masculinist and thus perilous non-urban areas, we have to appreciate the cultural singularities that urban life has created. Almodóvar's cinematic interventions presume an urban–non-urban divide; his films presume an urban culture's anti-nationalist effects. "Historically," "Francoism," as D'Lugo points out, "constructed its own ideal of the Spanish nation against the models of social and political deviance embodied as much by the urban styles of Madrid and Barcelona as by the external otherness of foreign political ideologies and social customs." He suggests (as noted above) that – despite Almodóvar's insistence that his films have no connection with Francoism – "Madrid has figured prominently in [his] cinema … [as a] cultural force, producing forms of expression and action that challenge traditional [Francoist] values by tearing down and rebuilding moral institutions of Spanish life … those related to religion, the family, and sexual expression."[95]

As I have noted elsewhere, state-centric "geophilosophy," exemplified in the writings of Hegel, "never effectively alighted at the level of city life … Rather than pondering the implications of the modern city's diversity and intense sensorium for city dwellers, or even the 'citizen-subject,' a key persona in his political musings, Hegel was discomfited by it."[96] He admitted, for example, that although "he was impressed by the sophistication of the cultural life of Paris, the city seemed maybe a bit too disorderly."[97] In contrast, for Walter Benjamin (as is the case for Almodóvar), the city occupies his space of attention. While Almodóvar mobilizes protagonists, Benjamin famously "mobilizes the observer, so that the experience of the urban sensorium becomes a series of shocks that disrupt habitual modes of consciousness."[98] Almodóvar's observer is the film viewer for whom he delivers a similar experience. The unsettling (aberrant) movement of his non-linear film narratives, along with their multiple genres of expression and decentered points of view, disrupts the viewers' positioning vis-à-vis the life world of the film and encourages a questioning of their position in their own worlds.

The difference between urban and rural life, in which the former features diverse modes of being against the recalcitrance to fluid selfhood on the peripheries of urban settlements, is the dominant theme in Elliott's *Priscilla*. Whereas the model of aberrant movement that energizes aspects of Almodóvar's plot is Pina Bausch dance performances, it's drag queen performances in *Priscilla*. However, Almodóvar's films and Elliott's *Priscilla* converge in that, for both, aberrant movement constitutes a confluence of modalities of fluid selfhood. Crucially, what distinguishes *Priscilla* from Almodóvar's embrace of urban identity diversity is the film's inclusion of what the urban geographer Edward Soja calls a "thirdspace," which he sees as embedded within the urban, but applied to Australia references a space outside both urban and town spaces; it is the desert space of Australia's Aborigines who are definitively "Other" within the national context. As Soja puts it, "Thirdspace is a transcendent concept that is constantly expanding to include 'an-Other,' thus enabling the contestation and re-negotiation of boundaries and cultural identity."[99] Australia hosts a fundamental exception to William Boelhower's narrative of the totalizing nineteenth-century Euro-American "ethnogenesis" on the American continent, the moving frontier which led to a whitened regionalizing of the continent that took over and recoded Native American space, confining the remnants of Native American nations to reservations on small tracts of land.[100] While Euro-American domination turned the U.S. landscape into a legally and administratively enforced grid, cross-hatched with policed territorial and identity boundaries, the ethnogenesis of the Australian continent has been incomplete. Thousands of square miles known as the "Outback" have remained as what Deleuze and Guattari call "smooth space," space that eludes the coding practices of the state apparatuses and is thus open to the identity-fluidity practices of "nomadic thought."[101]

Nevertheless, within Aboriginal culture, the desert (and indeed the rest of the continent) *is* "striated," albeit in a singularly cultural way. It is crisscrossed with invisible songlines known to Aboriginals as dreaming tracks, which are routes that reference mythological cultural beliefs, ontologies, and interpersonal obligations. Aboriginal space is performative rather than a place in which to settle. A songline contains the prescription of what is to be sung and memorized in order to do justice to the ancestral significance of the route along which one moves. That Aboriginal cultural geography sets the context for the most telling aspect of the spatial Odyssey of *Priscilla*'s three white performers. As their traveling performances, initiated in urban space's cultural diversity, carried on through non-urban spaces of intensified white male homophobic nationalism, finds its way to the extra-national desert space of Australia's Indigenous peoples, they trace the effect of Australia's cultural disjunctions. Moving through "two quite distinct notions of cultural space," as Paul Carter puts it,"[102] they encounter radically different receptions of their challenge to traditional sexuality and gender norms. In contrast with the Aboriginal populations for whom space is performative – a music-loving culture in which Aboriginal peoples were often on the move, traveling "great distances to learn new songs"[103] – Australia's white settlers have constructed space as a series of material and "symbolic enclosures."[104]

To summarize the narrative of the *Priscilla* Odyssey: When the film's gender-bending troupe – two drag queens, Tic (Hugo Weaving) and Adam (Guy Pierce), and one transgender person, Bernadette (Terrence Stamp) (Figure 5.6) – leave Sydney and head to Alice Springs in their bus, "Priscilla," to perform in towns, they attract life-threatening levels of hostility. The non-urban version of "hegemonic masculinity" (a "hetero-nationalism" that links hetero-normativity to homophobic nationalism), results in a markedly unwelcoming reception.[105] However, when the bus reaches the desert where the troupe has an unplanned encounter with a group of Aborigines, Elliott's road movie, a genre which, as M. M. Bakhtin suggests, portrays "events governed by chance,"[106] dramatizes a more welcoming intercultural possibility. In the seemingly smooth space of the desert, a space that predated Euro-instituted statehood and persists without the striations that inhibit identity fluidity, sexual and otherwise, the resident nomads, who have non-state practices of space, are unthreatened by and welcoming toward Priscilla's traveling performers. As I've put it elsewhere, what the viewer observes is a

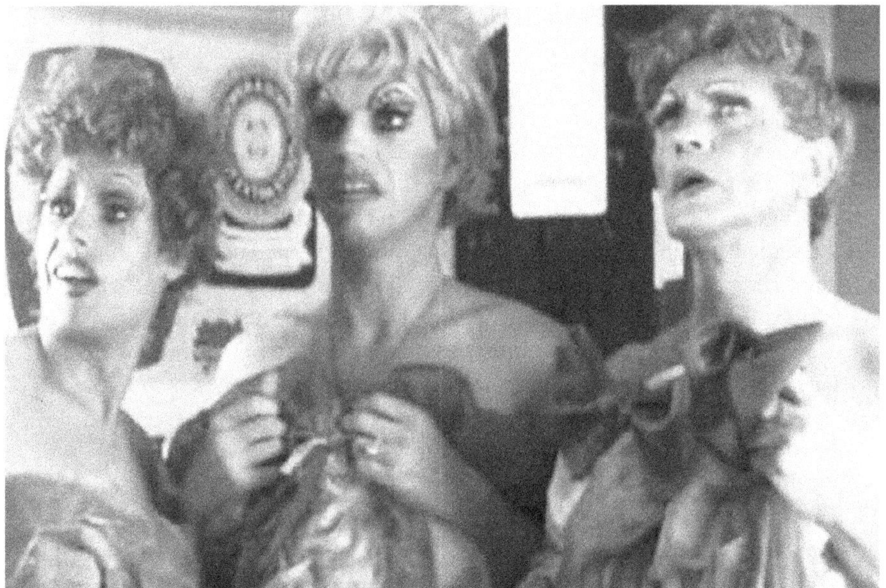

Figure 5.6 The Priscilla troupe in Stephan Elliott's 1994 film *Priscilla, Queen of the Desert*. Source: Twentieth Century Fox, DVD, 2005.

form of nomadism functioning in a space that has never been subdued, greeting with evident delight, a newer form [of nomadism] which is enabled by a spatial odyssey [begun] in … resistance to the power of a masculinist state that … proscribes transgender practices and same-sex sexuality.[107]

Most significantly for purposes of appreciating the landscape setting, once the film reaches the desert and Priscilla's performers are greeted by Aborigines, the film registers a space that is performative in two senses. On the one hand is the desert's invisible songline routes, a historically invisible marked space of performative obligations which from the beginning of Euro-Australian settlement has not been fully subsumed within the nation-state coding machine. On the other hand is contemporary Indigenous performativity, a situation summarized by Chris Gibson: "Indigenous organizations continue to challenge the geography of the nation-state and its grid-like maps of absolutist property markers, with demands [often in the form of musical and dance performances] for new fluid spaces of coexistence."[108]

The meeting between the Priscilla troupe and Aborigines is thus an encounter between two deterritorializing assemblages. Just as "Transvestites are deterritorializing personages … [who] intervene in the symbolic relays between personhood and nationhood,"[109] so too are Aboriginal nomadic practices of space which challenge the state's institutionalized territorial imaginary. Importantly for purposes of the chapter's focus, the Priscilla–Aboriginal encounter returns the analysis to the concept of monstrosity. In what turns out to be a music and dance festival, as the Priscilla troupe and their Aboriginal hosts perform together, the resulting con-sociality is between assemblages afflicted by different kinds of monstrosity assignments. While the Priscilla troupe's "monstrosity" is a function of Australia's masculinist heteronormativity, the Aboriginal monstrosity assignment is based on racism. As Gautam Anisha puts it, white Australia's racism has produced a "resignification of Australia's indigenous people as monstrous beings whose very presence within national space poses a threat to the nation's white identity." Quoting an Indigenous footballer who suffered racist taunts from the stands while on the pitch, he adds, "today monsters ... are a product of modern colonialism, a system supported by a specific dynamic of racism – 'anti-black racism.'"[110] In contrast, the monstrosities that Aborigines narrate are not invented to diminish the worthiness of outsiders. "Throughout Aboriginal Australia" there has existed "a rich inventory of monstrous figures ... roaming ogres, bogeymen (and bogeywomen)" among others. However, unlike white Australia's masculinist and racist use of monsters to disqualify LGBTQ and Aboriginal people from qualified civic personhood, the Aboriginal use of monstrosity has had a positive enabling dimension. Their monstrous figures and their attendant narratives provide a valuable source of knowledge about the hazards of specific places and environments. "Most important of all is their social function in terms of engendering fear and caution in young children, commensurate with the very real environmental perils that they inevitably encounter."[111] Elliott's *Priscilla* provides a model of an alliance among assemblages involved in what Felix Guattari calls "wars of subjectivity" which are ongoing in the contemporary postcolonial world.[112] The congeniality between the transvestite/transgender nomads and the Australian Aboriginals that Elliott's film stages suggests that a hospitality to gendered otherness (a main feature of Almodóvar's films) must be based on a critique of and active resistance to another alliance, that between nationalism and hegemonic masculinity.

NOTES

1. Georges Canguilhem, "Monstrosity and the Monstrous," in *Knowledge of Life*, trans. Stefanos Geroulanos and Daniela Ginsburg (New York: Fordham University Press, 2008), p. 136.
2. *Ibid.*, p. 134.
3. Deirdre McCloskey, *Crossing: A Memoir* (Chicago: University of Chicago Press, 1999), p. xv.

4. Jeffrey Weinstock, *The Ashgate Encyclopedia of Literary and Cinematic Monsters* (London: Ashgate, 2014), pp. 1–2.
5. Jessica Webb, "Herculine Barbin: Human Error, Criminality and the Case of the Monstrous Hermaphrodite," in Holly Lynn Baumgartner and Roger Davis (eds.), *Hosting the Monster* (New York: Rodopi, 2008), p. 153.
6. Michel Foucault, "Introduction" to *Herculine Barbin*, trans. Richard McDougall (New York: Pantheon, 1980), pp. vii–viii.
7. Michel Foucault, *Abnormal*, trans. Graham Burchell (New York: Picador, 2003), p. 65.
8. Judith Butler, *Gender Trouble: Feminism and the Subversion of Identity* (New York: Routledge, 2006).
9. Ellie Ragland-Sullivan, "Jacques Lacan: Feminism and the Problem of Gender Identity," *SubStance* 11, no. 3 (1982), p. 6.
10. Jacques Lacan, "Agency of the Letter in the Unconscious," in *Écrit: A Selection*, trans. Alan Sheridan (New York: W. W. Norton, 1977), p. 152.
11. *Ibid.*
12. German Lopez, "Anti-transgender Hysteria Explained," *Vox*, May 5, 2016, at https://www.vox.com/2016/5/5/11592908/transgender-bathroom-laws-rights (last accessed September 12, 2024).
13. *Ibid.*
14. *Ibid.*
15. Valo Vähäpassi, "An Imaginative Geography of Linear Gender: Bathrooms, Locker Rooms and Cis Vulnerability," *European Journal of American Culture* 42, no. 1 (January 2022), p. 38.
16. Ragland-Sullivan, "Jacques Lacan," p. 7.
17. Michael Arlen, *The Green Hat* (New York: George H. Doran, 1924), p. 31.
18. Thomas Laqueur, *Making Sex: Body and Gender from the Greeks to Freud* (Cambridge, MA: Harvard University Press, 1990), p. 11.
19. Quoted in my commentary on Laqueur's analysis: Michael J. Shapiro, *Cinematic Political Thought: Narrating Race, Nation and Gender* (Edinburgh: Edinburgh University Press, 1999), p. 141.
20. Laqueur, *Making Sex*, p. 8.
21. *Ibid.*, p. 10.
22. Louis Althusser, "The Underground Current of the Materialism of the Encounter," in *Philosophy of the Encounter: Later Writings, 1978–1987*, trans. G. M. Goshgarian (New York: Verso, 2006), pp. 163–207.
23. *Ibid.*, p. 170.
24. *Ibid.*, p. 173.
25. *Ibid.*, p. 174.
26. Harold Garfinkel, *Studies in Ethnomethodology* (Cambridge: Polity, 1984), p. 11.
27. All quotations in the paragraph are from the editors' Introduction to Garfinkel's Agnes chapter, reproduced in Susan Stryker and Stephen Whittle (eds.), *The Transgender Reader* (New York: Routledge, 2006), p. 58.
28. Harold Garfinkel, "Passing and the Managed Achievement of Sex Status in an 'Intersexed' Person," in *ibid.*, p. 68.

29. Foucault, *Abnormal*, p. 33.

30. Foucault, "Introduction," p. vii.

31. Michel Foucault, *Lectures on the Will to Know*, trans. Graham Burchell (New York: Picador, 2013), p. 4.

32. Michel Foucault, quoted in Paul Rabinow (ed.), *Foucault: Ethics Subjectivity and Truth*, trans. Robert Hurley (New York: The New Press, 1997), p. xi.

33. This convenient summary is in Tetz Hakoda, "Bodies and Pleasures in the Happy Limbo of a Non-identity," *Zinbun* 45 (2014): 102.

34. Foucault, "Introduction," p. viii.

35. Michel Foucault, "The Order of Discourse," in Michael Shapiro, *Language and Politics* (New York: NYU Press, 1984), p. 132.

36. Hil Malatino, *Queer Embodiment: Monstrosity, Medical Violence, and Intersex Experience* (Lincoln: University of Nebraska Press, 2023), p. 163.

37. *Ibid.*, p. 165.

38. *Ibid.*, p. 168.

39. Michel Foucault, *The Politics of Truth*, trans. Lysa Hochroth and Catherine Porter (New York: Semiotext(e), 2007), p. 47.

40. Ingvil Hellstrand, Line Hendriksen, Aino-Kisa Kaisa Koistinen, Donna McCormack, and Sara Orning, "Introduction: Promises, Monsters and Methodologies: The Ethics, Politics and Poetics of the Monstrous," *Somatechnics* 8, no. 2 (2018): 143.

41. *Ibid.*, p. 146.

42. Foucault, *The Politics of Truth*, p. 66.

43. Marvin D'Lugo, "Almodóvar's City of Desire," *Quarterly Review of Film & Video* 13, no. 4 (1991): 47.

44. Zavier Nunn, "Transliminality and the Nazi State," *Past & Present* 260 (August 2023): 124.

45. Robert Money quoted in Malatino, *Queer Embodiment*, p. 164.

46. Christopher Isherwood, *The Berlin Stories* (New York: New Directions, 1954), p. 86.

47. Linda Gershon, "Gender Identity in Weimar Germany," *Jstor Daily*, November 18, 2018, at https://daily.jstor.org/gender-identity-in-weimar-germany/ (last accessed September 12, 2024).

48. *Ibid.*

49. Matthew H. Birkhold, "A Lost Piece of Trans History," *The Paris Review*, January 15, 2019, at https://www.theparisreview.org/blog/2019/01/15/a-lost-piece-of-trans-history/ (last accessed September 12, 2024).

50. Barbara Creed, *The Monstrous-Feminine: Film, Feminism, Psychoanalysis* (London: Routledge, 2015), p. 11.

51. Gilles Deleuze, *Spinoza: Practical Philosophy*, trans. Robert Hurley (San Francisco: City Lights Books, 1988), p. 25.

52. William E. Connolly, *Identity/Difference: Democratic Negotiations of Political Paradox* (Minneapolis: University of Minnesota Press, 1991), p. 164.

53. Svend Ranulf, *Moral Indignation and Middle Class Psychology* (New York: Schocken, 1964; originally published in 1938), pp. 8–9. For a similar analysis,

see Slavoj Žižek, "Enjoy Your Nation as Yourself," in *Tarrying with the Negative* (Durham, NC: Duke University Press, 1993), pp. 202–3.

54. See Sarah Lippek, "Disrupted Values, Erupting Culture: Cabaret and Sexual Persona in Weimar Berlin," *SSRN*, online January 13, 2020, at https://papers.ssrn.com/sol3/papers.cfm?abstract_id=1079945.

55. Michael J. Shapiro, *Writing Politics: Studies in Compositional Method* (New York: Routledge, 2021), p. 64. The second quotation is from Andrew Dickson, "Culture in Weimar Germany: On the Edge of a Volcano," *Brewminate*, November 8, 2018, at https://www.bl.uk/20th-century-literature/articles/on-the-edge-of-the-volcano-culture-in-weimar-germany (last accessed September 12, 2024).

56. Laurie Marhoefer, "New Research Reveals How the Nazis Targeted Transgender People," *Smithsonian Magazine*, September 21, 2023, at https://www.smithsonianmag.com/history/new-research-reveals-how-the-nazis-targeted-transgender-people-180982931/ (last accessed September 12, 2024).

57. Gerna Pérez-Sanchez, "Franco's Spain, Queer Nation," *University of Michigan Journal of Law Reform* 33 (2000): 371.

58. "Six Survivors Remember Spain's Brutal Anti-LGBT Laws," *Equality*, August 1, 2018, at https://lacuna.org.uk/equality/six-survivors-spains-brutal-anti-lgbt-laws/ (last accessed September 12, 2024).

59. *Equality* August 1, 2018, at https://lacuna.org.uk/equality/six-survivors-spains-brutal-anti-lgbt-laws/.

60. Mary Ann Doane, *The Emergence of Cinematic Time: Modernity, Contingency. The Archive* (Cambridge, MA: Harvard University Press), p. 107.

61. Almodóvar quoted in J. Thomas, "Pedro Almodóvar's Serious Side," *Advocate* November 10, 2016 at https://www.advocate.com/current-issue/2016/11/10/pedro-almodovars-serious-side (last accessed September 12, 2024).

62. Julián Daniel Gutiérrez-Albilla, *Aestheticism, Ethics and Trauma in the Films of Pedro Almodóvar* (Edinburgh: Edinburgh University Press, 2017), p. 24.

63. I am quoting a Flaubert observation by Carlo Ginzburg, *History, Rhetoric, and Proof* (Hanover, NH: University Press of New England, 1999), pp. 97–8.

64. Theodor W. Adorno, *Aesthetic Theory*, trans. Robert Hulot-Kentor (Minneapolis: University of Minnesota Press, 1998), p. 88.

65. Leora Lev, "Women and the Staging of Rape in the Cinema of Pedro Almodóvar," in Marvin D'Lugo and Kathleen M. Vernon (eds.), *A Companion to Pedro Almodóvar* (New York: John Wiley & Sons, 2013), p. 222.

66. Pedro Almodóvar, quoted in the 2005 Sadler's Wells program for *Nelken & Palermo Palermo*, at https://sadlerswells.com/discover-dance/pina-bausch/pedro_Almodovar-on-pina-bausch/ (last accessed September 12, 2024).

67. Wim Wenders, "Speech for Pina," in *The Pixels of Paul Cezanne and Reflections on Other Artists*, trans. Jen Calleja (London: Faber & Faber, 2018), p. 96.

68. *Ibid.*, pp. 97–8.

69. Almodóvar, quoted in the 2005 Sadler's Wells program for *Nelken & Palermo Palermo*.

70. Malatino, *Queer Embodiment*, p. 193.

71. Donna Haraway, "The Promises of Monsters: A Regenerative Politics for Inappropriate/d Others," in Lawrence Grossberg, Cary Nelson, and Paula A. Teichler (eds.), *Cultural Studies* (New York: Routledge, 1992), pp. 295–337.

72. See David Price, "The Politics of the Body: Pina Bausch's 'Tanzheater,'" *Theater Journal* 42, no. 3 (October 1990): 329.

73. Johannes Birringer, "Pina Bausch: Dancing across Borders," *The Drama Review: TDR* 30, no. 2 (1986): 85–97.

74. *Ibid.*, p. 90.

75. Bracha L. Ettinger, "Matrixial Trans-Subjectivity," *Theory, Culture & Society* 23, no. 2 (2006): 219. I was alerted to the Ettinger–Almodóvar connection by Julián Daniel Gutiérrez-Albilla, *Aesthetics, Ethics and Trauma in the Cinema of Pedro Almodóvar* (Edinburgh: Edinburgh University Press, 2017).

76. Ettinger, "Matrixial Trans-Subjectivity," p. 219.

77. Those apropos phrases are belong to Chadwick Jenkins, "Aberrant Movements: Justifying Thought without a Ground in Deleuze's Philosophy," *Pop Matters*, September 27, 2017, at https://www.popmatters.com/aberrant-movements-the-philosophy-of-gilles-deleuze-by-david-lapoujade-2495380724.html (last accessed September 13, 2024). For an extensive treatment of aberrant movement in Deleuze's philosophy, see David Lapoujade, *Aberrant Movements: The Philosophy of Gilles Deleuze*, trans. Joshua David Jordan (New York: Semiotex(e), 2017).

78. Frederic Strauss (ed.), *Almodóvar on Almodóvar* (London: Faber & Faber, 1996), p. 213.

79. Adriana Novoa, "Whose Talk Is It? Almodóvar and the Fairy Tale in *Talk to Her*," *Marvels & Tales of Fairy-Tale Studies* 19, no. 2 (2005): 233.

80. *Ibid.*, p. 231.

81. See Abram de Swaan, *The Management of. Normality: Critical Essays in Health and Welfare* (London: Routledge, 1990).

82. Carla Marcantonio, "Undoing Performance: The Mute Female Body and Narrative Dispossession in Pedro Almodóvar's *Talk to Her*," *Women & Performance: A Journal of Feminist Theory* 17, no. 1 (March 2007): 19–20.

83. Almodóvar quoted in Annette Guse, "Talk to Her! Look at Her: Pina Bausch in Pedro Almodóvar's *Habla con Ella*," *Seminar: A Journal of Germanic Studies* 43, no. 4 (November 2007): 427.

84. Pedro Almodóvar, quoted in the 2005 Sadler's Wells program for *Nelken & Palermo Palermo*.

85. Foucault, *Abnormal*, p. 73.

86. Pedro Almodóvar quoted in Marcantonio, "Undoing Performance," pp. 19–20.

87. Novoa, "Whose Talk Is It?" p. 333.

88. Hellstrand et al., "Introduction: Promises, Monsters and Methodologies," p. 145.

89. Margrit Shildrick, "The Body Which Is Not One: Dealing with Differences," *Body & Society* 5, nos 2–3 (1999): 80.

90. Strauss, *Almodóvar on Almodóvar*, p. 219.

91. Malatino, *Queer Embodiment*, p. 177.

92. Those Deleuze and Guattari-inspired passages are from Malatino's chapter 5, "State Science: Biopolitics and the Medicalization of Gender Nonconformance," in his *Queer Embodiment*, p. 177.

93. I am quoting an analysis of the liberating consequences of Deleuze and Guattari's concept: Anne Shult, "Nomadic Thought and the Creation of New Utopias," *Journal of the History of Ideas Blog*, March 3, 2019, at https://www.jhiblog. org/2019/03/11/time-travelers-part-iii-nomadic-thought-and-the-creation-of-new-utopias/ (last accessed September 13, 2024).

94. Malatino, *Queer Embodiment*, p. 204.

95. D'Lugo, "Almodóvar's City of Desire," p. 47.

96. Michael J. Shapiro, *The Time of the City: Politics, Philosophy and Genre* (New York: Routledge, 2010), pp. 25–6. As I add, "disorderly was doubtless aversive for Hegel [because] ... the disharmonious global city was not in keeping with [his] commitment to the progressive development of the 'idea,'" p. 26.

97. Terry Pinkard, *Hegel: A Biography* (Cambridge: Cambridge University Press, 200), p. 552.

98. Shapiro, *The Time of the City*, p. 26.

99. Edward Soja, *Thirdspace: Journeys to Los Angeles and Other Real-and-Imagined Places* (Oxford: Basil Blackwell, 1996), p. 61.

100. "Ethnogenesis" is William Boelhower's term in his *Through a Glass Darkly: Ethnic Semiosis and American Literature* (New York: Oxford University Press, 1986).

101. Deleuze describes "nomadic thought" in several places. For a brief treatment, see Gilles Deleuze, "Nomadic Thought," in the collection *Desert Islands: and Other Texts 1953–1974*, trans. Michael Taormina (New York: Semiotext(e), 2004), pp. 252–61.

102. Paul Carter, *The Road to Botany Bay: An Exploration of Landscape and History* (Chicago: University of Chicago Press, 1987), p. 136.

103. Margaret Clunies Ross, "Australian Aboriginal Oral Traditions," *Oral Tradition* 1, no. 2 1986): 232.

104. Carter, *The Road to Botany Bay*, p. 168.

105. See Koen Slootmaekers, "Nationalism as Competing Masculinities: Homophobia as a Technology of Othering for Hetero- and Homo-Nationalism," *Theory and Society* 48, no. 2 (April 2019): 239–65.

106. M. M. Bakhtin, "Forms of Time and the Chronotope in the Novel: Notes Toward a Historical Poetics," in *The Dialogic Imagination*, trans. Caryl Emerson and Michael Holquist (Austin: University of Texas Press, 1981), p. 84.

107. Shapiro, *Cinematic Political Thought*, pp. 163–4.

108. Chris Gibson, "'We sing our home, We dance our land': Indigenous Self-determination and Contemporary Geopolitics in Australian Popular Music," *Environment and Planning D: Society and Space* 16, no. 2 (1998): 165.

109. Shapiro, *Cinematic Political Thought*, p. 161.

110. Gautam Anisha, "The Monstrous Other: Adam Goodes and the Colonial Legacy of terra nullis," *Social Alternatives* 38, no. 4 (2019), at https://socialalterna

tives.com/wp-content/uploads/2021/02/anisha_gautam_38_4.pdf (last accessed September 13, 2024).

111. Christine Judith Nicoll, "Mapping the Many Monsters of Aboriginal Australian Lore," *Atlas Obscure*, October 10, 2022, at https://www.atlasobscura.com/articles/aboriginal-australia-monsters (last accessed September 13, 2024).

112. Félix Guattari, quoted in Guillaume Sibertin-Biane, "From One Conjuncture, the Other: The Afterwardness of Guattari and Deleuze," trans. Cadenza Academic Translations, *Actuel Marx* 52, no. 2 (2012), p. 34.

EPILOGUE

Decades ago, I wrote this sentence fragment: "Ethical reflection becomes possible when negotiation with difference rather than security is the project ..."[1] Although I have since continually engaged artistic and cultural texts in which such negotiations have been imagined and staged, none have been as well articulated and as relevant to the investigations in this book as they are in James McBride's 2024 novel *The Heaven and Earth Grocery Store.* I want to think briefly with his novel in this afterthought because the complex negotiations it invents, a textual enactment of communal possibility, is a sustained imagining of what civic life could be at its best.[2]

The novel is situated in the ethnically splintered Chicken Hill neighborhood of Pottstown, Pennsylvania where three ethno-assemblages, Jewish, Black, and white, engage in contentious relations both among and within them. Written by an author from an ethnically hybrid family – his mother, a Polish Jewish émigré from whom he adopted a rich Yiddish vocabulary, and an African American father from whom he learned Black vernacular – the novel exemplifies the "heteroglossia" that M. M. Bakhtin famously attributes to that genre form. It features a mix of clashing "sociolects": Yiddish expressions brought to the U.S. by Jews from diverse places in middle Europe, Black vernacular issuing from diverse venues of African American dwelling, Spanish vernacular brought to the town by Latinx musicians, and styles of "white" discourse belonging to varied class and occupational types.

In the midst of the town's centrifugal ideational forces is one character who constitutes the novel's "moral engine."[3] Chona, the daughter of Jewish émigrés whose father is a rabbi, embraces and implements an ethos of care. In her role as a proprietor of the eponymous Heaven and Earth Grocery Store, which she runs as a charitable lending institution (extending credit to shoppers from the town's Black community), she serves as a centripetal force. Through sheer strength of character and by example she unites people from diverse ethnic groups into a cooperative civic assemblage that rescues a deaf Black teenager trapped in a punitive psychiatric hospital on the false presumption that his hearing disability is a mental disorder. However, before that event is underway, her empathetic ethos registers itself on her husband Moshe Ludlow's occupational and domestic situations. The care Chona dispenses on the local Black community convinces Moshe, a Romanian Jew who owns a local theater/dance hall, to open his establishment to Black patrons. After a friend makes the suggestion that a Black clientele would bring significant profits, he raises the possibility with Chona. In response to his worrying out loud about what the white Christian population in the town would think – "the goyim won't like it," he says – Chona responds in Yiddish, "Me ken dem yam mit a kendel mi ois' shepen (You can't ride in all directions at once)" and adds, "What does it matter what they think?"[4] Once he welcomes their business, the town's Black residents, who had formerly been excluded from downtown establishments as customers, "frolicked and laughed, dancing as if they were birds enjoying flight for the first time."[5] Moshe's dance hall/theater, like Chona's grocery store, functions as what Foucault calls a "heterotopia" (reviewed in the Introduction). They are places of reprieve from those that feature strictly competitive, uncivil aspirational motivations.

Once the profits from the "Negro" dance evenings roll in, Moshe is able to expand. He buys his theater outright, opens a second one nearby, and with the remaining cash surplus he buys his mother a house in Romania and constructs an apartment above the grocery store for Chona. Having become lifestyle aspirational as well as financially flush, Moshe tells Chona he'd like them to move from their apartment above her grocery store to a more fashionable residence in a more upscale neighborhood. "This area is poor. Which we are not. It is Negro. Which we are not. We are doing *well!*" Chona refuses to move, "because," she says, "we serve, you see. That is what we do."[6] Once Moshe has introjected Chona's communal sensibility, it extends to another ethnic assemblage. After his Black employee Nate welcomes a multicultural Latinx musical group, his ethno-musical imaginary amplifies. The lead composer musician, Mario, tells Moshe that the Spanish he hears in the dressing room is "the sound of the future. These people [Moshe's clientele] don't want swing music. They want decarga, ponchando, tanga, piano guajeo, mamba, Africano-Cubano." Once they began performing, "Moshe watched in awe as the Afro-Cubans proceeded to burn the wall paper off the walls of the All American Dance Hall and Theater."[7]

Moshe's dance hall/theater, a place of jouissance, and Chona's grocery store, a space of care, stand in stark opposition to a dystopic institution, the nearby Pennhurst, a psychiatric hospital where state officials have sent the Black teenager, Dodo. It is a place of despair, ruled by the violent "Son of Man," who physically and sexually abuses its inmates. Within Pennhurst, a disabled white roommate, "Monkey Pants," saves Dodo from a rape by the Son of Man on one occasion, using his only resource, shit, which he hurls at him. Dodo's last words on his dying day are "Thank you Monkey Pants."[8] What ultimately springs Dodo from Pennhurst is a collaboration between Black and Jewish members of the community. They accomplish a rescue that reverses the episode of capture in which the town's white assemblage (led by the racist Klan member Doc Roberts) was involved in reporting Dodo's whereabouts to the arresting authorities. The novel characterizes "Doc" and his friend Carl with a sardonic description of the way their habitus differs from those of struggling immigrant/Jewish and Black diasporic assemblages in their midst:

> Neither Doc nor Carl had interest in questioning their family lineage, for their childhoods were as full as much happiness as any descendent of the Mayflower might enjoy. They were white Christian men born in an America seemingly ready made for them ... They [and their Klan cronies] wanted to preserve America ... It needed to be saved ... The town, the children, the women, they needed to be rescued from those who wanted to pollute the pure white race ...[9]

Among what the novel models is a cross-ethnic caritas realized as a cooperative event that stands in opposition to the white supremacist political sensibility that McBride's passage captures. Because Doc and friends are the kind of assemblage whose politics has recently gathered momentum with the explicit blessing of a U.S. president during the period in which the novel was being composed, McBride's *Heaven and Earth Grocery Store* is a timely reminder of current danger as well as an imaginative construction of civic promise. McBride's contribution to my thinking evokes an observation that conveys the conditions of possibility for what my analysis throughout this book offers. In his monograph on the French essayist Montaigne, the late sociologist John O'Neill opens a chapter titled "Reading and Temperament" with this passage: "Writers are readers. This is not because they have no thoughts of their own, but precisely because they seek a thought that is their own; or rather, thought that becomes their own through the conversation of minds to be found in reading."[10]

NOTES

1. Michael J. Shapiro, *Cinematic Political Thought: Narrating Race, Nation and Gender* (Edinburgh: Edinburgh University Press, 1999), p. 119.
2. James McBride, *The Heaven and Earth Grocery Store* (New York: Riverhead Books, 2023).
3. The expression is in Ron Charles's review of the book in *The Washington Post*, August 8, 2023, at https://www.washingtonpost.com/books/2023/08/03/heaven-earth-grocery-store-james-mcbride-review/ (last accessed September 13, 2024).
4. McBride, *The Heaven and Earth Grocery Store*, p. 20.
5. *Ibid.*
6. McBride, *The Heaven and Earth Grocery Store*, p. 27.
7. *Ibid.*, p. 163.
8. *Ibid.*, p. 386.
9. *Ibid.*, p. 114.
10. John O'Neill, *Essaying Montaigne: A Study of the Renaissance Institution of Writing and Reading* (London: Routledge & Kegan Paul, 1982), p. 100.

INDEX

EU representative:
Easy Access System Europe
Mustamäe tee 50, 10621 Tallinn, Estonia
Gpsr.requests@easproject.com

www.ingramcontent.com/pod-product-compliance
Lightning Source LLC
Chambersburg PA
CBHW070947250726
48663CB00002B/118